P9-DFN-129

FERDINAND LASSALLE

Romantic Revolutionary

BY DAVID FOOTMAN

Man's temperament is his fate
Ferdinand Lassalle

GREENWOOD PRESS, PUBLISHERS
NEW YORK

Originally published in 1947
by Yale University Press

First Greenwood Reprinting 1969

Library of Congress Catalogue Card Number 70-90145

SBN 8371-2202-3

PRINTED IN UNITED STATES OF AMERICA

CONTENTS

FOREWORD

I

The fifteen or twenty years after the Congress of Vienna were for Germany a period of recovery from the exhaustion of the Napoleonic wars. The next four decades were a period of germination—to be followed, later in the century, by that output of national energy which has caused such disturbance to the rest of the world ever since. Ferdinand Lassalle belonged to the Germany of the middle period. It was a Germany of thirty odd separate principalities with, in each, a social structure of more or less separate and ordered castes. It was an age when a Minister of the Interior could still declare that "it was not becoming for subjects to judge the actions of the Head of the State by the measure of their own restricted understanding"; when a king, pressed for the grant of a constitution, could refuse to consent "that a written paper should intrude like a second Providence between our Lord God in Heaven and this country, to govern us through its paragraphs". It was a land of country gentlemen and unpolitical peasants; of petty capitals and little market towns; of small traders and master craftsmen, dependent for their livelihood on the good will of the local court, the local bureaucracy and the officers of the local garrison.

And yet there were seeds of change. Industry was in its infancy, but was already developing. When Lassalle was nine years old the North German Customs Union opened up a territory of thirty million people to free internal trade. One year later the firm of Krupp set up its first steam engine. In the Rhineland and the Ruhr, in Saxony, Silesia and the Berlin area, the rising class of merchants, bankers and manufacturers were no longer willing to acquiesce in the forms and controls of a bygone age.

The economic impetus towards political progress was reinforced by the emotional currents of the age. There was, particularly in Germany, an urge towards "freedom" and an urge towards national unity. The romantic legacy of the French Revolution inspired in young Germans a bitter dissatisfaction with the antiquated system of government under which their own lot was cast. National pride was piqued at the check to German prestige and German might imposed by the unwieldy structure of the German Confederation and by the jealousies and rivalries of Austria and Prussia, its two predominant members. Events in the world outside—the liberation of Greece, the change of régime in France of 1830—served to stimulate these feelings. Associations were formed and meetings held. There were demonstrations and popular outbursts. In some of the smaller states some form of constitutional government was established. Throughout the period the existing régimes were ever more on the defensive.

With the landed gentry for the most part in a natural alliance with the Courts, with the proletariat still small in numbers and politically backward, it was, inevitably, the middle classes which comprised the opposition. It was primarily to men of some education that the "new ideas" appealed; and it was only men of some means who could afford to smuggle past the censorship the literature in which these ideas were contained. The censorship operated, with greater or less rigidity and efficiency, all over Germany. The works of Börne and Heine were among those prohibited by the Federal Diet. One field alone remained comparatively free—philosophy. The young Hegelians brought the dialectical system of their master to bear on political science, and arrived at conclusions far to the left of any Hegel himself would have approved. But, to quote Marx (or more probably Engels) "the abstruse philosophical language in which these ideas were clothed, if it obscured the mind of both writer and reader, equally blinded the eyes of the censor. And thus it was that the young Hegelian writers enjoyed a liberty unknown in every other branch of literature."

2

IT WAS in this eager, active, frustrated atmosphere that Ferdinand Lassalle grew up. He was twelve when a first-class political sensation was caused by the dismissal of seven Göttingen professors for protesting against the repeal of the Hanover constitution. He was fifteen when Schneckenburger wrote *Die Wacht am Rhein.* He was a schoolboy when Frederick William IV ascended the throne of Prussia, and still at school as it became apparent that the hopes the liberals had centred on that monarch would not materialize.

The boy Lassalle is revealed in his early diary. He was quick-witted and precocious. He was capable of warm affection, but unscrupulous when something he really wanted was at stake. He was a voracious reader. His boyish dreams of knight-errantry and glory were of a passionate intensity such as affected the course of his life. He was highly sensitive, sensitive of the figure he was cutting before others, sensitive of being a Jew and son of a provincial tradesman. He was very conscious of being some one set apart from the crowd, of a vocation for leadership; he, Ferdinand Lassalle, was to lead the crusade against tyranny which the romantic poets of his age had proclaimed.

The first big milestone in his life was his discovery of Hegel when preparing for his matriculation. Hegel provided a creed in which he found full satisfaction. The romantic poets of his adolescence were set aside with other childish things and he became an apostle of the Idea. It was, he convinced himself, only by the dissemination of true philosophy that the individual could hasten the inevitable advent of a classless utopia within the framework of an ideal state; and he set himself, as his own contribution, to prepare a new philosophical system which should crown and carry further the work of Hegel. Hegelian dialectic not only indicated the course of his career: it permeated his whole mental process. It provided an instrument by which he could solve any problem to his complete satisfaction and in the sense of his own desires. It gave him the self-assurance that helped him to secure so many of his successes in later life. But it gave him this at the price of his sense of humour and proportion, of his power of self-criticism; and it thus contributed not a little to his ultimate disaster.

3

INTENSE as Lassalle's preoccupation with Hegelian philosophy undoubtedly was, there still remained his crusading spirit, his urge for action and for limelight. His meeting with Countess Hatzfeldt provided an outlet. This was the second big milestone of his career, and the next eight years were devoted primarily to the vindication of the Countess's claims against her husband.

For the rest of his life he looked back on his campaign with supreme satisfaction. He had, he felt, played the part of a knight-errant. It is certain that his client's beauty, her princely birth, the very considerable interests involved and the blaze of publicity endowed the case with an irresistible attraction for him. None the less, as the struggle dragged on and the difficulties and setbacks accumulated, he was called on to show courage, pertinacity and resource. His determination did not fail him, and he lived up to the spirit of his adopted motto: *Flectere si nequeo superos, Acheronta movebo*. One by one the courts decided against his client. The case seemed hopeless. And then, by an ingenious stroke of blackmail, he secured a satisfactory settlement.

The Countess remained, to the end, an important factor in his life. It was characteristic of Lassalle that he should identify his client's cause with his own political predilections. From quite early on the Countess came to share his views. Together they took part in the political upheaval of 1848. Lassalle's participation led to his arrest. He continued to conduct the Countess's legal and financial affairs from prison, and when he was let out again they both engaged in doing all that was possible to help the shipwrecked survivors of the democratic cause.

By 1854, when the Hatzfeldt case was finally decided, the

Right Wing régime was firmly in the saddle throughout Prussia, and police vigilance left no opportunity for oppositional political work. Thus the two burning interests which Lassalle and Sophie Hatzfeldt had in common lapsed together, and in the consequent reaction their relations came to a crisis. She did not resent his desire to make himself a career; she did not, actively, resent his liaisons with other women. And though he did resent her preoccupation with her family and with her former friends, the trouble came chiefly from a series of less obvious causes. The Countess was a tired woman. Very probably at this time she was going through her change of life. She was anxious about her son, about her health, about her investments. She was haunted by the spectre of a lonely old age. All this made Lassalle peevish and impatient: he shared the almost universal male conviction that woman's first duty was to be gay, light-hearted and appreciative. Irritations multiplied.

Largely to give their friendship a chance to recover, Lassalle undertook a tour to the Near East. He broke this off and returned to Germany to help steer her affairs through a slump on the bourse. Soon, however, there were more recriminations and quarrels. Lassalle was exasperating in his dictatorial demands, his self-assumed omniscience, his insistence on having the last word. The Countess was a woman of spirit and could and did reply in kind. But they had become necessary to each other. They were bound together by their years of common struggle. For him she was the one friend on whom he could implicitly rely, and he had the greatest respect for her judgement on matters which admitted a woman to be competent to judge. She had and retained complete faith in his intellectual pre-eminence and in his political ideas. It was to be her part, she felt, to stand at his side when the moment came to translate those ideas into action. And as her family and friends slipped further away from her it was Lassalle, and her pride in his achievements, that were to be the delight and comfort of her declining years.

It may well have been a shock to her to find Lassalle talking seriously of marriage, though the Russian girl to whom he first proposed refused him. In any case, not long after this episode, the Countess took up with Wilhelm Rüstow, an ex-Prussian regular officer, who, since 1848, had been living the drab life of a political *émigré* in Switzerland. Lassalle had no logical ground to object to this development. He was, nevertheless, angry and bitterly jealous. For many months he did not even write to her. But he became increasingly conscious that he had no other friend who could take her place; and the Countess for her part found that the devoted, high-minded, but rather dreary Rüstow was no effective substitute. News of Lassalle's literary successes filled her with an almost maternal delight. Their correspondence was resumed. Soon after the start of his career as an active politician she returned to Germany; she became his closest and, when occasion demanded, his most courageous collaborator. She was with him through all the storm and stress of his last campaign. When his health broke down and he left for a sanatorium in Switzerland their letters showed their friendship as complete as it had ever been—perhaps, indeed, more firmly established, for Lassalle's disappointments had mellowed him. Then came the entanglement which ended in his tragedy. Here again it was to Sophie Hatzfeldt that he turned for help and advice, to her that he cried out in his moment of humiliation and despair. Throughout those last few weeks she fought for his happiness and his sense of proportion. He died with his hand in hers; and the remaining seventeen years of her life she devoted, with fanatical persistence, to the defence of his memory and of his work.

4

IT WAS in the Rhineland in 1848 that Lassalle met Marx.

Lassalle was then, of course, deeply involved in the Hatzfeldt case; but he was also a revolutionary. Action made an irresistible appeal to his temperament. He quickly revised his previous conviction that it was only by the dissemination of philosophy that the cause could be furthered. He took an active part in the struggle, and thus came in contact with the editor of the *Neue Rheinische Zeitung*. Marx was thirty-one. Apart from *The Communist Manifesto* his major works were still to be written. But by the force of his intellect and personality he was an outstanding figure. He was as learned a philosopher as Lassalle, though he had renounced the "mystical nimbus" of the great Hegel. He was moreover at that time a practical revolutionary. Lassalle, for all his habit of playing the dictator, seems to have realized that here was one whose superiority he must recognize. That feeling lasted through all their years apart, through all their friction and disagreement; and even survived their final break.

The two seem quickly to have established a personal friendship. The letters between Lassalle and Marx's wife show their relationship was more than a political alliance. Marx was not blind to the younger man's foibles, to his vanity, ostentation and tactlessness. But they did not exasperate him as they did Engels (who always disliked Lassalle); and he appreciated freely (as Engels did only grudgingly) the resource, the vitality, intelligence and drive that were here being offered to the common cause. They were in contact for only three months. Lassalle was arrested in November 1848. On his release Marx had already left Germany for his long exile. Lassalle kept up a friendly correspondence with both Marx and Jenny. He did what he could to help the *émigré* household in their money troubles. At times he offended by his tactlessness, but the offence was passing. Marx recommended him for membership of the Communist League. The Central Committee in Germany turned him down. Much, perhaps too much, has been made of the fact that Marx took no steps to make the Committee reverse their decision. Marx was fully aware that the League was a delicate plant; he had ample experience of the harm that could be done by internal bickering in a central committee. However highly he may have thought of Lassalle there were excellent reasons why he should not, at that moment, try to force him into a group that did not want him. At any rate the friendly correspondence went on; and with the collapse of the Communist League, the arrest of its leading members and the persistent vigilance and activity of the Prussian police, it is clear that Marx regarded Lassalle as the one man in Germany on whose loyal collaboration he could rely.

By 1854, when Lassalle secured his settlement of the Hatzfeldt affair, Marx had spent six years in exile. They had been years of grinding poverty and bitter disappointment. He had been involved in the pettiness, treachery and intrigue inseparable from *émigré* life. All this had increased his natural suspiciousness; but it had not affected his faith in himself and in his mission. His experience of revolutionary activity and the situation of the world as he saw it had now led him to conclude that his own task was to provide a scientific and philosophical basis for the future of the movement and for the future of mankind. It was to this task that he devoted himself with ruthless energy and persistence, unsparing alike of himself and of others, for the whole of the rest of his life.

In 1853 he received an unfavourable report on Lassalle's behaviour, to which he does not seem to have attached much importance. Two years later Lassalle was denounced to him by a delegation of workers who came over to London from the Rhineland. We know now that the denunciation was inspired by personal malice. But the allegations contained some truth, and fitted in with what was known of Lassalle. Marx, though he respected the Countess personally, had always disliked the dirty linen that made up so much of the Hatzfeldt case. Since the settlement, Lassalle's manner of life and choice of friends were not such as would appeal to Marx as suitable for a collaborator in the movement. Of more import was the indication that Lassalle had estranged the Rhineland workers and made improper use of a letter from Marx. Marx asked for further evidence. None was forthcoming, but, all the same, he was "deeply impressed". Such feelings of personal friendship as he still retained were driven under. For the next two years he did not write.

It was Lassalle who, on the eve of publication of his first major work, re-opened the correspondence. Marx hesitated, consulted Engels, weighed the advantages and disadvantages, and finally replied. He had no other political correspondent in Germany; he had no one there to help him place his books and newspaper articles; finally he was always more or less in need of some one to lend him money—Marx's faith in the importance of his work was such that he had no compunction in tapping his friends to enable him to continue it. When the contact was re-established Lassalle did what he could to find editors and publishers. From time to time he backed bills for Marx or advanced him loans (which were usually repaid). In return Lassalle desired that his friend should show an interest in his literary output.

This interest was only grudgingly accorded. Lassalle was greedy of praise, and Marx's praise was luke-warm and perfunctory. But his criticism was too shrewd and too trenchant not to hurt. Lassalle sent back long pages of explanation and self-justification. There was often much point in them. But they were too long and too subjective. Marx merely became impatient. It must be remembered that by this time Lassalle had made himself a reputation. He had a very definite standing in Berlin intellectual circles. As such he felt he deserved more consideration than Marx accorded him. Meanwhile Marx's lot continued to be obscurity, ill-health and humiliating poverty. Through it all he retained his faith in his mission, his dignity and his caustic sense of humour: but he would not have been human had he not been touched by bitterness at the disparity of their positions.

In 1859 Marx's whole energy was taken up in defending his honour and integrity (and with them, as he saw it, his life's work) against the attacks of a Dr. Vogt. Lassalle contributed advice. But the advice, though sound, was too dispassionate to be welcome to Marx. It was given, too, with an air of complacent superiority (born of his knowledge of German conditions and of legal procedure), which finally exasperated Marx into sending him copies of the "denunciations" of 1855. This act brought Lassalle, already overstrained and ill, to the verge of a nervous breakdown. Marx brushed aside the flood of expostulation that followed; and the correspondence resumed its uneven course.

It is clear throughout that Lassalle had the discernment to remain convinced of Marx's genius and importance in his years of apparent eclipse; it is clear too that, notwithstanding Marx's treatment of him, he was big enough to desire close personal collaboration. At one time he nursed a project that they should together run a Left-wing newspaper. This was the subject of inconclusive discussions during Marx's visit to Berlin in 1861, where he stayed ten days as Lassalle's guest; but the visit served chiefly to emphasize their fundamental differences of temperament and outlook. When Marx got back to London he wrote to thank his host in a tone of cordial friendship. The contrast between this and the bitterly sarcastic private report to Engels has led to suggestions that Marx was either playing the hypocrite to Lassalle or else was pandering to Engels' old dislike. Such suggestions seem unnecessary. Marx may well have felt both the friendship and the angry exasperation that Lassalle was so capable of inspiring; but with Marx the supreme consideration was always the good of the movement—as conceived by Marx. And so his final judgment went against Lassalle.

The year that followed Marx's Berlin visit was of decisive importance to Lassalle. As the Prussian constitutional crisis developed the founding of a Left-wing paper became of minor urgency. The times were getting ripe for action, not for mere journalism; and Lassalle determined to enter the arena of practical politics. He came to London to make one more bid for the active co-operation of Marx. Once again the discussions proved negative. There was not only the difference of temperament. The two men were fundamentally opposed on questions of strategy and of principle. Lassalle's proposed campaign implied some measure of tacit alliance with the extreme Right against the bourgeois Liberals, thus running directly counter to Marx's theory of political evolution. Even more inacceptable to Marx, with his conception of the state as an instrument in the class struggle, was Lassalle's idea of socialization by means of the existing Prussian State. When Lassalle returned to Germany all prospect of political collaboration was gone, and a few months later a quarrel over the endorsement of a bill put an end to their personal correspondence.

It was then alone, without Marx, that Lassalle embarked on his political campaign. But, throughout, the two men were constantly in each other's minds. Lassalle had copies of all his pamphlets and speeches sent to Marx; certainly with the desire of displaying his own achievement, possibly with the hope of extracting some word of approval or support. But Marx remained silent. In the private correspondence with Engels we can trace the bitterness with which they watched Lassalle's movement, launched without them and conducted on principles of which they disapproved, assume an importance which no workers' movement in Germany had ever yet had. But there was no action they could take. To endorse Lassalle's movement would be tantamount to endorsing his ideas. Openly to oppose him would play into the hands of the Reaction, and would in addition lay themselves open to Left-wing charges of being pernickety doctrinaires, arbitrarily hampering the fighters in the field. Marx and Engels had no party, and, in the early 'sixties, no particular following. Memories of 1848 and of the *Neue Rheinische Zeitung* were growing dim; and the first volume of *Das Kapital* was still uncompleted.

Nevertheless the sudden news of Lassalle's death came as a shock to both of them. Both paid a spontaneous tribute to the man who had been "the enemy of our enemies". The impact of the tragedy brought back to Marx the memory, perhaps more than the memory, of their former friendship. "Quite apart from what he did," he wrote to Countess Hatzfeldt, "I loved him as a man." And then he added, in a rare burst of self-revelation, "the trouble was that we kept in hiding from each other, as if we were going to live for ever". This was a passing mood. Neither his nature nor his self-imposed crusade left Marx much scope for sentiment. In the toil and controversy of the next few years the rekindled embers of the former personal feeling flickered out again. Towards the end the ageing warrior found one more enemy added to all those others he had met or made. It was the Lassalle legend.

5

LASSALLE's General German Workers' Association grew up in the face of opposition from the established parties, from the large section of the working class under Liberal influence, from the whole German press, from the police and the Public Prosecutor's Department. His pamphlets were confiscated, his meetings broken up, he himself arrested. The shadow of imprisonment was never far away. Then there were all the growing pains of a young organization—administrative hitches, money troubles, friends who failed and the threat of mutiny within. Progress was slow, and patience a quality that Lassalle conspicuously lacked. Far behind were the days when he had regarded the dissemination of philosophy as the supreme revolutionary task. He wanted immediate success and effective power. He was increasingly obsessed with a hunger for some resounding triumph, or, failing that, at least for something he could pass off as one.

The history of his brief career as an active politician is in some measure a history of that obsession. His dynamic energy, his resource, his power of command were less and less guided by the fundamental principles of the proletarian movement, and more and more directed towards the attainment of some quick result. With a hectic opportunism he endeavoured to exploit episcopal denunciations of *laissez-faire* and royal platitudes to a workers' delegation. Above all he sought to further his ends through Bismarck. In their few confidential meetings, in the half-dozen letters that he wrote to him, in the formulation even of some of his public speeches, he strove with ever more eager insistence to induce the Prussian Prime Minister to bring in some measure for which he and his Association could claim the credit. But the young movement did not yet possess the momentum to force concessions from so ruthless a political realist. Bismarck held back.

It was Lassalle's fate to have to measure himself against the two outstanding figures of his generation. It has been said that he stood at a parting of the ways. To the Left Marx pointed along a hard and stony path to a distant and uncertain future. To the Right the road was blocked by the massive presence of Bismarck. There was no clear way to an immediate triumph.

As his dreams failed to materialise Lassalle became a bitter and frustrated man. In the end it seemed to him there was one card left, the card of nationalism. He determined to demand, in the name of the workers, the incorporation of the duchies of

Schleswig-Holstein. But he was worn out by the feverish tempo of his last campaign and the strain of his court proceedings. His health was near breaking point. Before he could make this final *coup* he was ordered to undergo a prolonged cure. He went off to a sanatorium in Switzerland exhausted in body and restless in mind. For a few days he fretted there amid mist-covered mountains and drizzling rain. Then Helene von Dönniges appeared, twenty-one, with gold-red hair, *la femme la plus femme du monde*; and the stage was set for the final tragedy.

6

IT IS unwise to attempt too exactly to assess the influence of any man's life on the succeeding age. We cannot isolate the imponderabilia of history—the moods, vanities and impulses of individuals and groups, their inner jealousies, urges and despondencies, the impact of seemingly irrelevant accidents that combine to determine the course of events. Of Lassalle we will only say that he came to his exuberant maturity when the time was ripe for a call to form a proletarian front. He put out the call with a passionate persistence and forced a hearing for it. The movement started, grew—far more slowly than he himself had hoped but none the less perceptibly—and with it the Lassalle legend. The power of this legend, and the clarity and force of his style, procured a wide circulation for his writings. When, eleven years after his death, his party amalgamated with the younger and rival movement under Bebel and Liebknecht, the joint Gotha programme was largely inspired (to the dismay of Marx and Engels) by Lassalle. The Gotha programme remained the official platform of German democracy for the next fifteen years.

It is true that the specifically Lassallean political and economic theories have not stood the test of time. His "Iron Law of Wages" is discredited, and his panacea of state-aided co-operatives is no longer taken seriously. Detractors point to his "Cæsarism", his readiness to collaborate with the powers of reaction, his uncritical German nationalism. Ominous comparisons can be and have been drawn with the N.S.D.A.P. But there remains what Marx admitted to be his "immortal service" of awakening the proletarian movement in Germany, in the teeth of bitter opposition. There remains his all-out battle against the exponents of unrestricted capitalism, which made him, in Engels' words, "the only man in Germany they were afraid of"..

We are not here concerned with Lassalle's position, as apostle or heresiarch, in the Left-wing movement after his death. This book is an attempt to give a picture of the man and his work. There are few nineteenth-century figures of whom we can know so much. In his boyhood he kept a diary. Throughout his life he was a voluminous and uninhibited letter-writer. All that he wrote, for publication or otherwise, bears the stamp of his personality. There has been little posthumous tampering with his papers, little censorship or suppression by relatives and pious executors. There are few whose qualities and weaknesses lie so patently exposed as do Lassalle's, for he was rather larger than life and rather more vivid. We, of posterity, are brought up in other fashions of thought and behaviour. Modern psychology has taught us caution in the manner of our self-revelation, and encouraged us to complacence in our judgment of romantics. We may smile at Heine's image of the stern young gladiator, marching so proudly to his doom. Yet perhaps there are few of us, politicians or others, who will not find in Ferdinand Lassalle some disconcerting echo of our inner selves.

Chapter 1

BRESLAU

I

Ferdinand Lassal—"Lassalle" was a form of spelling he adopted later—was born in Breslau on the 10th April 1825. His family were Jews, originally domiciled in Poland, who moved into Prussian Silesia in the latter part of the previous century. His father, Heymann Lassal, was a fairly prosperous wholesale silk merchant. Store and office were on the ground floor, and Heymann and his wife née Friedländer, Ferdinand, a daughter Frederike (Riekchen) and the servants occupied the rest of the house.

For the New Year of 1840, Ferdinand's father gave him a diary with lock and key, and the boy, not yet fifteen, opened it with an introduction:

"These pages will give an account of all my activities, my faults and my good deeds. I wish to set down, conscientiously and objectively, not only what I do but also my motives. It is desirable for everyone to know his character. Just as one knows the characters in a novel by reading what they say and do, so anyone can get to know his own character by reading his diary, if he describes himself strictly and accurately. Suppose I do something wrong, will I not blush when I write it down? And will I not blush even more when I read it afterwards? It is with this moral end in view and also for the future pleasure of reading and recalling what I have enjoyed and suffered that I start this diary."

He kept his diary, on and off, for eighteen months; he lived up to his resolve to describe himself strictly and accurately; and the diary gives us a vivid picture of the boy who grew up to be Lassalle the man.

The first entry is for New Year's Day. The Gerstenberg

brothers mentioned were his closest school friends—especially Isidore who later settled in England, amassed a fortune and became one of the founders of the Council of Foreign Bondholders. Hein was another friend. Manatschal, Hesse and Häsel were Breslau cafés. Thirty groschen went to a thaler—Ferdinand's finances figure largely throughout—and one thaler was worth about three shillings.

"*1st January.*

"Got up at eight, feeling very cheerful although I was late last night. Went to see Isidore Gerstenberg. When I complained of having no money—I only had five groschen left—he offered to lend me some. But I refused. I went on to Manatschal to breakfast, spent three of my groschen and read the *Journal des Débats*. Before that I had been with Hein to Hesse to play billiards, but billiards are not allowed while church services are going on, so we could not play. After breakfast I went home and then to Samuel Gerstenberg. He had just got out of bed. He dressed and we went to Häsel and played billiards. We both played very badly and took a long time over it. Some of the people looking on got impatient and laughed at us. This embarrassed me, so I only played two games though I won both. Then I watched the others. One man played extremely well, like a professional. He mostly betted on individual balls. He was a Christian, not of good family. He offered Samuel a start of forty and challenged him to a game for four groschen. I told Samuel I would play if he put up the money. Samuel wanted me to put up two groschen myself, but I wouldn't. Finally we arranged that I should play the man for two groschen a game, Samuel going fifty-fifty with me. I lost the first game but won the second, third and fourth. I then wanted to stop in spite of the fuss made by my opponent. I had not really wanted to play the first game—it was against my principles—and did not want to go on. Although I still like billiards it is no longer a passion. However my opponent who had lost four groschen insisted on double or quits. I refused, but let myself be persuaded by Samuel, though only on the express condition that this was the last game. I won, divided my eight good groschen with Samuel and went out, laughing at my extremely exasperated opponent. I arranged to go to the Gerstenbergs at two. Then I borrowed eight more nice groschen from Isidore so as to have money for the afternoon and went home. . . .

"In my room I found this diary and a scarf. I guessed they were both for me. I had told my father I wanted a scarf and he had got me one, though it was not the sort I wanted. I made up my mind, however, not to say so to my father. His aim was to please me, and I am too thoughtful to say 'Father, you made a mistake, I don't want this sort of thing'. I am not like my mother in these little matters. I was especially touched by my father's kindness because I had been playing billiards which he has forbidden me to do. Why do I play billiards? It is a fault of mine that I do not obey my father's orders blindly but always think them over and ask myself 'Why does my father forbid this?' In this case I had reached this conclusion: my father would not object to my playing billiards now and then. He forbade me because he was afraid it might become a passion with me—which was quite possible in view of my sanguine temperament. I used at one time to ignore his order because billiards was a passion with me. Now it is no longer so, and can never become a passion again. Apart from love one never has the same passion twice. Therefore I can play without going against the spirit of my father's order. I believe in the saying 'The letter killeth, but the spirit giveth life'. Though what I do is against the letter of my father's order, I am not acting against the spirit which caused him to make it. I do not really know if I am right or wrong."

We have here a pre-view, quite apart from the "sanguine temperament", of many of the parts later to be played by the grown-up man: the man about town, the gambler—albeit with a sharp eye to his money—the critic, the casuist, the affectionate son. In an entry a few days later the boy of fourteen reveals yet another Lassalle—the Man who knows about Women. The people mentioned were various friends of the family:

"Mother had asked Herr and Fräulein Skutsch, Madame N. and Cousin Dorchen to come on an expedition to Kroll and later to have supper with us. They arrived at our house at two. Dr. Shiff also came. I dressed and went into the drawing-room. 'Dr. Shiff,' I whispered, 'how do you like Madame N.?' 'She's marvellous. If only I could . . .' 'Nothing easier,' I answered, 'I'll tell you what to do and you go boldly ahead—

'If you treat her gently
Probably you'll get her
But if you act boldly
You will do much better.'

'You're an angel,' cried Dr. Shiff, and took me across to Madame N. where he proceeded to make himself agreeable.

"We came back from Kroll at about six. . . . After supper Madame N. sat on the sofa, Shiff pulled his chair up close and I sat on her other side. Shiff and I proceeded to open fire from both flanks. The Doctor is clever, and the N. had her work cut out to counter him. I was also in good form.

"Madame N. broke into a flow of compliments about me. Then Shiff turned to my sister. 'Your brother is extremely clever,' he said. 'Who ever doubted it?' she answered proudly.

"Suddenly Shiff said to the N. 'Madame, if only I had seen you at your wedding.' 'I had that pleasure,' I called out excitedly. 'I shall never forget her. Just think of those soulful eyes half-opened, half cast-down, ringed with tears that made them seem still darker, a myrtle wreath in her bridal hair, a white shimmering dress over these lovely limbs. . . .' 'Enough, my son, you're getting too poetical,' called out my father half in fun and half in disapproval. Madame softly pressed my hand and the thought came to me if only I were twenty years old."

Later in the evening Shiff asked Ferdinand to suggest a definite plan of campaign.

" 'Listen,' I said. 'Take the N. home. On the way ask if you can call on her to-morrow. She won't say no. To-morrow you call. Her husband is away. Brother-in-law will be in his office. Probably she will be alone. And then, full steam ahead and I don't mind betting Monsieur N. will soon deserve our pity.'

"When it was time to go it turned out that Lachs had

already offered (through my sister) to take Madame N. home and she had accepted. On my advice Shiff went with them. Here the rest of the story. As Lachs was there Shiff did not ask if he might call. All the same next day he did call. Unluckily the N.'s sister was there. A story reached us that the N. was surprised that Shiff should be so forward. I heard this from two sources, and so suppose she did say something of the sort. But I explain it like this; the N. must have been rather friendly to Shiff, and her sister-in-law afterwards tackled her with this in the presence of Lachs. Quite possibly she—the N.—may have then said something against Shiff so as to put herself in a good light. Shiff told me she had been very nice to him and pressed him to come again. But when I told him what she was supposed to have said he felt insulted and decided not to make a second call. But for this Monsieur N. would no doubt by now be in a state deserving of our pity."

2

IT WAS not a restful household. All four of them were quick-tempered. "My mother, so good in other ways, cannot get rid of a tendency to quarrel and nag, which makes both herself and my dear father unhappy. She will even quarrel about a piece of ribbon." Riekchen the sister was of not dissimilar temperament. There were frequent rows between mother, daughter and Emilie, the family dependant who lived with them. There is a record of one such occasion in late January. Riekchen burst into tears and Ferdinand realised she was deliberately prolonging the scene so as to involve their father who was then due back in the home.

"In a moment I thought it all out. . . . Foaming with rage I threw myself on my knees, wringing my hands wildly and shouting so that my voice became hoarse. 'Oh God, oh God,' I screamed, 'let me remember this, grant that I never forget this moment! You serpent with your crocodile's tears! You will repent of what you are doing by God, I swear by God you will! If I live to be a hundred I shall remember it to my death bed and you will remember it too!' I was completely exhausted. My mother held on to me, and my sister, now really frightened, dried her tears. They had great difficulty in soothing me. But it is only by war that peace can be obtained and this outburst of mine had been the only possible means of securing calm. My proud sister was sobered. She went off to her room."

In this atmosphere father and son became natural allies. Old Heymann was disappointed whenever the boy (who wanted to play billiards in a café) made some excuse to avoid joining the family on some expedition. "But what am I to do?" we find him saying on one occasion. "Your mother is deaf. Riekchen is just an ignorant girl. If you are there at least I have some one to talk with."

But Heymann himself was quick-tempered and the wilful, precocious and sensitive boy was by no means easy to manage. Ferdinand's dressiness was an ever-latent cause of friction. An incident which started over a pair of trousers ended by frightening both of them.

"*29th January*

"This afternoon I wished to change my inexpressibles. There were no buttons. Then a row began. No one had time to sew on buttons for me. Father told me to change back into my old trousers. 'I cannot bear your being so vain,' he said. 'All right,' I said, 'both pairs are only fit for scarecrows.' This made him angry and he hit me. He told me not to cry. Every word I said only made him angrier. 'I won't allow myself to be beaten like that,' I shouted through my tears. Then he completely lost his temper. He rushed at me and beat me horribly. This stopped my crying; I dried my tears and looked at him contemptuously. I was so pale it frightened me to see myself in the glass. Whatever he said my only answer was a contemptuous smile. It made him want to hit me in the face, but he controlled himself. Calmly I dressed myself, said I had to go to tuition with one of my teachers and went out. I intended to throw myself into the river. When I reached the parapet I stopped. I considered how I was to set about it. 'Go down the steps,' I said to myself. 'When you get to the bottom put one foot into the water and then raise the other. You will fall forward and then it will be over.' Then I began to think of my mother and of my father too. But I walked on towards the steps, as my excitement had taken hold of me. Someone called 'Ferdinand.' I turned round. It was my father, even paler than I was.

" 'What are you doing?'

" 'Looking at the river.'

" 'You needn't go to school. Go into the office.'

"I did so. I sat on the sofa and within half an hour I realised I had done wrong to want to kill myself and give my father such a fright. Because he obviously knew what I meant to do; hence his paleness, his telling me not to go to school—he wanted to give me time to calm down. Also the fact that he came to the office three times to make sure I was there. 'My God,' I thought, 'if I had taken my life what misery I would have caused my parents.' I shuddered. Tom's a cold. All the same I did want to do something wrong to-day, so I then went to Samuel to get him to come and play billiards. . . ."

Heymann seldom made the mistake of trying to talk down to his son. We find the boy taking part, as an equal, in family discussions which then were mostly centred round the problem of marrying off Riekchen. There had already been one suitor, with whose family negotiations had reached an advanced stage. But, luckily as it turned out, the match did not materialise. Ferdinand put the matter very realistically:

"Benoni Herrman & Co. have gone bankrupt. We were all talking about it this evening. My father, rightly, pointed out how fortunate it was that he had not committed himself. If he had, Marcuse would have managed to hold off the crash till after the marriage, and then my father would have had to carry the whole burden. To save his good name he would have paid for his son-in-law, paid and paid until—horrible thought—he was bankrupt too. . . . Thanks be to God and to my father's pertinacity that this devilish scheme never came off."

A cousin, Ferdinand Friedländer, was now under consideration. Young Lassalle did not think much of this connexion.

"Uncle Friedländer", he records, "brought us cakes from Manatschal. The things one does to get a daughter-in-law!" He did what he could to influence Riekchen. " 'I would like to marry Ferdinand,' my sister said to me, 'but when you start frightening me that I would have to live like a clerk's wife——' 'Worse, worse, dear sister,' I answered, 'believe me you will be immeasurably unhappy if you take him. You have no idea.' "

He keeps a keen eye open for possible alternatives:

"A relation of Mme. Paierl, young, speaks four languages, very rich family, has himself 30 to 40,000 Thalers—wants a wife with 15,000, since as a wife, according to the Bible, is to be considered as the half of her husband, she ought to have a fortune equal to half of his. But if the girl is pretty and well educated he would take 10,000."

But Madame Paierl's relation apparently showed no interest. Ferdinand Friedländer remained the most probable bridegroom.

3

YOUNG LASSAL was not of the type that is happy at school. He did not run easily in harness of any kind; and the routine of even a day school is apt to be unkind to little vanities.

"*16th February*

"Dr. Tschirner [the classics master] was taking the class. We were doing the *Odyssey*. He asked one boy a grammatical question. The boy did not know the answer. I did. Tschirner asked another boy, and another. None of them seemed to know. I was burning with joy. The question came nearer and nearer, at last to the boy next to me, and he answered it! In my disappointment I lost the place in my book, and then Tschirner asked me a question. Of course I could not answer and he abused me so roughly that it was horrible. I felt the blood run in my cheeks. I almost cried at having to endure being insulted and abused and made a fool of for a little thing like that. Patience, patience. The time will come."

A few days later there was a similar incident and we find

him writing "Rage took possession of me. In that moment I could have drunk Tschirner's blood."

It was natural that the masters should regard him as a boy in need of discipline, and natural, too, that his reports should often be unsatisfactory. Reports at this particular school were entered in a book which the boys were supposed to have countersigned by their fathers. Young Lassal devised a method of his own to deal with this regulation.

"After dinner my father asked me suddenly: 'Tell me, Ferdinand, what about your reports? It seems strange I haven't seen any for six months.' I felt uncomfortable, but took pains to appear at my ease. I answered 'You know why it was you never saw the last one and the one before.' 'No,' he said, 'I don't know. And the teachers insist on reports being signed by the parents. I must write to the Rector.' My God, if my father writes to the Rector. . . .

"I don't know how it is. I play billiards every Saturday, which my father has strictly forbidden, I forge the signatures on my reports which is also wrong, and yet I love my father with an ecstasy of which only a son is capable. I would willingly give my life to help him. And yet. . . . It is due, I suppose, to sheer light-heartedness. Fundamentally my character is a nice one."

But the report problem was recurrent.

"*28th February*

"To-day Schönborn [the Rector] gave us our reports. Mine, as I could have foretold, was bad. The Rector called my name. I stood up and when he had finished reading the bad entries I replied that I didn't think I had deserved them.

" 'Yes, yes, Lassal,' said Schönborn. 'Your merits never seem to meet with justice. But tell me'—he handed me my report book—'why do I always see your mother's signature and never your father's?'

" 'Because my father is often away,' I said. I turned over the pages. 'But his signature is there too,' I added.

" 'Let me see.'

"I gave him the book again.

" 'Your father has signed once, and that was last year. Is your father away a whole year, or only when you get bad reports?'

" 'No,' I said. I felt sure the Rector would send to my father and ask him to sign the reports himself. 'Even when my father's at home,' I said, 'he sometimes gets my mother to sign the reports.'

" 'That I can explain,' Schönborn shouted, 'by your showing your reports never to your father and only to your mother.' (The man did not realise that my virtuosity was such that I showed them to nobody.) 'That', Schönborn continued, 'I will not allow. Your mother's signature is not enough.'

"He gave me back the book. A vast weight fell from my mind when I got the book in my hand again. But the whole thing was unpleasant. Up till now I had always written my mother's name as a certain sense of respect had prevented me from forging the important 'Heymann Lassal'. But now I had to take the plunge, so next day I brought back my report signed by my father, that is to say by myself, as I am father, mother and son as required.

"In truth, if my father had the right ideas about reports I would show them to him, even if it meant severe punishment. But my father would worry about them, they would be on his mind for weeks and he would never believe me when I told him not to worry about the cackle of fools."

For the moment the crisis had been averted. But it is clear that he knew that it had only been postponed. Sooner or later disclosure was inevitable. He was, not for the last time, caught up in the net of his own cleverness. Characteristically he decided on a drastic remedy. He would have to leave Breslau. He set to work to persuade his father to send him to a commercial school at Leipzig.

4

MEANWHILE, outwardly, life went on its course. Ferdinand's friend Dr. Shiff showed signs of becoming a rip and attracted unfavourable notice in the stricter Jewish circles of Breslau:

"My father said 'My son, a man who knocks up a restaurateur in the middle of the night and makes him open his business just because he wants to eat oysters—there's no good in him.' I said nothing, but thought it was not so bad a thing to eat oysters. My father thinks it the sign of a wastrel. It would be rather nice to be that sort of wastrel."

There are also indications of the boy's more serious side, of his inner convictions and daydreams. For instance this, in early February:

"... I had a talk with Bloch. He wanted to give himself airs and called himself an atheist. But when he saw I didn't agree with him he changed his tune. We talked about the transmigration of souls, about Geiger [a Breslau rabbi], and about Jewry. He was surprised I held so fast to the Jewish faith. Idiot, as if one could not be a good Jew without insisting on kosher food!

"I told him so, and in fact I believe I am one of the best of Jews and that without bothering about ritual. I could risk my life—like the Jews in Bulwer's *Leila*—in order to free the Jews from their present position. I would not even be afraid of the scaffold if I could only make them once more respected. When I go back to the dream of my childhood it has always been to lead the Jews, sword in hand, along the path to their independence."

On his way home from this talk there was an unfortunate anti-climax. "Near our house I fell over so hard that my nose and mouth began to bleed. Some man picked me up and helped me (I could hardly walk) to my father in the store. He was frightened beyond description. As he heard Mother was out he took me upstairs himself and made me bandages with cold water. Nose and mouth were horribly swollen, the skin had been rubbed off and it was very painful. My father kept asking where it hurt; he was almost in tears, the good father.

"He told me not to go to Hiller [one of the schoolmasters]. But I went because I had missed the last lesson. As it was I was sorry I went because Hiller said that if the air got to my wounds the marks would always show. The thought of this made me uncomfortable. I met Isidore who was very upset at my appearance and was very sympathetic.

"When I got back home Mother was there. She knew nothing about it, and was horrified when I told her my adventure. Later my father sent for the doctor who ordered bandages with vinegar. I have a very real fear that my nose will remain swollen like it is. My sister keeps on telling me so. Well, if that were to happen my face would be done for, though I believe that in the end I would not mind so very much. One thing I am certain of—if it does happen I must avoid all female society: for the sight of a woman would make me think what triumphs I might have had but for this damned accident. I would limit myself to male society. In spite of my temperament I would set myself apart just because of my nose. But a certain streak of brutality would appear in my character, as happens to everyone who does not move in the society of ladies."

But fear of a crisis in the matter of the school reports was never absent for long:

"*12th March*

"If I don't manage to be in Leipzig by Easter—God forbid that anything should happen to prevent it—I shall find myself in a very difficult position."

5

THERE ARE frequent references to Ferdinand's finances. He usually won his games of billiards in the cafés, but his winnings were more than swallowed up by what he spent on coffee and cakes. However his pocket money was supplemented by card games for small stakes in the evenings at home. Once when a cold kept him indoors for some days he was very successful in persuading his parents to play with him, and notes: "One's purse flourishes when one's health is weak." But there were other sources of income:

"*15th March*

"On Friday I managed to sell my pocket knife to my mother for ten groschen—two good groschen profit."

for the boy's removal from the Breslau school and his transfer to the Commercial Institute at Leipzig. When, weeks later, Ferdinand resumed his diary all he says of these last Breslau days is this:

"What a curious thing the human heart is! I, who had committed the crime of forging my parents' signature, and who had kept on telling more and more lies to my father, I now prayed in desperate earnestness to God to help me: if he would ensure that my deceit remained hidden I would undertake never to deceive anyone again. After praying I felt relieved. Just as if I could seriously believe that God answers prayers to hide our deceit! But I did feel relieved.

"For safety's sake I decided to stop keeping my diary. I did in fact stop keeping it, and have written all this in some time later."

Chapter 2

LEIPZIG

I

In early May father and son set out from Breslau, spent four days in Berlin, of which Ferdinand records "I will only say I have never had such happy days as those in Berlin," and finally arrived in Leipzig.

The Commercial Institute at Leipzig was not a boarding-school. Pupils had to make their own arrangements about lodgings, and the first task of Heymann Lassal was to find a family with whom Ferdinand could live.

"Among other suggestions as to where I was to live someone mentioned to my father a certain Herr Hander, headmaster of a *Realschule*. We went to his house, and all that we saw there—Herr Hander himself, his wife, the children, the rooms—delighted us. I had not taken to any of the places we had seen before, but this one pleased me enormously. We left, with a promise that he would write to us about the price. Next day he sent a note demanding the enormous sum of 400 thalers. A Herr Rothe had only asked 250, and this my father found too much. But as he liked the Hander house, and as he thought, rightly, that I ought to have the best, he did what I had never expected. Love triumphed over prudence, and my father, in spite of the pain it caused him, agreed with Herr Hander for 300. Every day I see more and more how good my father is and yet I have caused such pain to him!

"I have now been ten days with Herr Hander and like it. . . . My position in the house is most satisfactory. I am not regarded as a boy of fifteen (which might have happened elsewhere) but as a grown up young man of twenty. I have spent all the money my father gave me and have written for more."

2

FERDINAND in his fifteen months at Leipzig was often homesick, often exasperated but seldom bored. An early discovery was the lake in one of the parks, and one of his first letters home contains a carefully drafted request for permission to take swimming-lessons. "I feel my dear mother will have nothing against my learning, as she will realise that not to learn to swim would expose one to more dangers than learning. It will not interfere with my school work: I propose to get up an hour earlier, at 4 a.m., and take my swimming lesson between four and five."

The diary records his daily life and thoughts.

"*21st May*

"This evening Frau Hander's brother came in and brought us the news about the Jews in Damascus. [Note: the massacre of 1840.] It is dreadful to read and dreadful to hear about. . . . There is a horrible truth in one sentence of the reporter's: 'The Jews of this town submit to cruelties that none but these parias could endure without being provoked to terrible attempts at reprisals.' That means even the Christians are surprised at our mean spirit, that we do not rise and prefer death on the field of battle to one in a torture chamber. Were the Swiss more oppressed when they revolted? Could there be any juster revolution than if the Jews of that town were to rebel, set fire to every quarter of Damascus, blow up the powder magazine, and meet death with their tormentors? Cowardly race, you deserve no better fate! Even a worm will turn: you crawl more abjectly. You do not know how to die, or how to destroy, you know nothing of just revenge, or how to go down to the same grave as your enemies, tearing their flesh from their bones in the last death struggle! You were born to be slaves!"

"*19th June*

"I had a letter from Isidore Gerstenberg full of sense, wit and love. But it also said we had drawn a blank in the lottery.

O fate, o fate, why have you done this to me? Isidore enclosed one thaler because I had told him I was short of money. He is, as he writes, very short himself as he lost ten thalers in the lottery. What he sent gave me no pleasure. It is too little to make any show on. In a month and a half I have spent thirteen thalers. What use can one be to me? But I was deeply touched by this proof of his affection."

"*24th June*

"I did a deal with Philippsohn: his new scarf in exchange for my old walking-stick and 12 groschen, which I still have not paid him. What an idiot! The poet Heine was very right in saying 'Fools are my best friends.' "

[Note: Philippsohn and the boys named in the next entry were all fellow-pupils at the Commercial Institute.]

"*26th June*

"This afternoon I went with Fritz to Pfaffendorf. As I had no money I got a thaler from Herr Hander and borrowed eight groschen from Fritz. Soon after we arrived the races started and I lost Fritz. I looked for him till half-past eight without success. I was bored. But all the same I had not spent my money. I went into a restaurant and found there two lads from our Institute, Krager and Glier—half seas over. On their table was an empty wine bottle and some grog glasses. Siegmund joined us. We each put up twelve groschen and had a bottle of champagne. Siegmund left us, and as we had not the money for more champagne we had a bottle of Lunel. Krager was already fuddled and went on drinking grog. We made a hell of a noise and kept drinking to the health of the Commercial Institute. Then we went to see the fireworks. I was drunk, Glier was drunker and drunkest of all was Krager. I felt bitter remorse because all my money was gone except four groschen. When we got to the stand Krager broke away from us. I heard afterwards he was taken home by a policeman. Glier sat down and was sick. The champagne had its effect on me too, but quite a different one. I became poetic. I danced about and shouted 'Long live Bacchus! Long live champagne! Champagne and women!' Every now and then I added 'If you've never been drunk you're not a real man.'

"Someone asked me not to tread on his foot and at once I became quite sober. I made friends with the man whose toes I had been treading on and found he was a shoemaker. We carried the sleeping Glier home; and then to reward the shoemaker I went with him to the Café Français and spent my last four groschen. If I was not a scholar of the Commercial Institute I would have written a fine ode to champagne. But as it is . . ."

3

THE SUMMER HOLIDAYS were now approaching. Ferdinand had so recently arrived that he was to stay on with the Handers. Very possibly, with the shame of the Breslau discomfiture still fresh he had acquiesced in the arrangement; but as the time grew near he was homesick.

"*7th July*

"I don't know what is the matter with me. I have such a yearning for my father, mother and sister, that every time I think of home I burst into tears."

"*13th July*

"I don't know how it is that I get on so badly with the other boys in the school. I never say anything nasty to any of them and try to be friendly to all. Were it not for Isidore and a few more like him I should develop the idiotic idea that I am an idiot."

"*19th July*

"[After going to the theatre to see the play *Fiesco*.] By God this Count Lavagna is a great character! I don't know how it is, though I am as thorough a revolutionary democrat and republican as anyone can find, yet, if I had been in Count Lavagna's place I should have acted just as he did. I should not have been satisfied by being Genoa's first citizen but would have stretched out my hand for the crown. On consideration this boils down to the fact that I am an egoist. Had I been born a prince I would have been an aristocrat heart and soul. As it is I am one of the middle classes, and, therefore, a democrat."

23rd and 24th July

"I am reading Börne's letters which I find very impressive. One sees that Germany is just one great prison where human rights are trodden under foot and thirty million people are oppressed by thirty tyrants. One could cry at the stupidity of these people. They do not break their chains although they could if they had but the will. I admire Börne. But when he says 'No European monarch is so blind as to believe his grandchildren will ascend his throne' I must, I'm afraid, remain sceptical. Things will get worse before they get better."

"*26th July*

"I went on the lake with Fritz. He fell in twice and tore his new trousers. *Sic transit gloria mundi.*"

"*1st August*

"Swimming and boating on the lake, though very respectable occupations, are not in the least cheap. Although I don't play billiards and don't go to confectioners' shops I seem to be spending a lot of money."

"*6th August*

"I am reading *Wilhelm Meister*. Remarkable. With a few differences Meister might be a portrait of myself. Three months ago I too was at the crossways. My heart too beat only for Art —Art which I must put aside, or seem to put aside, in order to learn a trade. But what a difference! Meister was pressed by father and mother and friends to give up his so-called dreams. They made him a tradesman and yet he ran away and devoted himself to Art. But I, although my parents begged me to go on to a university, of my own free will I renounced the æsthetic life in order to become a counter-jumper. And yet I had no illusions. The point is I matured young; I reached my crossroads even earlier. And though my parents exerted no pressure the pressure came from my horrible position which I would have given anything in the world to escape from. I realized I could not go on with that tangle of lies: it was impossible. I wanted to escape from the school and from Breslau before the truth came out. But the truth did come out and then it was too late for me to retract. Anyhow, now, to tell the truth, I do not feel myself bound in any way to give up the thought of public, literary or political life. I have only taken on a temporary occupation; and I firmly believe that fate, or rather Providence, will take me out of the counting house to some scene where I can do my work . . . that I shall be concerned with Freedom rather than markets, and that I shall hate the aristocratic swine who rob mankind more than price-cutting competitors. But I will not let it stop at just hating!"

4

THROUGHOUT the summer and autumn we can watch his boyish ambitions crystallize.

"*24th August*

"I have an indescribable yearning for my parents. There are two extremes at war within me. I want to launch out into the world and win my way by my own effort; and yet again there are times when I can think of nothing better than the peaceful calm of home and my old friends. There are two other warring opposites besides. Shall I aim at cleverness or at virtue? Shall I take the line of least resistance, ingratiate myself with the eminent, win position and importance through subtle intrigues? Or shall I cling to virtue and truth like a stubborn republican, heed nothing else and only strive to give aristocracy its death blow? No, though I have all the talents for it I will not become a smirking cowardly courtier! I will proclaim Freedom to the Peoples even if it costs me my life. I swear it by God and beneath the stars . . . the blood of princes shall flow."

Meanwhile life in the Hander household was not so agreeable as Ferdinand at first expected. Little by little the landlord revealed himself as pompous, shifty and a bore. At first there was no open trouble. Ferdinand became fond of the two small Hander children; and when one of them, Marie, fell ill there are frequent mentions in the diary of the progress of the disease. Early in August Marie died, and on the following day there was an interview with Hander which, as Ferdinand remarked, gave food for thought:

"*6th August*

"This morning Herr Hander started off as follows: 'Lassal,' he said to me, 'I regard your arrival in my house as an act of Fate. I had never thought of taking paying guests. Before I really knew what was happening you were installed. You have seen yourself how cramped we are for space. Our Toni, poor little invalid, who used to be in your room, must now sleep in the vestibule. In summer there is no harm in that, and I thought that before winter came we should be able to devise some arrangement. But neither my wife nor I have been able to do so as all available space is occupied up to and even above its full capacity. My conscience would not have allowed me to expose little Toni to the rigours of winter in the cold vestibule; and it was my intention to write to your father at Christmas to tell him, much as I regretted it, that I could keep you no longer. Now God himself has provided accommodation. Marie is dead, and a room is available.' "

The school reassembled. On the first day of term the boys were told to write an essay on any journey they had made in the holidays. Young Ferdinand produced a paper "A journey from my favourite corner to the front door." He was sufficiently satisfied with it to preserve it: and his masters do not seem to have resented his flippancy. But as the autumn wears on there are signs of friction. As at Breslau he resented the efforts of the teaching staff to keep him in his place. Early in November he was reprimanded by the Director, Schiebe, in front of the class, whereupon "I said to him, quietly, but with a firm look: 'Sir, you should not forget yourself.' This made him very angry." A few days later he records "But for thoughts of my father I would tell him truths he never heard before." Schiebe and Hander were personal friends and the boy often suspected that they were discussing him.

On the 26th Ferdinand was ill, and stayed in bed reading Byron:

"I have to get out of bed at the risk of catching cold to prevent the fire going out. If I want anything I have to get out of bed and go to the stairs to call Emily who generally does not answer till I have stood there shivering for half an hour. I am fed on watery soup and treated like a dog. On top of all which my chimney smokes and when I complain their only answer is that it always smokes when the wind is that way. . . . I have never come across anything so surly, unhelpful and stupid as Emily. She is too far beneath me for me to quarrel with her, but I will punish her at Christmas."

He was still in bed three days later and four of his friends came to see him. One of them worked as junior clerk to a wine merchant. The boys pulled his leg by maintaining his firm did not stock any real French champagne. The victim pulled out as evidence a genuine champagne cork which he had in his pocket. "We looked at the cork, and then I threw it into a corner with the idea that if anyone found it they would think I had had champagne."

Things took their course.

"Frau Hander came to me and after a lot of roundabout innuendoes came out at last with 'Didn't you have champagne here on Sunday?' I said 'Yes,' partly because I see no harm in having champagne and partly because I wanted to punish her inveterate suspiciousness which is always making her imagine mysteries and want to show off by spying them out. My unexpected avowal disconcerted her. But when I went on to explain this was just a joke, no one had thought of drinking champagne and the cork was just an accident, she at once convinced herself that I had in fact been drinking. That is how a suspicious mind works. She made a long speech and said she would not tell her husband, though I know perfectly well she will spread it round all over the place. I answered politely that she could tell whomever she liked."

"*2nd December*

"Zander [one of the four] came and told me Schiebe had been holding an enquiry at the school as to whether or not there had been a champagne party in my room on Sunday. Of course he got no evidence and the only result is to make Frau Hander look foolish."

"*3rd December*

"I had a serious talk with Herr Hander. He admitted, *pauvre diable*, that his wife is wearing him down, day and night, by continuous complaints about my behaviour; in particular that I do not treat her with due respect in the presence of others. I explained quite clearly that it was Frau Hander who was invariably rude to me in the presence of my school friends, which, I said, I could not tolerate, particularly when she proceeded to make unprovoked attacks on my friends. Herr Hander admitted I had right on my side. All he could say was that his wife was wearing him down and that for the sake of peace and quiet he must write to my father: 'Herr Lassal, I am very sorry but your son and my wife cannot get on. Please take him away.' I agreed that was all he could do, expressed my sympathy, and began to hum

" 'Honour be to Woman,
Woman who contrives
To weave Heaven's roses
In our earthly lives.' "

5

BUT EVEN the daily round had some compensations. He struck up a friendship with some of his schoolfellows, especially Wilhelm Becker and Zander, although there were others, like Moewes, of whom he did not approve. And there was the intoxicating experience of making a first public speech, on the departure of Hülsse, one of the masters at the Commercial Institute.

"*Late Autumn*

"I am getting better acquainted with Wilhelm Becker. Once one really knows him he is good company. He has spirit, but is not nearly such an egoist as Moewes, and I believe he is capable of real friendship. We often go and play billiards. He is fond of the other sex and this sometimes raises the animal in him, though not so much or so often as with Moewes. I don't know how it is but I could never go with a prostitute. I have to be roused by a woman's beauty, I have to be in love or believe I am in love (which is much the same thing), I must want to possess a particular woman. I could never be moved by a crude animal urge. But I would not blame anybody for wanting to possess the charms of someone who had really aroused him, and for doing anything (as long as it was not dishonourable) in order to possess those charms."

"*19th December*

"The hour strikes and Hülsse makes his farewell speech. I look round to see if any one is going to reply but no one stirs. ... I stand up to save the honour of the class and make a speech. I don't really know what I said as it was quite extemporary—just what came into my head. But the emotion it caused in Hülsse and the applause and thanks of the whole class were proof that I had done the job well."

"*20th December*

"To-day I met Zander's family. His sister made a great impression on me. She is extremely pretty, just right for kissing. Most unluckily I am still too young for that sort of thing. Patience, *mon petit ami*, the moment will come. Meanwhile I made myself as agreeable as I could."

At the end of the year Herr and Frau Lassal had their silver wedding. It had not been suggested that Ferdinand should go home for it, but when the time came the desire to go was overwhelming. He approached the Handers who interceded with Schiebe. Permission was granted and off he went, arriving in time for dinner on the day of the anniversary, to the surprise and delight of his family, and the delirious joy of himself. He stayed three or four nights in Breslau and travelled back to Leipzig by himself. He had to wait in Görlitz for a connexion, and there he met a family friend, one Reissner. He wrote to tell his father about this meeting:

"Herr Reissner and I passed the time as best we could, ate, chatted, etc. I suggested we should change roles, i.e. that he should go on to the school in Leipzig and I return to Breslau as Herr Reissner. He refused, saying his wife would not like it; so I said I would do all in my power to console Frau Reissner, which made him laugh very heartily, but he still would not agree."

Soon after his return to Leipzig there was trouble. On the 5th January Zander came to see him and the two boys broke a lamp. Two days later Ferdinand broke a chandelier. He came back from school to his midday meal to find Hander very angry.

"Hander announced:

" 'Zander is not to come here any more.'

" 'Why not?'

" 'Because you two are as rowdy as a pair of common guttersnipes.'

" 'No, we aren't.'

"Hander sprang up in a fury.

" 'You impertinent, ill-bred, conceited puppy, how dare you say that you are not when I have told you that you are? Go to your room. You will have your meals by yourself there till Easter. I will write and tell Schiebe.'

"I tried to calm him but he only got angrier. He followed me up to my room and saw where the broken lamp had made a mess on the carpet.

" 'Idiot,' he screamed, 'Dirty little beast! The only thing to do is to smack your head!'

"He went out and came back again with the chandelier.

" 'That's a nice thing to do,' he said.

" 'I was clumsy.'

" 'You wait. I shall get even with you.'

" 'My God,' I said, 'it isn't a crime to break a chandelier.'

" 'Not a crime? That's the sort of idea you get from your poet Heine.'

"I looked at him contemptuously.

" 'I am going to take the lamp and the chandelier to Schiebe. You'll see. And don't look at me like that or I'll knock you straight through the window.' "

Ferdinand records that he reached for the inkpot and meditated drastic action. But then he thought of his father and restrained himself. Two days later the storm had blown over.

"*18th January*

"Apart from school my stay in Leipzig has not been unpleasant. And even the dreary hours in class are made more tolerable by my friend Wilhelm Becker. On Saturdays and Sundays there are generally skating or whist parties, or visits to Rosalie (Zander), so that life goes on happily till Schiebe gets tiresome again. Meanwhile I have taught myself to regard him with humorous contempt, so he can bark as much as he likes. Unfortunately I can't prevent his biting....

"It is depressing that my friend Wilhelm is one of those who thinks my enthusiasm for ideal friendship is a form of emotionalism."

"*28th February*

"To-day there was a crisis that I have long been thinking would come. The point is my clothes are so shabby that my acquaintances stare at me, and that Wilhelm, who is completely frank as a friend ought to be, either laughs or gets angry.

"Before I ever came here my father was annoyed at my thinking so much about clothes, and made a point of not giving way to me. He would say I was vain etc. which used to lead to long arguments. But my wardrobe was never so bad as it is here at the Commercial Institute. . . . Wilhelm got sarcastic. But what could I do? One has one's little vanities, even *vis-à-vis* one's best friends. I was ashamed to confess to Wilhelm that I ought to dress properly and it was only my father's whim which forced me to have, like God, only one coat and a very poor one at that. All I could do was to imitate the fox and the grapes and say I cared nothing for clothes; which engendered a form of cynicism quite foreign to my nature. I am not a mere dandy or tailor's model: but I wish to allot due care to my dress. The nineteenth century view is that clothes make the man; and it is foolish for a man, who depends on and gets his living through other men, to mock at the views or even prejudices of his generation. He can despise and laugh at them in his innermost heart: but openly defy them, no. If he does he is a fool.

"It is obviously a pleasure to everyone to look in the glass and see himself well dressed. But to dress smartly simply in order to look at a mirror is the sign of a fop or a fool. My clothes are to please others. I dress smartly for the sake of others. And my father is wrong to oppose me. Anyhow my wardrobe is so wretched that even Frau Hander has often said: 'Really, Lassal, if you didn't carry it off so well you would look like a tramp.'

"To-day I made a bold decision. . . .

"I said to Wilhelm: 'Come along to your tailor's.' We went and I ordered a coat, trousers, waistcoat, boots even, all so smart that even Wilhelm could want nothing better. And I promised myself that from now on—come what may—I will always dress smartly. I will not call this promise a solemn oath; but perhaps it will be easier to keep it just because it isn't a solemn oath."

6

A MORE serious crisis arose out of the visit of his cousin Friedländer. Ferdinand Friedländer had now been finally approved as the bridegroom for Riekchen Lassal; and he stepped off at Leipzig, on his way from Paris to the betrothal ceremony at Breslau. In Paris he had been laying the foundations of his career as a resourceful international company promoter, a career which led to his ennoblement as the "Chevalier de Friedland". Most of those with whom he was associated—including his wife and his future brother-in-law—found sooner or later good reason to mistrust him. But for the moment he was in high favour. The diary records:

"*9th March*

"Originally, when the marriage was first suggested, I was one of Ferdinand's keenest supporters. When he left Breslau my views seemed to change . . . all the unfriendly gossip about him, even though I didn't believe it, must have aroused my suspicions. I also doubted whether Riekchen would go on being fond of him. Things went so far that I even opposed his suit. But in Leipzig I returned to my original attitude. . . .

"Nothing did me so much good as Ferdinand's arrival. After six months among *cretins* and *canaille* it is a real joy to be with someone who can understand one."

Friedländer's arrival made him stay away from school, and although his cousin both wrote and called to explain the circumstances it was unavailing. Young Ferdinand was called before the Synod of the Commercial Institute.

"*11th March*

". . . I went in. The Director Schiebe sat in the middle, the other teachers in a semi-circle round him. I stood by the door with folded hands. . . . Hate, contempt, mockery, pain, grief, rage, indifference, swept one after the other through my breast. But I gave no sign of what was going on inside me, and forced my features to a calm quite out of keeping with my position.

" 'Come nearer.'

"The Director then read out my so-called crime. Then began a drama well worth seeing. Schiebe, Schierholz and Feller were the speakers: the others said nothing. These three however went on and on. In spite of the contempt I felt for them I became depressed. I pictured myself as a dead eagle, lying on a field, with crows and starlings picking out my eyes and nibbling the flesh from my bones. But suddenly life came back to me and I arose; the crows and starlings flew squawking away and I soared upwards towards the sun. . . .

" 'Gentlemen,' said Feller, that personification of falsity, '*Messieurs*, we must realize that Lassal regards things with the eye of a philosopher. We are not his superiors. He will not admit the conception of superiors. We are his inferiors because we are paid. Lassal takes no cognisance of Love, Respect or

Gratitude. The Heart and all emotions of the Heart mean nothing to him. He cares for no one. His basic principle is to pretend love so long as he can make use of anyone.'

" 'A nice basic principle,' said the Old Man. 'In this way he manages to create a *façade*.'.

" 'A *façade*,' repeated Schierholz.

" 'A *façade*,' said Feller like an echo.

" 'Your best course,' said the Old Man, 'would be to go on the stage. You could play Shylock one day and another bad part the next, since you are capable of playing any bad part.'

"And so on and so on.

"They told me to go out. When I was called in again Schiebe read me out the sentence: three weeks' house arrest. When I got home Hander had already had a letter from Schiebe notifying him of my house arrest."

" 12*th March*

"The first day of my house arrest. Wilhelm Moewes and Zander came to console me. Luckily I had little need of consolation. I do not take the punishment seriously; it is hardly a punishment at all. The opinion of Schiebe, Schierholz etc. is of even less interest. I think of the great poet banished to Asia Minor and say with him:

" '*Hic sum barbarus quia non intelligor illis*.' "

(It should of course be *Barbarus hic ego sum*, etc. Lassalle had a lasting weakness for not verifying his quotations.)

7

FROM NOW on there was no prospect of young Ferdinand ever being reconciled to his life as a pupil of the Leipzig Commercial Institute. The glimpse of the great world brought by his cousin Friedländer and the show-down with the school authorities came at a time when his mind was inflamed with eager day-dreams born of the writings of Börne, Heine and the revolutionary romantics. His restlessness came out in various ways. There was the familiar homesickness.

"To-day was the Passover. . . . Memories of happy past days came back to me. I saw us all sitting at the long festive table, my dear father at the head with his fine sonorous voice, next to him my dear pious mother, looking anxiously round to see that all the ritual was being observed as strictly as it had been in her childhood; at the bottom Riekchen with smiling rosy cheeks, inwardly giggling at the unintelligible ceremonies, busily intent on trying to avoid the bitter *Moraur*; and then Lachs, Schaitzer and Orgler holding up their big *Haggadahs* to hide their laughter at some joke. And then a sharp look from my dear mother's watchful eyes, after which she returns to her pious calm."

There was a time when he dreamed of setting up as knight errant on behalf of Frau Hander: Hander, he found out, had been up to dubious manœuvres to get possession of his wife's dowry, and Ferdinand's urge to champion the oppressed made him forget the real or imaginary indignities he had suffered at his landlady's hands. There were times when he endeavoured to work up a revolutionary spirit among his fellow-pupils: we have the fragment of a letter to his father—undated but obviously belonging to this period:

". . . Robespierre . . . and set flame, with all the fiery eloquence I can command, to the damp cold hearts of German youth. I work everywhere and with every means; but, alas, our Commercial Institute is no *Ecole Polytechnique*. With the mid-day meal my best speeches are forgotten, and all the courage I have inspired is snuffed out by one threatening look from the headmaster. Yet thanks to my efforts the revolutionary feeling still endures. . . ."

But the main, the concrete problem was this: was he or was he not prepared to complete the course at the Commercial Institute and take his place in the family business at Breslau? He faced the issue squarely, made his decision and carried it through.

"*5th April*

"Now I am at the cross roads. I still have time to turn back. Woe, woe, if I ever have to suffer the self-reproaches of a wasted life, if some voice called to me: 'God gave you noble powers for a noble task and you have let them rot.'"

Undated (*Summer* 1841).

"A very important period has just gone by. My father was here. I told him my wish, my irrevocable decision to study at a university. He was at first surprised; then said he would think it over. I went so far as to say he need not think it over, he need only give his consent, for I would never retract from my decision.

"It was admittedly going too far on my part to leave my father no choice. In any case I had a severe internal struggle. My father told me how he had hoped I would take on the burden which now weighed so heavily on his shoulders. He was old and tired and had wished to end his days in peace. Now, if I persisted in my resolve, he would have to start the struggle afresh for the sake of Riekchen and Ferdinand. That made it very hard for me. . . .

"He asked me what I wanted to study.

"'The greatest subject in the world,' I said. 'The subject bound up with the holiest interests of mankind. The study of history.'

"My father asked me how I expected to live, as I could not hope for any school or academic post in Prussia; and I would not wish to cut myself off from my parents. [At that time in Prussia no Jew might hold an academic post. To obtain one therefore he would have to cut himself off from his family by becoming baptised.] If that could only be avoided! I told him I would make a living somehow.

"He asked me why I would not study medicine or law.

"'Doctors and lawyers,' I said, 'are tradesmen who sell their knowledge. So are some professors.'

"I wanted to study my subject for its own sake.

"My father asked me if I felt I was a poet.

"'No,' I said, 'but I want to write. Now is the time to fight for humanity's highest ideals. Up to the end of the last century the world was bound in the chains of superstition. Then there arose a physical power, engendered by the might of the spirit, which shattered the existing order into fragments. This first outbreak was terrible. It had to be thus. Since then the struggle has continued uninterrupted. It has been fought not with physical weapons but with those of the spirit. In every land and every nation men have arisen with the sword of the word, have fallen or conquered. This struggle for the noblest aims is being fought with the noblest means. It is true that later on truth must be backed by force; the crowned heads will not have it any other way. Meanwhile we will not excite the peoples. No, we will enlighten and illumine them.'

"My father was silent for some time. Then he said: 'My son, I do not deny the truth of what you say, but why should you, personally, make yourself a martyr? You are our only hope and support. Freedom must be won; but it will be won, even without your help. Stay with us. Make us happy. Don't throw yourself into the battle. Even if you win, we shall lose. We lived for you. Make it up to us. You, just yourself, can make no difference to the struggle. Let those fight who have nothing to lose, people whose parents' hearts do not depend on their fate.'

"He is right. Why should I become a martyr? But if everyone spoke like that and withdrew, would any fighter be left?

"But why should *I* be a martyr?

"Why? Because in my breast there is a voice from God that calls me to battle; because God has given me the strength to fight. Because I can fight and suffer for a noble cause. Because I will not deceive God who has given me this strength for one special purpose. Because I cannot do otherwise.

"Finally we reached a point at which my father said he would make up his mind by Michaelmas. Till then he will think it over. But we are, to a certain extent, at cross purposes. He is not against my studying at a university. He is against my state of mind. That is why I say he doesn't understand me. He allows me to study and yet he tries to oppose the great, holy, all-pervading Idea that he calls Liberalism. As if it was not just that which is driving me to study, for which I mean to fight, and but for which I should have been content to remain as I am!"

Chapter 3

THE STUDENT

I

We have little knowledge of Ferdinand's life at home between school and university. Years later he appears to have told Countess Hatzfeldt of frequent quarrels with his father. We are told that on one occasion old Heymann banished him from his presence; so that Ferdinand took up quarters in an attic where his mother and sister brought him food and where, day and night, he read for his examinations. In any case there is evidence that he took tuition in certain subjects from various Breslau teachers. One contemporary has left a record of him: "He developed an iron determination to study. For days on end he never left the house. When we went to see him he received us in an elegant velvet dressing-gown amid piles of books and papers. He did not limit himself to the set subjects, but already went in for all sorts of literary and philosophic studies."

Early in 1842 he applied for permission to sit for the matriculation examination. On the 20th January his application was refused on the grounds that the requisite period had not elapsed since his entry into the proscribed secondary school grade. On the 19th February he appealed to the Prussian Minister of Education. Some weeks later, when the examinations had already started, his appeal was allowed and permission was accorded for him to sit. He seems to have done well both in his written work and his *viva.* Greatest scope for self expression was given by the German essay: "The Development of the idea of the Humane". He pleased his examiners: "Lassal, who has been influenced by modern, principally Jewish, writers, showed a not unnatural tendency to confuse 'humane' with 'tolerant' and with 'liberal'. But his intelligence and his facility of expression marked him out from the other examinees, and in these respects we considered his effort to have been the best."

In spite of this Ferdinand failed to pass. He had aroused the hostility of Dr. David Schulz, the Commissioner presiding over the examining body. It is suggested that the motive was personal; Schulz had a son, older than Ferdinand, who had not yet matriculated. In any case Lassal was of the type to inspire mistrust in an orthodox professor. Schulz refused to accept the examiners' favourable reports. "His German essay," wrote Schulz, "on the conception of the Humane is a hotch-potch of undigested and misunderstood phrases, devoid alike of any appreciation of subject or of form; and with a number of errors both in grammar and spelling. I would particularly emphasize his faulty punctuation, which is also noticeable in his other work." Schulz proceeded to browbeat the examiners into reversing their decision. Ferdinand was ploughed. Again he made an elaborate appeal to the Minister of Education; his appeal spent five months going round the Ministry and was finally rejected. He had to wait till the following year.

2

FERDINAND'S university career was divided between Breslau and Berlin. The year from Easter 1843 to Easter 1844 he was in Breslau, and the following year in Berlin. He spent the summer of '45 in Breslau, returning to Berlin that autumn. It was in his early days as an undergraduate at Breslau that he became a Hegelian, and, as he afterwards wrote, "changed my skin for the third time. Philosophy took possession of me, and it was in this spirit that I was born again. This second birth gave me everything, gave me clarity, self-assurance . . . made of me self-containing Intellect, that is self-conscious God." Ferdinand's language about himself was always extravagant, but it is true that the impact of Hegel was of decisive and lasting influence. Hegelian dialectics were for him an instrument that enabled him to solve, in his own favour and to his own satisfaction, all intellectual, moral and political problems that confronted him. It was here that he obtained that self-assurance—so exasperating to so many of those around him—that was at once his main source of strength and his ultimate weakness. Incidentally it was Hegelian philosophy that emancipated him from the revolutionary romanticism of Heine. It made him a "determined socialist", but one within the limits of Hegelian evolutionary idealism. For him the new social order was to come not as a consequence of barricades, of risings or conspiracies but in the train of the inevitable triumph of the Hegelian idea.

This is not to imply that his life as a student was a peaceful one. Given his temperament that would have been impossible. He joined a Breslau student association—the Raczeks—devoted to the study of Hegel and his successors, Feuerbach, Ruge, Echtemayer. A contemporary has left a picture of young Lassal with his pale cheeks and "Grecian profile", his high voice, his complete self assurance and his uncanny quickness in argument. The Raczeks were of a decidedly Radical tendency, and on various occasions, in which Ferdinand played a prominent part, came into collision with the authorities. But when, in the middle 'forties, distress among the Silesian weavers led to a series of disorders in Breslau we find him indignant that the troops were not called out. "Public order and peace are too holy to be exposed to the arbitrary assaults of the mob."

In April 1844 he moved to Berlin. His first letter to his father is chiefly concerned with the difficulty of finding rooms. Rooms in the centre of the town were expensive; rooms in unfashionable suburbs were inconvenient, uncongenial and also not cheap. He solved the problem by taking a large room at 52 Unter den Linden with an impecunious student cousin who made a small contribution to the rent. "It is always an advantage," he wrote, "to have some trustworthy person living in the house with one. And in this particular case I shall be more or less in the position of having a servant."

A subsequent letter, dated 13th May, gives details of his studies and his way of life:

"I wanted to attend a lot of lectures. I got a list and marked those that seemed most interesting. . . . For a fortnight I went to Gabler and Trendelenburg on Logic; and you can class me as an idiot if they did anything but mumble the dreariest of platitudes. It is not the professors' fault, it is the whole system here of philosophical education that is wrong. . . . It would have been a deadly sin against my so precious time to attend such lectures. So I tore up my list and dropped the whole philosophical school except Gabler on Logic. That is I don't go to his lectures but I am keeping my name on the roll and paying the fees—one has to be enrolled for one course. . . . As it is I only go to two lectures—Benary, five days a week, on the Books of the Old Testament, and Panofka, twice a week, on Monuments of Greek Art.

"My normal programme is like this. I get up a little before 4 o'clock, work on Hegel till 9, go to my lecture; come back at 10, undress and put on nightshirt, dressing-gown and slippers and work straight on till 10 at night. About 10 I go to bed. I undress on coming back from the lecture at 10 in the morning because I don't go out again. I usually have my midday meal at home—only about twice a week do I go out for it. When I eat at home I have bread and butter. In general I have accustomed myself to eating very little. At home I used to take three rolls and butter for breakfast; now I just have a cup of coffee at 4 and eat nothing at all till twelve noon. Then I have some bread and butter; I have a cup of coffee during the afternoon and then supper of bread and butter at seven. I never feel hungry and am in excellent health. I don't go out to meals partly to save money but chiefly because staying in saves time and gives me an uninterrupted day's work. I am very pleased with my work and that is saying a lot because I am my own severest judge. In the summer I intend to give up coffee, which is expensive. That I can do easily, but my attempt to give up smoking was a failure. It is strange, I can give up anything else, but not, apparently, that. I am also playing with the thought of doing without butter."

Four days later he sent his father his monthly budget. Rent, six thalers, was the largest item; meals out and food at home together came to four. This last was made possible by his having already given up coffee. Three thalers were allotted to cigars. The total budget, including 15 groschen for "unforeseen expenses and pocket money" comes to just over twenty thalers, or about £3. He required no new clothes for the current year, and so envisaged a substantial saving on his monthly allowance of 33 thalers. He finished his letter, characteristically, by requesting an immediate advance of 80 thalers (to buy books) to be refunded in monthly instalments out of this saving.

3

OTHER LETTERS to his father tell of his inner thoughts and aspirations:

"Since you seemed anxious, in your last letter, about my 'subversive tendencies' I can and must reassure you that there is no cause whatever for such fears. There is not the slightest risk that I shall be inspired by revolutionary emotion to rush out into the street. On the contrary, I, as a Hegelian, know perfectly well that one must wait; and that the only way in which an individual can hasten the march of events is by disseminating culture and philosophy. And there is no call for you to worry yourself about my studies. I am concentrating exclusively on the task of working out my system, a task I can only begin in two years' time. For I shall need at least two or three years in preliminary studies and researches—indeed I shall be lucky if two or three years will be enough: the field to be covered is enormous. . . ."

In September there was an international Industrial Exhibition in Berlin, and young Lassal made it the occasion of a declaration of faith.

"For me" (he writes to his father) "the Exhibition had an interest quite different in kind from that of the gaping throng who crowd the halls. It is my aim now to set out the essential Idea of industry, its connexion with and its importance for the Age in which we live."

He begins by explaining that Christianity was a milestone in human development in that it established the concept of justification of the individual personality as such, in opposition to the Greek and Jewish concepts of justification by race. But this fundamental Christian concept was incompatible with the structure of medieval society, based on hereditary castes. Thus there came the French Revolution with its insistence on the unrestricted freedom of the individual ego. But the French Revolution gave only "formal" liberty: it did not guarantee to the individual that modicum of property necessary for the satisfaction of individual needs, and without which real liberty is impossible. Society therefore became an arena, with every individual struggling for the acquisition of property. Out of the idealism of the Revolution there grew materialism. "Modern Materialism is only the inevitable result of an abstract Ideal, the ideal of abstract freedom. And at the same time it is the direct negation of all idealism and freedom. This is the so-called Dialectic of History." The error of the French Revolution was not fully to realise that the human individual is not isolated. The individual can only attain perfection as member of a community.

Ferdinand goes on to consider industry which he defines as the symbol and instrument of man's internecine materialistic struggle. Industry provides the means of reconciling the old feudal class differences with the new spirit of "abstract" equality introduced by the French Revolution. At the same time it contradicts the principles of the Revolution in that it reduces subjective personality to dependence on material objectivity, i.e. money. Further, there are two sides to industry—the subjective "human" side, i.e. the workers, and the objective "dead" side, i.e. the capitalists made dependent on their capital by the workings of free competition. Finally by a complicated process of Hegelian reasoning he deduces the inevitable end of the system of free competition and its supersession by the Communist State. Then industry will be an organised totality, entailing the negation of the principle of property, and man's subjective individuality will come to real fruition in the conception of the State as an organised whole.

Such is the bald outline of this formidable forty-page letter. We have no record of the effect it produced on old Heymann, but Ferdinand himself had no doubts of its importance. "I have" [he concludes] "spent three days writing this letter, used seven nibs and smoked 39 cigars. I would like to write a lot more, but I would miss the post. When are you going to Leipzig? We might meet there. Bring this letter with you. It contains much that was hitherto only in my head and I want to have a record of it. It would mean time and trouble writing it all down again."

4

BUT HIS LIFE did not always proceed with the austere and scholarly calm which these particular letters would suggest. His cousin seems soon to have left the lodgings; and thereafter Ferdinand became embroiled in a series of quarrels with the landlady, who tried to put up the rent, made a fuss about bringing up water, and wanted to charge one groschen a day for cleaning the coffee machine and a further five per month for use of the commode (there being no water closet). Then there were his clothes. A contemporary has recorded how he would spend an hour at a time in front of the mirror, "adjusting his tie to the right degree of negligence." The houses he frequented were mostly those of well-to-do Jews, who in these early days of their intellectual and social emancipation were beginning to make their mark upon Berlin. This society, however, was not sufficient. On the 30th July he wrote to his mother:

"And now a request. I am taking riding lessons. I would have done so before but I was deterred by the expense. That, however, is no longer so important now that the gas business has been put through. Also I was much moved by your anxiety that I should have some exercise: the Breslau doctors declared riding to be good for the abdomen. Again, I would like to learn now, as later I may have neither the wish nor the opportunity. Finally I don't disguise the fact that after my strenuous work I want and indeed need some recreation."

Then follows an eight-page dissertation on Hegelian lines on the subject of recreation, social recreation, society in Berlin and Jewish and Christian society generally.

"All this", he continues, "is to explain why social life does not afford me recreation and why I have to seek it in things which may not excite the intellect, but at least do not repel and insult it. All these considerations led me to expend the sum of twelve thalers and I took a course of riding lessons, which gave me much entertainment and taught me a good deal. My seat is nearly perfect. But I still find great difficulty in controlling the horse. To remedy this and to make sure I do not forget what I have learned already a second course of lessons is essential. The state of my finances makes the cost prohibitive. Therefore I am asking you for twelve thalers. But just as you wish. I shan't be upset if you can't send it."

Then there was his love affair with a girl musician, Lonni Grodzka. He was introduced to her at a picnic on Ascension Day by Arnold Mendelssohn, an impecunious young doctor and a cousin of the well-known banking family. Mendelssohn had been in love with Lonni for years, indeed "so much so he could hardly bear to look at her". He was a sensitive young man, full of inhibitions, which may have been all the stronger because of his lack of income. He felt that no good could come of his connexion with Lonni and, lacking the strength of mind to break it off, seems to have deliberately arranged for Ferdinand to supplant him. This duly happened but Ferdinand grew tired of her, whereupon she showed a tendency to fall back on Mendelssohn, to the latter's acute embarrassment. Luckily a small landowner from Lithuania made her an offer of marriage. We find both Lassal and Mendelssohn eagerly pressing his suit. The newcomer was plain, but kind-hearted and eminently safe. Lonni finally accepted him and the wedding took place in the summer of 1845.

Lonni Grodzka provided only one among many less reputable affairs. Lassal was highly sexed, with little natural caution. He was, for the first time, living in a big capital and independent of parental or any other control. Among his papers after his death were found a number of drafts of letters—it is characteristic of him that he should make drafts and preserve them—to various women dating from this period:

"Since I saw you the Devil has entered my blood and I am shaken as a ship caught by a hurricane: this Devil I cannot and will not resist for that would be a sin against the supreme God, the God of Desire and of the Flesh. Since I saw you my blood has curdled and gone dry: my flesh is parched. My every minute is like an age. You must *must* quench this arid furnace. I want one night, and for that night I will give eternity. In that night I will dissolve in your arms. Drop by drop you will drain my manhood. I promise you ecstasy for that night, but that night I must have. I will beget a son in your body who will be the God of future generations. The yearning, moist desire in your eyes tells me your senile husband's embraces do not satisfy you—Come to me and your lust shall strive with my lust till I wear your lust to death. . . ."

A complete record of Ferdinand's love life is (perhaps fortunately) no longer available. A year after his death Lothar Bucher, one of his literary executors, wrote to Countess Hatzfeldt: "I have destroyed certain letters to Lassalle from a number of women and girls. I burnt them because they were compromising for the writers, dangerous for the peace of mind of their families, and, in part, of so indecent a nature that it would be impossible to hand them over to a lady. This course I took after considerable reflection which confirmed my view that, as a gentleman and a friend of Lassalle's, it was the only one open to me."

It was a tactless form of approach to the Countess who was then over sixty, had never been squeamish, had read most of the letters and regarded them as hers. She answered Bucher by return of post, accusing him "if not of stealing at any rate of clandestinely and arbitrarily destroying other people's property. It is ridiculous for you to plead prudishness in burning correspondence which, as you know, I have already read. What right had you? Are you my guardian? I find your pose as 'gentleman' disgusting. The first thing, remember, is to be an honest man. A gentleman is one who shows even more scruples than his duty as an honest man requires."

5

FERDINAND quickly established a complete ascendancy over Arnold Mendelssohn, though the latter was seven years older. We have a letter from Mendelssohn to his Uncle Joseph, the head of the banking house, dated early January 1845:

"It was last November that Lassal invited me to share his rooms, an offer I accepted with pleasure. I had long wished to leave my parents' house in the Oranienburger Strasse: I had long realised—as will be obvious to a man of your experience —that an address so far from the centre and the poverty which marked my surroundings would handicap my working up a practice in a society that pays such heed to externals. But I had an inner, and more important motive for accepting Lassal's offer. You will doubtless have noticed a change in me since I made his acquaintance. It was through him that I was drawn to philosophy; and not only that. He made himself my Mystagogue and introduced me to the mysteries of learning.... As a result my attitude to my profession has become quite different. Before it was, to me, just a means of livelihood: now I have learned to recognise the thought behind the science of medicine. . . . I hope and trust you will realise this is not a case of 'youthful enthusiasm', against which my character and my mature age should be effective safeguards. . . . Not only has he shown me the path to learning, it is through him that I have learned peace of mind.... Serious philosophy is a joyous science, for it leads us away from jaundiced liberalism to the joys of contemplation. I can say of philosophy and of Lassal— I cannot think of one without the other—those words of Hegel's 'They have reconciled me to the world of reality.'

"I have seen how much more quickly I have been able to work since I joined him in his lodgings. Indeed it is only by living under one roof with him that I get through the work that I do. By making use, without too much disturbing him, of every available hour I am able to overcome the handicaps due to my age and the calls of my medical practice.

"Recently Lassal told me that in view of the many and

undeniable inconveniences of living in furnished rooms he proposed to take a flat and invited me to join him. I accepted very gladly, without thinking of the implications. It was only when I found Lassal was buying some luxurious furniture that I realised that we were taking an unfurnished flat and that I would have to provide my share of the furniture and household effects. And here was I, completely devoid of funds! It is true that Lassal with his accustomed generosity at once asked me to allow him to furnish my room. . . ."

For a variety of reasons, which he sets forth at great length, Arnold Mendelssohn could not bring himself to accept this offer. He had therefore to request his uncle for a loan or gift of 250 thalers.

The appeal made no impression on the banker. Arnold should, he replied, be making a living by his practice, and his friendship with Lassal was interfering with his medical career. "Lassal is a young man with money, and he can afford to philosophise or do anything else he wants. I am no philosopher and you know my views on the subject. Philosophy is an intellectual game, better perhaps than cards or chess, but no more likely to pay the butcher's bill."

Lassal acquired two other, if less devoted, disciples—Alexander Oppenheim, a young lawyer, also his senior, of a well-to-do Königsberg family, and Albert Lehfeldt, a student. On his return to Breslau in early April 1845 he kept up a brisk correspondence with his *Triumviri* as he called them.

Mendelssohn's letters are the most revealing. In April he wrote:

"Cassandra said 'what is fated must happen' and now you have left Berlin. Your widows and orphans turn their gaze reverently and longingly towards Breslau just as the Moslem looks to Mecca. Let us hope that your Hegira will also be but the prelude to your return, a return as terrible for your enemies as was the Prophet's."

The same strain continues throughout the summer. "People are noticing how much better company I am now that you are gone than I was when you were here and when I used to sit in silent admiration of you." And again, "I am yearning for you just as the stag that pants for cooling streams." In August Mendelssohn wrote: "Your letter shows that, wise as you are, you still keep that gift of sympathy which I have so often experienced but which, from you, comes as such a blessed surprise—it is sympathy tempered in the fire of thought, the pure gold of human nature. . . . You found in me a plastic substance and my life to come will be a proof that you have known how to mould the clay."

Oppenheim's letters are less emotional, and mostly confined to his own philosophic studies. We find him, for instance, asking for Lassal's notes on Feuerbach and Ruge. Lehfeldt seems to have written very little.

In mid-September Lassal indited a ten-page manifesto to his followers. It starts by elaborating his already quoted thesis on the Industrial Exhibition: his father had evidently returned it and it had come to be one of the group's main text-books. The manifesto goes on to be, in his own words, "a declaration of war against the world", the present world of "organised robbery". "Can I conquer in this struggle?" he asks. "I must. For the power which I oppose, i.e. money, is but the dead and disembodied being of my own Ego. That Ego am I, but not as a dead and passive being. . . ."

Towards the end the language becomes more than ever extravagant. "There is no real existence but in the thinking mind: my body is but appearance, proceeding from the thinking mind, and I have brought it about that my body changes with the changes of my thought. From head to toe I am nothing but Will. Sleeping and waking are as one to me. Arnold may have told you, Klex [Oppenheim] of his alarm on noticing that my body was merely the selfless reflexion of the glow within me. . . ."

Much of this had, no doubt, the sincerity of exaltation. But there was, equally certainly, a conscious desire to impress his readers. A few years afterwards we find him writing:

"When people have preconceived ideas one must take a very extreme line so as to startle them into mental activity. In order to shake prejudice one must use paradox."

Lassal's ambition, as we have seen, was at this time to formulate his own philosophical system. As a preliminary step he was already planning a work on Heraklitus, the sage of Ephesus, which work was to establish his academic reputation. But the retired life of a philosopher offered little scope for his irrepressible urge to be a leader, to be a power in the lives of others, and it was the devotion of his *Triumviri* that helped to satisfy this urge.

One of them, however, turned out disappointingly. In November 1845 Lassal had to write to Albert Lehfeldt's cousin a letter "which will cause you no less pain to read than it causes me to write". He enumerated the various steps he had taken for Albert's good, not the least of which had been introducing him to Mendelssohn and Oppenheim.

"I had hoped that the serious, ordered and industrious manner of life of these two gentlemen might inspire your cousin to follow their example. . . . But in late September my friends informed me that Albert had adopted a dubious manner of existence, was doing no work, frequently stayed out all night, and disregarded their remonstrances. I at once wrote him an extremely serious letter, to which I received a repentant reply. However, at the end of October, Dr. Mendelssohn informed me that Albert's behaviour had been most disreputable, he had run up debts with waiters, was in the habit of gambling in low society etc.—in short my friends could no longer consort with him without becoming compromised themselves. . . ."

The little sect of Lassalians was thus reduced from three to two, and we do not know that Ferdinand ever seriously tried to increase their number. He was, however, free with his advice to any he thought might profit by it, and we have an eight-page exhortation of his to a Baron Hubert von Stucker, a progressive Silesian aristocrat, who had expressed the intention of retiring from public affairs to look after his estates. Ferdinand expressed horror that any one should "arbitrarily choose to devote his life to manure, irrigation and cattle fodder". He implored the Baron to take up philosophy, or, failing a vocation for that, to enter the Prussian Government service and do what he could there to prevent the repression of liberal ideas. But he did not feel his advice would be followed. "I fear, Baron, you will merely smile and go your way. As you will. I have done my part. *Dixi et salvavi animam meam.*"

6

HIS MOVE from Berlin to Breslau in the summer of 1845 may have been to have more leisure for his *Heraklitus*. But he was also interested in the gas business, mentioned in the letter to his mother. His cousin Friedland (ex-Friedländer) had, a little while before, come to Breslau, talked old Heymann into participating, secured a contract from the municipality and formed a local gas company. Friedland and Heymann then negotiated a contract for Prague. There was some difficulty at first in finding capital for the Prague company, and Ferdinand Lassal approached the Mendelssohn Bank. In August he wrote a formal letter to Arnold's uncle Joseph:

"With regard to the latter enterprise, Prague, which, in view of the more favourable contract and the larger consumption, offers a prospect of greater profit than Breslau, we propose to provide the capital ourselves in collaboration with only one bank. Although we have already been approached from various quarters, we—in particular the undersigned—would prefer to be associated in this profitable enterprise with your distinguished firm. Allow me to give you a brief outline of the proposed business. . . ."

Lassalle proceeds to give details emphasising, among other advantages, the low cost of constructional labour in Prague as compared with Germany and the fact that the Prague contract contained no clause limiting the prices to be charged to the consumer.

In September he returned to the attack.

"The present position is no longer as described in my previous letter, in so far as our negotiations with another financial house have reached an advanced stage. I felt it my duty, however, to hold open our offer to you. . . ."

In the attempt to overcome the banker's reluctance to doing

business with a philosopher he made a personal visit to Berlin. Old Mendelssohn was away, at his country house in the Rhineland, so all that could be done was to discuss estimates of costs and income with the Berlin office. More inconclusive correspondence passed and in late October we find Ferdinand taking a firmer line:

"In your honoured letter of the 15th you expressed the fear lest we should break off our discussions with other firms on account of our negotiations with you and thus expose ourselves to a setback in the event of failure to conclude an agreement with your bank. I hasten to express my deep appreciation of this proof of your regard for my interests and for those of my associates. Meanwhile I can assure you that your fears are ungrounded. We, as business men, can in no circumstances allow our personal inclinations and sympathies to stand in the way of the conclusion of business. . . . I have no need to remind a man of affairs of your calibre that all personal considerations, however great, must remain within the limits set by our practical interests. On my return [from Berlin] we resumed our negotiations with the parties concerned; though, in order to give you time for final consideration, we proceeded somewhat less expeditiously than we would otherwise have done. You may be assured however that we are fixing the tempo to suit our convenience: there is no reason to fear precipitance on your part out of personal regard for us; and just as little to fear loss of time or opportunity on our part out of personal regard for you."

In the end the Bank Mendelssohn declined to participate, and finance for the ultimately profitable Prague Gas Company was found elsewhere.

7

IN THE WINTER of 1845–46 Ferdinand spent a few weeks in Paris to work in the libraries there on his *Heraklitus*. There is no full record of his other activities. Marx had already left the French capital, which was no longer the centre of Left-wing thought and activity that it had been in the days of the *Deutsch-*

französische Jahrbücher. But Ferdinand met Grün, the émigré apostle of "True Socialism", and, through Grün, Proudhon. Ferdinand de Friedland was in Paris at this time; and it may have been his cousin's example which induced our Ferdinand to take the step, which he did at this juncture, of gallicising his surname to the more imposing and distinguished Lassalle.

Friedland gave him some introductions to the smart and semi-smart world. In after life Lassalle told the story of his first morning call on a French lady whom he had not yet met. After waiting some time he was shown to the boudoir where Madame, in her dressing-gown, offered him her foot. He said "*Charmé, Madame, de cette nouvelle manière de faire connaissance. C'est plus joli et surtout plus intime que d'embrasser la main.*" And kissed the foot. There was a flurry, and explanations; and it turned out that by mistake he had sent in, instead of his own card, the card of a pedicurist who had called at his hotel. Characteristically he hinted that this incident had led to a successful little adventure.

Of more interest and more consequence was his meeting, also arranged by Friedland, with Heinrich Heine. The poet was no longer in his prime; he was ailing, more than a little shop-soiled and preoccupied with his undignified quarrels with his relations over money matters. The meeting was a success. Heine was genuinely impressed by Lassalle; he also had hopes that he might be of service in his private affairs. Lassalle no doubt retained a sentimental regard for the literary idol of his school days. He was always susceptible to admiration, and ever ready to accept the role of champion of the poor and oppressed. He left Paris promising to do what he could to secure permission for the poet to return to Berlin and to have pressure put on his rich Hamburg cousins. He carried with him a letter of introduction from Heine to Varnhagen von Ense:

"My friend Herr Lassalle is a young man with remarkable intellectual gifts, with the greatest devotion to study, the widest knowledge and the keenest judgment I have so far met. He unites, to a degree that astonishes me, a power of exposition, a strength of will and a practical sense of business that will, if I continue to enjoy his friendship, be of the greatest value to me. . . . This new generation is determined to enjoy and to attain concrete success; we, in our time, bowed meekly before the invisible, we snatched at shadowy kisses and the thin perfume of flowers; we renounced and smiled a bitter smile. And yet perhaps our lot was happier than that of these stern young gladiators who march so proudly towards their doom."

Varnhagen's house in Berlin was a centre for intellectuals; it was also frequented by the aristocracy and by people about the Court. Lassalle met Professor Boeckh and the great Alexander von Humboldt. He met Prince Pückler-Muskau, whom he found willing to take an interest in Heine's affairs. The Prince sent him the draft of a letter he proposed to dispatch to Heine's banker cousin in Hamburg. In returning it Lassalle wrote:

"Your Highness, How can I find words to express the admiration your letter has aroused in me? I am sure it will have the effect desired; but quite apart from that the high moral feeling that inspires the letter has moved me most deeply. I have read it again and again."

We must remember that it was an age of elaborate politeness; also that Lassalle was deliberately flattering the Prince to encourage his efforts on behalf of Heine. Lassalle was often flowery, but never obsequious. He sent a very sharp note to Baron von Stucker who omitted to show him proper attention on a visit to Berlin. And he horrified the assembled company one evening by flatly contradicting Humboldt on a point of erudition. Humboldt looked up the point at issue on returning home, and sent a letter saying Lassalle had been right. The young man further appalled his new acquaintances by the offhand manner in which he accepted this triumph. But Humboldt himself bore no grudge; and Lassalle was soon established, more or less on his own valuation, in those academic and social quarters he most wished to impress. His course seemed set fair towards the career he had planned for himself. But then he met Countess Hatzfeldt.

Chapter 4

THE COUNTESS

I

Sophie von Hatzfeldt was born in 1805, third daughter of Prince Franz Ludwig von Hatzfeldt, head of one of the richest and most influential noble families of North-West Germany. There were two sons, Prince Hermann and Count Max, the latter subsequently Prussian Ambassador to France. For family and property reasons it became desirable that one of the daughters should marry a cousin, Count Edmund von Hatzfeldt-Kinsweiler. The Count's choice fell on Sophie and the wedding took place in 1822. They had two sons and one daughter.

The marriage was from the start an unhappy one. The Count was unfaithful and was unscrupulous in money matters. Later on he removed the two elder children and denied their mother access to them. The Countess appealed to her brothers for help, but they feared a public scandal and merely advised her to be patient and tolerant. She appealed to the Palace, but the Palace took a similar line. Things went from bad to worse. The Countess in desperation took lovers. One of them, a Count von Bassenheim, wanted to marry her, and it was hoped to secure a Papal decree that the marriage to Hatzfeldt was nul and void. Nothing came of the project. Bassenheim drifted away. The years went by and, at the age of forty-one, Sophie von Hatzfeldt was a lonely and embittered woman.

However, in the spring of 1846, she wrote to her elder brother:

"Up till now I have managed my affairs badly. I listened to my feelings, and feelings are no weapon in a struggle. This phase is now over, and I intend to let the law take its course. ... From now on I take no steps without the advice and help of third parties. You may notice the assurance of my present attitude. Having, thanks to you, lost confidence in my own judgment I have found certain experts and will make use of their services. . . . I shall go to law for the restitution of my rights. If this can be arranged without my going into court I shall be glad that my family should avoid legal proceedings which must inevitably compromise one of its members. If, however, I am forced to take this step the responsibility is not mine."

2

THE EXPERTS to whom the Countess refers were Lassalle, Oppenheim and Arnold Mendelssohn. Lassalle had been introduced to her at the end of January by one of the young noblemen he had met at Varnhagen's: and for the next eight years he devoted himself, to the exclusion of all his personal, academic and family interests, to the vindication of Sophie von Hatzfeldt's claims against her husband. Later in life he gave this account of how he first embarked on his crusade:

"Quite by chance I happened to be at hand when the Count committed a new outrage. Late in 1845 there had been a reconciliation, as always as far as he was concerned only an apparent one. The idea was that they should come together in April 1846. Instead, shortly before that date, the Count wrote to the second son of the marriage, Paul, whom the Countess loved deeply and who returned her love—the Count wrote secretly to tell his fourteen-year-old son that he would disinherit him unless he clandestinely left the Countess. Paul brought this letter to his mother. I found her bowed down with tears and anguish, and little by little I heard the whole story.

"I have always been a revolutionary of the school of Robespierre who wrote: 'Social oppression exists so long as one single individual is oppressed'. I saw fully the egoism and cowardice of the aristocratic world which sacrificed this noble being to its heartless and rotten prejudices. . . . I felt shame for humanity.

"I said to myself: 'Let it never be said that you knew all this and that you calmly left the woman to her fate without going to help her. If you do that, what right will you ever have to denounce cowardice and selfishness?' . . .

"And I, a young powerless Jew; rose up against the most formidable of powers—I alone against the world, against the power of rank and the whole aristocracy, against the power of unlimited wealth, against the Government and its officials—the natural allies of rank and wealth—against all possible prejudices. . . ."

On another occasion he wrote: "If it had not been the Countess I would have found some other cause to show my opposition to the world as it is to-day. Man's temperament is his fate." Lassalle's temperament contained an irrepressible urge towards knight-errantry, and we can accept his explanation as sincere. At the same time the cause he was adopting was not any the less congenial because of the publicity involved or because it was on behalf of a good-looking woman. And it is certain that the exalted rank of his client and of her opponent made an immense appeal to the obscure young Jew from the provinces.

The precise nature of Lassalle's personal relations with the Countess became, of course, a matter of burning interest to the various women in whose lives he subsequently played a part. One of them, Helene von Dönniges, he asked straight out: "What do you think were my relations with the Countess?" Helene said: "I suppose she was still attractive then and you were very young, so you fell in love and had an affair with her. Now she's old and you're still young, so you're just friends." To which Lassalle replied: "Thank heaven you take it so sensibly. It was more or less as you say: but there is one unbreakable bond that unites us—gratitude."

We must remember that it was not in Lassalle's nature to deny that he had "had an affair" with any attractive woman. Furthermore in the early 'fifties he wrote the Countess a letter which has been quoted as evidence that there was no physical relationship. The letter is a characteristic effusion, immensely long and packed with Hegelian arguments to convince the

Countess she was the protagonist of female emancipation. The proofs include the fact that help came to her not from a lover, but from "your Three Musqueteers . . . the flower of manly youth, in comfortable financial circumstances, a lawyer, a doctor and a philosopher, men of the highest intelligence and education, men motivated not by personal considerations but by the idea inherent in the spirit of the age." Again, in 1857, when the Countess was suspected by the Queen of Prussia of having been Lassalle's mistress and when, in consequence, the Berlin police were making difficulties about allowing the two to reside in Berlin at the same time, we find him protesting against an insinuation supported by "no shreds of evidence" and giving his word of honour that no intimacy had ever taken place. It is also significant that in her will, drawn up in 1852, the Countess declares her "warmest motherly love for my son Paul, also for Herr Ferdinand Lassalle, who has behaved to me as the best of sons and whom I regard as a son."

Caution, policy and convention may have played their part in all these statements. In 1860 Lassalle wrote to the Countess: "You are the only person I have ever loved." Here again posterity can only guess at what these words imply. The relationship between any two people is, more often than not, known only to themselves. We cannot tell what passed between Lassalle and Sophie von Hatzfeldt. We only know that each remained a major factor in the life of the other. She gave him a crusade to embark on, an entrance into a bigger world, and a trust and friendship that lasted all his life. He gave her devoted service, a philosophy, a political creed and, in the end, something very akin to a religion.

3

BY MARCH 1846 Lassalle was already active on her behalf as an amateur private detective: an attempt to intercept Hatzfeldt correspondence brought him into collision with the Countess's brother-in-law, General Count Nostitz, and there was an inquiry by the university authorities which trailed on for months. In the summer he moved with the Countess to the Rhineland, to be nearer the Hatzfeldt properties and the courts in whose jurisdiction the various issues lay. He brought with him Oppenheim and Mendelssohn. The latter had misgivings, more than justified by the event. Eighteen months later he wrote to Lassalle from prison, recalling the words he had used when first asked to embark on the venture: "I said: 'I will go with you wherever you go. I will do whatever you tell me, because you are wiser than I. I know that once you have gained your end you will throw me aside. I foresee that my obedience to you will bring me no good. But all the same I will do as I say.'"

The campaign opened with a series of law suits which grew ever more numerous and complicated. The Countess sued her husband for alimony. She brought a charge of "prodigality", regarding his misuse of her dowry. There were proceedings for the establishment of domicile in the event of a petition for divorce. Both parties inserted or inspired polemical articles in any paper that would publish them—most papers did for the case was news—and there were the consequent libel actions. Old scandals were raked up and embellished. Witnesses were bought, suborned or terrorised. The struggle was conducted by both sides without mercy, inhibition or scruple.

In late August affairs took a sensational turn. Lassalle later gave the following account of it:

"The Count was in Aachen. I got my two friends to go round the neighbourhood to collect and prepare valid evidence of the Count's extravagance and dissipation. This I required for a legal injunction on his property and for the coming divorce proceedings. I myself went to Aachen to see what steps the Count was intending against his wife. I soon found out. He was in Aachen with his mistress, Baroness von Meyendorff, *née* Hagguère, who had worked as a spy for the Russians in Paris. Now she had got hold of Count Hatzfeldt. Soon we had evidence not only of their adulterous intimacy, but also of the fact that the Count had made her a gift, under the guise of a loan, of such a nature as financially to ruin the Countess's son Paul. . . .

"News came that the Meyendorff was taking the train to Cologne. I instructed Oppenheim and Mendelssohn who were with me to follow her, if need be to the end of the world, and if possible to discover if she still had the deed of gift. They left. They arrived at Cologne at the same time that she did and put up at the same hotel. Next day, shortly before the departure of the steamer, Oppenheim saw the Meyendorff's servant bringing her luggage out of her room. He noticed a box or casket such as one uses for keeping papers. A sudden idea occurred to Oppenheïm. When the servant went back to the Meyendorff's room he seized the casket. He himself had no trunk to hide it in, so he hurried to Mendelssohn's room. Mendelssohn was dumbfounded over this mad *coup*, but he would not fail his friend.

"Meanwhile Meyendorff's servant had missed the casket and raised the alarm. Mendelssohn packed the casket into his trunk but as it was already full he had to take out some of his clothes. The two friends left, for different destinations. The hotel was searched. Suspicion was aroused against Mendelssohn when they found the clothes left in his room and he was followed. He was sitting in the train when he noticed the police were watching him. He got out of the train and disappeared, leaving his luggage behind him. . . . But as he had, at Oppenheim's request, taken Oppenheim's suitcase with him and left it behind with his own trunk in the compartment, the police discovered papers identifying Oppenheim and arrested the latter on a charge of theft."

Mendelssohn escaped over the frontier and went to England where he took out a passport in the name of Goldsmith. He came back to Belgium and then on to Paris, having spent all his money. He sent a series of imploring letters to Lassalle, most of which went astray. It was not till the 29th September that Lassalle replied to him:

"Under separate cover I am sending you twenty Napoleons. You are a complete idiot. It is too much, now when I have so many troubles, that I should have to waste money, time, care and nervous energy simply on account of your stupidity. How could you imagine I should leave you in the lurch?"

It may have been Mendelssohn's presence there that suggested the use of Paris as a base of operations against Count Hatzfeldt. Heine, already under an obligation to Lassalle and with his position in the literary world, was the obvious collaborator to start a press campaign in the French and English papers. Lassalle wrote to him in early October:

"The first essential is that the *Journal des Débats*, the French press in general and also the London *Times* should print a series of fulminating articles. Their object should be (*a*) completely and ruthlessly to discredit and ruin the Count, and (*b*) to show the Countess's brothers, hitherto supine through fear of scandal, that their betrayal of their sister is becoming notorious throughout Europe; and thus drive them into making effective efforts to help her."

Heine did not answer, and a fortnight later Lassalle wrote to Mendelssohn. There had, he said, been some mention of the case in some of the smaller boulevard papers, the *Constitutionel* and the *Corsaire-Satan*; also in the English *Galignani Messenger*. "But that is not enough. Why doesn't Heine write? Look after his health."

On the 24th he wrote to Humboldt with the preposterous suggestion that Humboldt should intervene with the King to secure the release of Oppenheim. By return of post came Humboldt's refusal: "I must request you to stop writing to me about this most unpleasant affair." On the same day news came from Mendelssohn that nothing could be expected from Heine; and Lassalle proceeded to write to the poet a letter that must be accounted a classic of its kind:

"When I read Mendelssohn's letter, telling me, in a cloud of vague verbiage, that you could or would not do me the small favour for which I asked, I was, for the moment, struck dumb with astonishment. But only for the moment. A useful tag is *Nihil admirari.* Why should you not be just the same as so many others? . . . Shall I remind you of what I did for you? Shall I send you back your letter 'never has anyone done so much for me as you have'? At that time in Berlin I was beginning to make a career. But after the *démarches* by Pückler and

Humboldt the rumour started that I was the declared friend of Heine. I had then a great deal to gain by a prudent retreat, by disavowing your cause, by writing the sort of letter I have now received from Mendelssohn. I did not take that course; and the eminent and influential began to turn their backs on me....

"I repeat, I see no cause for astonishment at your finding your ease and comfort, your social position and your distinguished connexions as of more importance than any use you may or may not be able later on to make of me. We all have the right to be weak in our principles. I do not grudge you this right.

"Mendelssohn writes that you were very upset at the postage you had to pay on my letter. I apologize. The idea never occurred to me that this aspect of a letter from a friend would mean so much to you. I enclose the sum involved....

"With greetings,

LASSALLE."

All this time lawyers' fees and other expenses were mounting up; and, for the moment, the only visible source of funds was Lassalle's father. Old Heymann bore his son's peremptory demands with remarkable patience. In October he wrote from Breslau:

"I am hurt by your continual references to 'mistrust', and by your remark that a business man is only satisfied by a mortgage. You know perfectly well how fond I am of you, and how I have always let you have more money than my financial position justified. But what is impossible is impossible. I now remit 500 thalers, all I have been able to raise."

In November Oppenheim came to trial and was acquitted: Lassalle had succeeded in securing and destroying certain papers that might have helped the prosecution. Oppenheim was persuaded by his family to return to Berlin, and he took no further part in the affair. Meanwhile a new complication arose. Lassalle was threatened with arrest in connexion with a libel action arising out of one of his press articles. So he went to Paris to look for a journalist who, being out of range of the jurisdiction of the German courts, would agree to pose as the author of the article in question. Such a man was found, but he wanted a fee of 5,000 francs. Lawyers' and other bills continued to mount, and old Lassal received a demand for 5,000 thalers. He felt it time to speak his mind on the whole Hatzfeldt connexion:

"You ask me to send you thalers 5,000 and tell me that otherwise the world would hold nothing for you and you would have nothing worth living for. If I were not so fond of you I would send you a sharp answer. . . . As it is, if I had this sum or could raise it—credit here is very tight since Schiller went bankrupt—I swear by God I would send it to you; not that I think it would serve your purpose, you have three times already been completely wrong about the sum of money you require, but because I care for money only to spend for things that are dear to me, and nothing is so dear as you. . . . If some one, who has always had an easy life, leaves his own circle out of pure presumption, mixes himself, out of pure presumption, in a quarrel that has nothing to do with him, and does not get results as quickly as he imagines he should, has he any right to talk about life holding nothing for him? You young idiot!"

Ferdinand wrote back on New Year's eve: "Your letter did not help me, but it made me very happy and immensely proud of you." Nevertheless with his usual persistence he went on pressing for money. The Countess arrived in Paris bringing with her some jewellery. But to get top price for these jewels required time and negotiation. Present needs were pressing. Lassalle tried his brother-in-law Friedland, then also in Paris, and reported to his father on the 6th January 1847:

"I went to call on Friedland, kissed him, told him of my difficulties, and, as I went away, asked him for 40 francs. I told him I could not even stamp my letters to you without some money. He refused, on the grounds that you would not pay him back. I laughed and he replied with a stream of abuse about you and the way you had treated him. I said if he did not expect to get the money back he could give it to me as a present. He said I wasn't worth that much to him. So I quickly took my hat to go, and he gave it to me. Next day I went back to him and asked for 5,000. He not only refused but refused in the most offensive and insulting manner, told me he could easily do it but I was not that much worth to him and he began to abuse you and accused you of letting him starve in Breslau, so he intends to get his own back off me now. As I saw there was nothing doing I went and fetched the diamonds and asked him to sell them for me. When the damned Jew saw I had some diamonds he became more polite. . . ."

In February Lassalle and his client went back to the Rhineland and stayed with an old friend of hers, Count Clemens von Westphalen. Westphalen was a wealthy man and lent them 17,000 thalers, so that, for the moment their position was easier. Following the acquittal of Oppenheim, Mendelssohn was anxious to return to Germany. In early March Lassalle wrote to him. "I asked Holthoff [the lawyer] if I should let you come back. He thinks there is no danger, but it would be more prudent to wait another six or eight weeks." On 26th March Lassalle himself was arrested for having purloined the papers in the Oppenheim case. Six weeks later he was brought to trial and acquitted. He next organised a deputation of peasants on one of the Hatzfeldt estates and took them to Berlin: on 14th May he and his peasants were turned out of the Landtag. June he spent mostly in the country, where the pro-Count and pro-Countess factions of the peasants were waging what was more or less a civil war. That same month Mendelssohn came back to Germany; and was promptly arrested. On 8th July he wrote a plaintive letter to the Countess from Cologne prison, complaining of the way Lassalle had treated him.

Throughout the summer and autumn litigation proceeded and multiplied. The results were not unsatisfactory as far as they went. Lassalle had succeeded in creating the impression that his client was the victim of the injustice of a privileged caste, and, with the rising tide of popular democratic feeling, courts, and particularly juries, were ready to accept her case. But the Count invariably appealed; procedure in both lower and higher courts was cumbersome and slow; new actions were initiated. After eighteen months the affair had become immeasurably more complicated, and a final settlement seemed more remote than ever.

In November Count Clemens von Westphalen went to Berlin, and we find Lassalle sending him frequent and peremptory instructions as to what he should do there to further the Countess's case. The Count, considering his age and position, showed remarkable patience. But he was getting tired of the affair, and in late December he reminded his young friend that the Countess's case was "not so crystal clear". This provoked a diatribe in the true Lassallean manner. "There are three ways", he replied on 1st January 1848, "in which woman can commit sacrilege against the purpose of her being", i.e. sexual abstinence, marrying for money, or promiscuous relationships "without spiritual or emotional content". Surrender to real love was, on the other hand, "the highest form of chastity". Meanwhile, "besides the three sins mentioned there is a fourth, a sin against the Holy Ghost, the case of a woman who, while she really loves and surrenders to love, nevertheless puts on an outward show of prudery and preaches on texts from so-called Christian and bourgeois morality. How much more noble is one who can openly proclaim the doctrine of free love! Such is the Countess. . . ."

To which Westphalen replied: "When I said our friend may have some episodes in her life that she regretted, referring to her relations with men, I did not mean it was for me to judge—that is solely her business—whether she had committed any of what you rightly call the mortal sins against love. What I did mean was that if, out of all these relationships, not a single friend remains to her, then she must regret them and be ashamed of them. . . . I would rather our friend thought seriously of her past than have her count on figuring in future calendars as a Red Letter Saint and Martyr to the cause of Free Love."

Chapter 5

1848

I

In January 1848 there was an insurrection in Sicily. Constitutions were proclaimed in Naples, Turin and Florence. On the 11th of that month Sophie von Hatzfeldt and Lassalle were sentenced by a Rhineland Court to two months' imprisonment and a fine on a charge of criminal libel. They lodged an appeal. At the end of the month Arnold Mendelssohn came to trial; on the 11th February, to the astonishment and dismay of the Countess's adherents, he was found guilty and sentenced to five years' imprisonment. A week later revolution broke out in Paris and Louis Phillippe was deposed. Lassalle went to Berlin. In February he was arrested in Potsdam on a count of having instigated the theft of the casket. He was transferred under guard to Cologne, and there he sat impotent in prison during the months that followed. On 13th March there was revolution in Vienna; on 18th March revolution in Berlin. In April Karl Marx arrived in Cologne and the *Neue Rheinische Zeitung* was started. In June the Paris workers were decisively and bloodily defeated in the streets of their capital—a grim omen for the immediate future of the proletarian revolution. Meanwhile Arnold Mendelssohn's friends had been active on his behalf and he was released on condition that he left the country. He went to Austria, then on to Hungary. He joined up with the Hungarian national revolutionary movement, and on the defeat of that movement was one of the little band of refugees to escape to Turkey. Lassalle never saw him again.

Lassalle, unable to take part in world events, found his sole emotional outlet in planning his forthcoming trial.

As he afterwards wrote, he "wanted an opportunity to state my case to the country—a criminal trial, a solemn opportunity to annihilate the slanders against me, and to disclose the true nature of my campaign on behalf of the Countess. Further, this was necessary in the Countess's interests. Here was an occasion to proclaim to the world the nature of her dispute with the Count and, by this disclosure, to destroy him morally.

"The lawyers begged me not to do so. . . .

"I determined not to listen to these cautious counsellors. I mounted the dock not as a defendant, but as a victor marching towards certain triumph. I launched an offensive against the Count and against his accomplices the judges. Fourteen witnesses had been suborned to give false evidence against me. That I had foreseen. I exposed the false witnesses, I destroyed once and for all the slanders, I demonstrated beyond all doubt the true history of the Hatzfeldt marriage, and on the final day in a six-hour speech I struck the Count and his accomplices to the ground."

In more pedestrian language it is a fact that, when the trial was held in the first week of August, Lassalle made a spirited counter-attack on his client's husband and skilfully identified his own cause with that of Liberty and Democracy. The Cologne jurymen were susceptible to this appeal to the spirit of 1848. Lassalle was acquitted; and his acquittal was hailed throughout the Rhineland as a triumph for the Left. There were demonstrations in Cologne. When he and the Countess arrived in Düsseldorf a cheering crowd unharnessed the horses and dragged their carriage through the streets. The trial, the acquittal and the ovation remained Lassalle's most vivid and proudest memories. "The newspapers", he wrote twelve years afterwards, "spread my fame throughout the Kingdom. I was recognised as a man able to fight alone against the whole world. Since that day the democrats of the Rhineland have regarded me as one of their principal leaders."

There were, of course, others who regarded him merely as the leading figure of the most publicised scandal of the decade.

2

AFTER HIS ACQUITTAL Lassalle took up residence with the Countess and her son at her Düsseldorf house. He was at once immersed again in the Hatzfeldt case—the Count still refused any acceptable settlement—and joined up with the Left-wing of the Rhineland democrats in the Prussian constitutional struggle of 1848. To him, as to the Countess, these two issues were allied, if not identical. "I have left all to help the people", the Countess declared to a group of Düsseldorf workers, "I am now a proletarian. Here is my friend and here is my son. Protect us from the fury of the aristocratic reaction."

It was at this period that Lassalle met Marx and Engels.

Marx was seven and Engels five years older than Lassalle. Marx had left Berlin before he went there, and he did not meet either during his visits to Paris. A letter from Arnold Mendelssohn mentions Engels's book on the Working Class in England: but there is no record of the Three Musqueteers having come across the Communist Manifesto or the *Deutsch-französische Jahrbücher*. When Lassalle was acquitted Marx was editor of the *Neue Rheinische Zeitung* and the biggest personality of the extreme Left in Cologne. We have no details of the first meeting. Engels disliked Lassalle from the start. He disliked his glibness, ostentation and self-importance, and he disapproved of the trail of the Hatzfeldt scandal being dragged across the austere path of revolution. Marx, though alive to all this, was more tolerant. His own Jewish blood may have given him more understanding of the young man's foibles. He liked him personally, and he appreciated the substantial contribution that his drive and his intellectual capacity might render to the cause.

Lassalle made his first public political speech on 29th August, at a protest meeting in Cologne against the arrest of the revolutionary poet Freiligrath. For the next two months he was constantly on the move in the Rhineland and in frequent touch with Marx. It was a critical period for the revolutionary cause. In October the forces of order, or reaction, scored a decisive victory in Vienna. Meanwhile the democrats of the Rhineland, fearing a similar course of events in Prussia, organised an armed citizens' guard, Lassalle taking a prominent part. In early November the Royal Government of Prussia instructed the Constituent Assembly to leave Berlin for Brandenburg, declared a state of siege in the capital, and ordered the disbandment of the citizen guard. On the 19th Lassalle addressed a meeting in Düsseldorf. "Passive resistance is over", he declared. "We appeal to the Assembly—Give out the call to arms!" On the 21st he advised a meeting at Neuss to "get ready to strike as soon as the word is given". On the following day he was arrested on a charge of inciting the populace to arms against the royal power. He remained in custody for six months.

He was soon in trouble with the prison authorities. He was found to be smuggling out letters to the Countess and in consequence permission was refused for her to send in his meals to him. But by dint of hard arguing he obtained facilities to continue to conduct her affairs from prison; he was even allowed to go out and plead in the Courts.

On 25th February he wrote to his mother:

"I shall come before the Assizes some time in March. I am delighted at the prospect. I shall hurl my lances like an Apollo; and shall have no pity for those poor wretches who have the dismal task of preferring this ridiculous charge against me. The political crisis will soon come to a head. Either Germany will return for ever to medieval darkness—in which case science is a lie, philosophy a joke, Hegel an idiot escaped from a madhouse, and there is no sense in history—or else the revolution will celebrate a new and decisive triumph. . . . Then there'll be something doing! This spring will find Europe in fire and flame. Whoever does not realise that is a fool."

Meanwhile he was asking Marx to do all in his power to put pressure on the Public Prosecutor Nicolovius to speed up the hearing. On 28th February he wrote:

"Don't be annoyed at my pestering you with these requests; but God knows it isn't just a trifle to have to sit here for another four months. And I promise you that when you are next locked up—which is certain to happen sooner or later—my personal laziness will not prevent me from setting all the wheels in motion that I can."

On 3rd March a deputation, with Marx and Engels at the head, went to see Nicolovius. But the hearing was still deferred. Three weeks later Lassalle wrote to Marx asking for more publicity for his case in the *Neue Reinische Zeitung*. He went on, with a surprising lack of discernment, to plead for a series of polemical articles on the Hatzfeldt case. Nothing, of course, came of the latter request but in early May the paper had two leading articles on Lassalle's detention. They appeared on the eve of the hearing, fixed at last for 5th May.

Lassalle prepared a long speech for his defence and had it printed for subsequent distribution. It took the form of a counter-attack on the authorities.

"On 18th March the People of Berlin fought for and won a Constitutional State. The fundamental principle of a Constitutional State is that it is not the will of the monarch that is supreme but the popular spirit, the will of the nation as a whole, as expressed by the people's representatives. . . .

"It is ridiculous to bring, on legal grounds, a charge against the People who have been a shining example of loyalty and devotion to the law, who saw it their duty to take to arms to defend the law, and were ready to risk their lives. . . .

"Every revolution has existed, for months, in the heart of society, before it bursts into the open with the rattle of gunfire, . . . Law is never master of the community, only the written expression of its will. Should a community have new needs and new desires, from that moment the old codes belong to a historical museum, and in their place comes the pattern of the present. . . .

"The Crown has lost for ever the monopoly of legality: this belongs to me and mine. We set our seal upon it last November. . . .

"Passive resistance would have been treachery. Passive resistance is a contradiction in terms—unresisting resistance is no resistance. Passive resistance is like a knife without a blade. . . ."

Some copies of this "speech" came into circulation in Düsseldorf on 4th May. Accordingly on the following day when Lassalle rose in Court to deliver it the Prosecution raised an objection which the Court upheld. Lassalle then refused to plead. Nevertheless the following day he was acquitted. The authorities, knowing the temper of the Rhineland juries, had foreseen this possibility and he was at once rearrested on a charge of inciting to violence against the authorities. This lesser charge could be dealt with summarily by the police magistrates. He remained in custody for two more months, in the course of which the German revolution flared up for the last time and was finally extinguished.

Lassalle came up for trial in early July and was duly sentenced to six months' imprisonment. He did not serve his sentence till more than a year later. For the moment he was set at liberty; and he returned to a world in which the *Neue Rheinische Zeitung* was no more, Marx an exile on his way to London, and Engels a volunteer in what remained of the doomed revolutionary army in South Germany.

Chapter 6

THE LAST OF THE MOHICANS

I

But for the fact of his being in prison Lassalle would certainly have been involved in the disturbances of May and would have shared the fate of the other Left-wing leaders—exile, penury and all the risk of demoralisation inherent in being a refugee. As it was he remained behind, "the last of the Mohicans" as he once called himself, with the tide of reaction rising all round him.

The last of Marx's private fortune had gone in paying off the debts of the *Neue Rheinische Zeitung*. In July he wrote to Lassalle from London asking for a loan. Lassalle, who had little money to lend, set about organising a subscription, news of which got back to Marx. "Lassalle's behaviour surprises me", Marx wrote to Freiligrath. "I made a personal approach to him as I knew of his friendship to me, and I had myself once made a small loan to the Countess. I had no idea I would be involved in all this. I would rather suffer any poverty than go round begging."

Lassalle sent Marx a long explanation and the matter was buried. Meanwhile Countess Hatzfeldt's affairs were becoming more difficult; the spirit of reaction had pervaded the judiciary, and favourable judgments passed in 1848 were being regularly reversed on appeal. Lassalle's inherent optimism was put to a heavy strain. "I have never", he wrote to Marx, "believed in a lasting success of the counter-revolution . . . but who can guarantee that the present régime will not last another two years? The psalmist says a hundred years are but an instant in the sight of God. But for a lone soldier, in an advanced post surrounded by the enemy and in the thick of battle, waiting for reinforcements, for him two years is a damned long time! That is my position. And then the poison and gall poured out by our judiciary in their judgments in all my Hatzfeldt cases. . . . Every Red democrat in Germany knows what it means to be a Red. He is either dismissed or put in prison or robbed of his livelihood, or annihilated. . . .

"Nevertheless I still believe revolution will break out in France in the spring or summer of 1850. . . . I greet with joy your prognosis of a trade crisis in England. May it come surely and soon!"

The correspondence of this period between Lassalle and Marx and his wife shows a real and warm friendship. The *émigrés* were already involved in that bitter poverty which was to dog them for years. On 7th June Lassalle wrote to Jenny Marx:

"Your letter touched me deeply: I could see half-suppressed tears behind your gay smile. Kiss your little son for me. Though now he drinks tears and cares with his dear mother's milk, yet when he is older he will find a world from which his father's blood and sweat will have banished that penury now pressing so heavily on the best of us. He is lucky to live through this time of doubt and sorrow in unconscious childhood."

The secret police of course were showing interest in this correspondence. Lassalle wrote to Marx in late June:

"I share your dislike of Prussian police noses sniffing into our letters even when there is nothing in them. Also it can happen that there *may* be something in them. So from now on I shall address everything to my old school friend Gerstenberg, who will be punctilious in forwarding them. And you will write to me with an outer envelope addressed to Herr Wetter. . . . I would indeed like to make a flying visit to London. But prospects are bad. A few days ago we lost our appeal at the Berlin Supreme Court and so sailed safely into the harbour of complete ruin. There is a certain relief about having lost everything: no more need to worry over one's chances."

An undated letter (also to Marx) of about this period gives a pointer to Lassalle's views on immediate political tasks and possibilities:

"I still think there is something, and something not unimportant, that one can do. One can educate a number of workers to act as leaders and *points d'appui* of the proletariat in as many towns as possible. This may help to prevent, on future occasions, the proletariat from acting merely as a chorus to the bourgeois leads."

2

LASSALLE served his term of imprisonment from 1st October 1850 to 1st April 1851. In his first letter from prison to the Countess he says: "So long as I can resign myself to it my position is not unbearable. The Governor is quite human. On his advice I have put in a fourfold request—1. Writing material (as it is I can only get it for some specific purpose like writing a letter or petition). 2. Permission to smoke. 3. The *Deutsche Reform*. 4. Permission to play chess with Mirbach." [Another political prisoner.]

Apparently these requests were granted. The Governor allowed him an extra blanket (Lassalle always felt the cold); and the Countess sent him his fur-lined coat. Now and then she was allowed to come and see him. For one as ready to complain as he was he had few complaints. "If", he wrote, "one can vegetate and still be happy, then I am happy. A Dutchman would find it the summit of bliss to be as I am now." He spent much of his time on a project, destined never to be fulfilled, of working out a full-length treatise on economics. He continued to conduct the legal affairs of the Countess. And he could still write to his family (27th November) "I go to bed with the happy thought that the world will be standing on its head in one year's time."

Meanwhile in London there was friction within Marx's party, the Communist League, as a result of which the party's headquarters were, in the spring of 1851, transferred from London to Cologne. The new committee in Germany was, inevitably, composed of men whose role during the revolution had been too obscure to entail their exile or imprisonment. One was Heinrich Bürgers, ex-tutor to young Paul. Marx suggested that Lassalle be admitted as a member. The Committee unanimously turned down the proposal "in view of Lassalle's reputation".

There may have been a personal motive on the part of Bürgers: there had, we know, been friction over salary and status between the Hatzfeldt tutor and the Hatzfeldt man of affairs. But at the same time there were many serious democrats who sincerely disapproved of the seamy side of the Hatzfeldt imbroglio, and many more who disliked Lassalle's personality and manner of life. Lassalle himself knew nothing of the committee's decision. Marx neither informed him nor took any step to have it re-considered. When Lassalle was released, in April, he gave a party and invited Bürgers to come and drink to the Red Republic. Bürgers wrote in reply: "Show us that you fulfil all the conditions for joining us. First you must win our confidence, which can only be won little by little and in course of time." Lassalle, bewildered and indignant, wrote back: "Are you talking as a supreme chief to a raw recruit, using the royal plural?... I know of no special ways of winning confidence—only the natural way, by devotion to one's cause and not flinching from any sacrifice or suffering. That is my way. If, in spite of this, anyone does not trust me, I have no wish for him to do so."

In the late spring of 1851 relations between Lassalle and the Cologne committee became more and more strained. Meanwhile the Prussian authorities turned their attention to the London end of the Communist League. One Greiff, a police officer, was attached to the Prussian Embassy, and he recruited two agents, Fleury and Hirsch. Hirsch established touch with the London Communists and a series of long reports were sent to Berlin. They were patchy in quality, as the two spies soon realised that Berlin was not in a position to check what they wrote, and when they had no facts to report they invented. But at least the Prussian police obtained enough material to carry out a number of arrests in Cologne during June; and in October and November the trial of the Communists took place. It was not difficult to expose the flimsiness of much of the evidence of the prosecution. But a case was there. The authorities neglected no precautions, the jury was packed, and

Bürgers and his associates were sentenced to various terms of imprisonment.

Lassalle was not involved. Once again he owed his immunity to pure good fortune, this time to the refusal of the Cologne committee to admit him. The police had seized some of his acrimonious correspondence with Bürgers at the time of the latter's arrest, and decided that, though a social democrat, Lassalle was "not a Communist".

The trial and its aftermath showed Lassalle at his best. His personal quarrels were at once forgotten. He did all that he could to help Bürgers and his fellow-prisoners; sent them books and comforts while under arrest; looked after their dependants during their term of sentence. All the time he remained the rallying point of the Left-wing Düsseldorf workers in their hour of defeat—so much so that the secret police watched him with an ever-increasing closeness. A confidential police report of late 1851 describes him as a man of "remarkable intellectual qualities, persuasive eloquence, tireless energy, great determination, wildly Left ideas, a very wide circle of acquaintances, great practical adroitness, all supported by the considerable financial means of which his client [the Countess] disposes".

The "considerable financial means" is an exaggeration. The Countess possessed little but the uncertain issue of her suit. She could and did from time to time succeed in raising a loan, but the proceeds were mostly swallowed up by legal expenses and by the cost of her Düsseldorf establishment. There was not very much left over to devote to the needs of ship-wrecked democrats. Lassalle, on behalf of the Countess, made another appeal to Count Clemens von Westphalen. But Westphalen was not inclined to throw, as he thought, good money after bad. Besides he was a Catholic and a nobleman of the old school. He had been profoundly shocked by the revolutionary movement in the Rhineland and the part the Countess and her man of affairs were playing in it. After 1848 the old friendly relationship was never restored. Meanwhile Lassalle could expect no help from his father as the family fortunes were passing through a difficult stage.

3

OLD HEYMANN had been persuaded by his son-in-law, Ferdinand Friedland, to invest nearly all his capital in the newly formed Prague Gas Company. Friedland settled in Prague, installed himself in a big house, entertained lavishly and did all he could to make himself popular with the local magnates. He took great pains to hide his Jewish origin. Before his first grand dinner party he took aside old Lassal, who happened to be in Prague, and enjoined on him not to disclose their race. Heymann was angry, but said nothing at the time. However as soon as the company was seated he got up, asked for silence, and inquired if those present realised that they were guests of a Jew. "It is my duty", he said, "to announce that I am a Jew, my daughter is a Jewess and my son-in-law is a Jew. It is an honour for me to dine in this company, but I do not want such an honour if obtained by fraud." This speech was received with cordial applause. But it caused acute embarrassment to Friedland, and he never forgave the old man.

The Gas Company had its teething troubles. Friedland, of course, had other resources, but old Lassal, always easily alarmed, wrote in the gloomiest strain to his son. Lassalle thereupon wrote to his sister Riekchen, urging her to use all her influence with Friedland. "I gathered from what he [Heymann] wrote that he has lost all or nearly all and is now completely dependent on you and your husband. . . . As far as I know your husband, I would say, without denying his good qualities, that he is inclined to be narrow-hearted in money matters. In the world of to-day that is necessary, and indeed more of a quality than a defect. But it would be horrible if such narrow-heartedness were to appear in his relations to our parents. . . ." Lassalle goes on to express his sorrow at being himself able to do nothing for his parents in view of the present position of the Hatzfeldt affairs. "It is a point of honour with me not to desert a beaten cause. The captain is the last to leave a sinking ship. The iron clamp of honour holds me here."

Friedland appears for the time to have been reasonable. But

a year or two later came the threat of a crisis. Riekchen, who had never been particularly happy with her husband, caught him *in flagrante* with one of the housemaids and began to talk of a divorce. Lassalle called up all the worldly wisdom of his twenty-eight years to bring his sister to a sensible mood.

"I have," he wrote, "just heard of that most unfortunate incident. I quite understand your having every reason to feel humiliated and pained. F. was inexcusable in doing such a thing in your own home and at a time when your health was so precarious. But I feel you are taking it all more seriously than it really deserves. I myself do not remember any man who was strictly faithful to his wife, but I have known a great many happy marriages. A sensible woman should not mind little side steps on the part of her husband, so long as he is careful to hide them from her and provided that his treatment of her, in other respects, is all that she could desire.

"I can understand a woman being really unhappy should her husband have a permanent liaison. She feels herself supplanted by the mistress; she has reason to fear her own treatment and position will be affected. But a little dirtiness like this . . .

"If he had been treating you so badly that you already wanted a divorce and were looking out for an excuse for one, here would have been an excuse. But, since I gather you were living fairly happily together, I would not think of letting such a thing upset me. . . . You should realise how these matters appear to a man. I can assure you that very few men attach any more importance to this sort of thing than a woman does to relieving herself. It would be fatal if you pressed for a divorce. The most I would do in your position would be to make F. promise—perhaps in writing—never to do such a thing again in your house. I would not ask him to make any promises about what he does elsewhere."

4

CORRESPONDENCE with Marx in London remained close and friendly. The outstanding political event of that epoch, the *coup d'état* of Louis Napoleon, was of profound interest to both parties and in December 1851 the Countess wrote to Marx: "... Try and find time to write and tell us what you think about this disgusting affair in Paris. Lassalle seems to me to be blinded by his wishes. That is, while he correctly assesses the causes and effects of the catastrophe, he deludes himself as to how long the scoundrel's régime will last. I can't suppress the fear that it may last for years. Lassalle says that would be impossible."

Marx considered, not for the last time, that the Countess's political judgment was better than that of her man of business. Meanwhile his own affairs were going badly. In February 1852 he wrote to Lassalle:

"My health is better, though I still have eye trouble. Otherwise my position has got worse. The publishers have definitely refused my book on economics. My anti-Proudhon MS. which has been wandering round Germany for a year has equally failed to find a home. My financial crisis is as acute as the general trade crisis in New York and London. Unfortunately, unlike a business man, I can't even go bankrupt. Herr Bonaparte was in the same kind of situation when he risked his *coup d'état*."

To which Lassalle replied by return:

"It would hurt me to send you a completely empty reply in your desolate circumstances. Enclosed is a miserable three pounds sterling. These three pounds, on their journey from *misère* to *misère*, ought to have, as far as poetry and affection go, the worth of thirty...."

Lassalle exerted himself in trying to find a German publisher for Marx. For the time being he failed; his own position was not yet such that his recommendation carried weight with publishers, and he could not even find a home for Marx's *The 18th Brumaire*. But he tried, and he went on trying in spite of all the difficulties involved in smuggling in the manuscripts without the knowledge of the Prussian police. "The way you sent *The 18th Brumaire*," he wrote to Marx, "is not, as Dronke said, the cheapest. On the contrary it is hellishly expensive. I had to pay one and a half thalers. Tell Dronke to find some cheaper way." Later in 1853 we find Marx writing to Engels in Manchester "Lassalle is now the only one who has the courage to keep up a correspondence with us Londoners. We must see he does not suffer for it."

5

IN 1854 there came a sudden and complete change in Lassalle's circumstances. After eight years of persistent and bitter struggle he forced Count Hatzfeld to come to an acceptable financial settlement.

The campaign was finally won, as it had been waged, by intrigue and blackmail. Marx wrote later:

"The case came to an end in this way: Count Hatzfeldt's estate agent, Stockum, later sentenced to five years hard labour, had fallen out with the Count. He let Lassalle know he had documents in his possession which would land the Count in chains for perjury, forgery, etc. Lassalle promised him 10,000 thalers; and then persuaded the Public Prosecutor, Kösteritz—since resigned on this account—to let the Count know a charge lay against him. Hatzfeldt was just off to Paris when Lassalle produces the documents and agrees to withdraw the charge on condition the Count signs an agreement with the Countess. Kösteritz of course acted merely as Lassalle's tool."

The sum that thus came into Countess Hatzfeldt's possession was rather over 300,000 thalers, a substantial fortune in the Germany of that time. There were of course debts to be paid off, to Stockum, Kösteritz and the money-lenders. There was also the loan of 17,000 thalers from Westphalen to be settled, and we still possess a lively exchange of letters between Lassalle and Westphalen in which Lassalle attempted (unsuccessfully) to make Count Clemens renounce any interest on that sum.

Ten years later Lassalle explained, to the girl he was wanting to marry, how he himself came to benefit:

"My relations with the Countess, my complete absorption in her affairs and in her lawsuits, interrupted my career and caused me trouble with my family. It was necessary, both for my sake and for that of the Countess, that I should receive some compensation for my sacrifices, that she should not be under too great an obligation to me. So we made an agreement that once our case was won I should receive, in consideration of my time and labour, an annuity to be paid from the Hatzfeldt funds recovered. On my death these payments revert to the Countess."

The annuity fixed was 4,000 thalers—half the salary of a cabinet minister. For the rest of his life he could live as a rich man.

Chapter 7

THE MAN OF MEANS

I

For the time being Lassalle stayed on with the Countess at Düsseldorf. The new prosperity simplified a number of his problems, including that of his sister's private affairs. "The Countess", he writes, "wishes me to invite Riekchen to come to us for the winter. I feel the Countess would have a good influence on her. The financial position arising out of the settlement makes the idea of this visit practicable." The visit apparently did not come off. But in the autumn Lassalle took the waters at Ems and arranged for his family to join him there, though not without some anxiety over his mother's strict Jewish orthodoxy. "It is essential", he warned his father beforehand, "that my dear mother should eat everything that we do. There is no kosher cooking here, and I refuse either to see my mother go without or to have a fuss made about the food."

For the time being prosperity had no effect on his close relations with the Düsseldorf workers. This surprised the Prussian police. That the Countess had previously, to quote one of their reports, "devoted part of her income to the corruption of the working class" could be explained as part of the campaign against her husband. But that she and her plenipotentiary could continue, when rich, to hold Left-wing views was "almost inexplicable". By 1854, however, there was little scope for serious political activity. The last active revolutionaries had been long since arrested or assisted (in many cases by Lassalle and his client) in their flight over the Dutch frontier. There remained only evening classes, the lending of books, an occasional meeting with ostensibly cultural aims. It was inevitable that much of the time which Lassalle now had on his hands should be devoted to other circles.

He and the Countess struck up an acquaintanceship with one Georg Klindworth, a man then in his fifties, ex-teacher, ex-actor, ex-journalist, and now making a good if precarious living as secret political intelligence agent. He had no particular loyalties. He was at one time or other on the payroll of Guizot, Manteuffel, Nicholas I of Russia and Louis Napoleon. He was of the type naturally to gravitate towards the rich. No doubt he also felt that the Countess, whose brother was then Prussian Ambassador in Paris, had valuable political contacts. For Lassalle Klindworth was a useful source of information on international affairs, which he could pass on to Marx in London. Such information had another use, that is, for stock exchange transactions. Throughout the 'fifties speculators were busily exploiting the influence of international politics on share quotations. This appealed to the gambler in Lassalle and was a game which, thanks to his annuity and the favourable progress of the gas industry, he could now afford to play.

Klindworth had a daughter—Agnes Dennis-Street. Little is known of Dennis-Street, the husband. He may have been already dead. In any case he did not interfere with his wife who had a flat in Brussels but mostly travelled with her father. If ever there had been any physical relationship between Lassalle and the Countess it was now over, and she made no attempt to discourage his affair with Agnes. In 1855 Agnes gave birth to a daughter whose father was Lassalle.

2

THE CORRESPONDENCE with Marx remained, for the time, very cordial. Friedland had now acquired interests in the newspaper world, and Lassalle did his best to have Marx appointed London correspondent. In January 1855 he sent Marx 200 thalers. In the same month he asks for his views on the effects of the repeal of the Corn Laws in England, and Marx sent a detailed reply, packed with statistics. He was deeply affected by news of the death of Marx's little boy, and had a letter from Marx which ran: "Bacon says that a really superior man will find too much of interest in the world to be seriously affected by any one loss. I am not in this class. I am deeply shaken in heart and mind by the death of my son. I feel the loss as acutely now as in the first few days."

In the summer Lassalle wrote to Marx:

"A few weeks ago I wrote to Hinkeldey [Chief of the Berlin Police] to ask if there was any objection to my settling in Berlin. He replied that permission would on no account be given. *Sic stantibus rebus*, I propose to go to Italy for a couple of months. After that will be quite soon enough to get back to Düsseldorf. In the event of my not being able to live in Berlin —though in view of my connexions I don't think it will come to that—I am playing with the idea of settling provisionally in either Paris or Heidelberg. Gala performance or idyll. Or can you suggest anywhere else for me? London is too expensive. It's still of course doubtful whether they will allow me to live in Heidelberg."

He did not go on the suggested trip to Italy but went instead to Paris with his family. There Marx wrote to him: "I was surprised to hear you were so near to London and yet did not come over. I would certainly come over to Paris and surprise you if France were not hermetically sealed to me."

Lassalle intended to make the visit, but the Countess called him back to Düsseldorf where he soon became very immersed in his private affairs, and the correspondence with Marx languished.

3

LASSALLE had not only written about permission to reside in Berlin. He had, in March, journeyed to the capital, been arrested on arrival as an unauthorised visitor, been transferred from police post to police post and finally sent back to the Rhineland. He had bombarded the authorities concerned with letters, appeals and memoranda. He had begged all his friends to use their influence. But the authorities remained adamant.

There were various motives behind his urge towards Berlin. Berlin had always held an attraction for him. He was the type that could never be happy living away from a capital. Then he had decided to devote his newly acquired leisure to his long-projected work on Heraklitus; he wanted the Berlin libraries for research and the Berlin *salons* in which to play the lion after publication. Finally his relations with the Countess were coming to a crisis.

There was no definite issue at stake or quarrel. The old affection and esteem remained, perhaps more strongly than either party realised. But they were both difficult, both temperamental, both nervy. Both were feeling the strain of the eight-year struggle. Lassalle was ambitious. Sophie von Hatzfeldt was afraid of a lonely old age, and apt to hanker after her old friends and her old position in society. Lassalle knew how she felt and was jealous. He was jealous, too, of her love for her son Paul. And Paul was growing into a smart young nobleman, naturally resentful of his family name being coupled with that of Lassalle. The joint household at Düsseldorf was becoming impossible. In August the Countess wrote from Wildbad where she was taking a cure: "Our ways must part. The real reason for our differences is this—you are young and I am old. You are brave and pressing forward, and I can no longer follow you. How proud and glad I would be if I could. . . . You want to move to Berlin. That I understand and wish: though I am afraid of your doing foolish things when I am no longer there to warn and plead with you. . . ."

The winter and spring they spent at Düsseldorf together, Lassalle busy on his *Heraklitus*. Friction and squabbles persisted. To make a break Lassalle planned to join Friedland on a tour to Turkey and Egypt later in the year. In June the Countess went off to her spa, and Agnes Dennis-Street came to Düsseldorf to stay with Lassalle. The two of them went on to Bonn, where Lassalle made use of the university library. His eyes were hurting him and Agnes acted as secretary. As the time for his Eastern tour drew near he began to regret he had promised to go. He asked the Countess to write to Friedland and make excuses for him; instead they would go for a tour in Switzerland—the Countess, himself and Agnes. "Don't imagine I suggest this for Agnes's sake or for my own. It is for the principle. Also it will be pleasanter for you. There will be someone to stay behind with you when I go mountaineering."

However the Eastern tour was not cancelled, though Lassalle still protested that he did not want to go. His correspondence with the Countess becomes more affectionate. "No one since Goethe has written letters like yours," he wrote, "and not even Goethe had your warmth and liveliness. You are so natural, so naïve and so childlike in the way you pour your heart out —so much wit, so much intelligence, and so much touching absurdity. . . ."

The Countess, fearing loneliness, suggested that Agnes should stay with her for the winter. Lassalle put it to Agnes, but "that loathsome creature her father won't allow it. He is going to London and wants her to stay in Brussels. A ridiculous pretext. She can't be any use to him there and Brussels doesn't suit her."

In mid-September Lassalle joined his brother-in-law in Prague. He made much of his eye trouble, whereupon Friedland took him to a specialist who declared that the tour would do him good. Lassalle raised no more difficulties and two days later they set out for Budapest. On the eve of his departure he wrote to the Countess: "What really decided me to go was the wish to improve the relations between our two selves. If our friendship were to come to an end it would be a great misfortune, a defeat for love, friendship and truth, a crime against all ideal bonds that unite two human beings. . . ." But he continues: "After thinking it over very seriously I am convinced that you are almost solely to blame for our difficulties. All you can reproach me for is my natural impatience, which, however, never comes out except under strong provocation."

4

LASSALLE's correspondence with Marx had ceased some time before his departure for the East. Lassalle had written, Marx had not answered, Lassalle had been preoccupied with other matters. It is certain that Lassalle had no notion that Marx's attitude towards him had in any way changed.

It was natural, with Lassalle's personality, that many people did not like him. He had, as we have seen, personal enemies among his political allies. In 1853 Marx received a report on him from a certain Wiss, describing him as a "clever *roué* who would stick at nothing, not even betraying his friends, so long as he could twiddle his thumbs, live like Lucullus and play the big man." Marx took no notice of the report; but he preserved it. A life of exile is apt to make for suspiciousness, even, or perhaps especially, within one's own political circle.

Meanwhile, in the Rhineland, with the change in Lassalle's manner of life, the feeling against him increased. His old collaborators objected to his friendships with people like Klindworth. The workers objected to his intention of moving to Berlin. At first they had no spokesman. But then one Gustav Lewy, a small business man and one of the most active of the Düsseldorf democrats, applied to the Countess for a loan. Lassalle advised the Countess against it. A few weeks later Lewy arrived in London, and on 5th March Marx reported to Engels in Manchester that Lewy had been sent over by the Düsseldorf workers to denounce Lassalle.

"After a very sharp cross-examination I think they are right. . . . They accuse him of having constantly exploited the party for his private dirt—even of trying to make use of the workers for private crimes in the interests of his law suits. . . . They have produced a mass of unsavoury personal details which I cannot repeat because I forget them one after another. . . . Now that he has won his case, instead of letting the Countess pay him for his work and making himself independent, he lives under her yoke as a kept man without any pretext whatsoever. . . . In a deliberately provocative way he flings the workers aside as superfluous tools. . . . They say his plan is to go to Berlin, play the great gentleman there and open a *salon*. . . . To show how dangerous he is, moreover: in order to smuggle one of the workers' party into the police as a sham spy he gave the man one of *my* letters and told him to establish his credentials by saying he had stolen it from Lassalle. . . . He seems to regard himself as something very different from what we took him for. He thinks he can order the world about just because he rushed into a private intrigue. As if a man of any worth would give ten years of his life to that sort of rubbish! It has made a definite impression on me, much as I used to think of him."

Engels, with the generous air of a man who had foreseen it all, replied: "A pity, in view of his very real talent. But he was always a man one had to watch very closely."

Marx asked for further evidence. None was forthcoming. But the minutes of the denunciation were filed away to await such time as they might be required.

5

LASSALLE, unaware of all this, went on his way. The other members of the party were Friedland, one Haase—one of Friedland's big business friends in Prague—and Weitling, a pianist. They spent a few days in Budapest where they drank a lot of champagne, admired the girls, and "listened in the gardens to the wild music of the gipsies, who were, unfortunately, in evening dress." They went on by river craft to Zemun. For one brought up in Byronic traditions the Danubian plain was disappointing after the beetling crags and Gothic ruins of the Middle Rhine. But there was champagne on board and they played cards with the ship's captain. At Zemun they came into conflict with Austrian bureaucracy over a faulty endorsement on two of the passports, and three days were spent in exasperated argument. Finally matters were put right, and the party went across the river to spend a day of sightseeing in Belgrade, then still under Turkish rule. Lassalle describes the outing in the first of the long letters home to be passed round his family and friends which he intended as the record of his tour:

"We landed with great expectations. It was our first glimpse of the Orient. But our expectations were more than surpassed. I cannot describe the riot of colour, strange, varied, picturesque yet always tasteful, of these costumes that emphasised the beauty of the bodies they clothed. And the faces, the sharp-cut noses, the fiery eyes, the noble profiles—it was a real joy to wander through the steep and ill-paved streets of Belgrade."

They called on the Pasha, and were so embarrassed by his unbroken silence during the interview that they committed the gross breach of Turkish etiquette of leaving before coffee was served.

The following day they continued their journey by river. The scenery was again dismissed as unromantic and their interest was centred on their fellow-passengers—on the magnificent beard of the Orthodox Bishop of Bucharest, on "a real boyar"—Prince Ghika—and in particular on the Princess. At Orsova the water was too low for the steamer to put in to the quay, and the passengers were dumped on the bank two miles down. Lassalle found this behaviour of the Austrian steamship company typical of the rottenness of all Austrian institutions. After a night in a verminous hotel they went on to Bucharest by carriage. They were not impressed by what they saw along their journey.

"The Wallachian peasant women's clothes are really remarkable. There is no trace of the gay colours of the Serbs. Indeed I can declare that an American Indian's feathers show not only a greater sense of beauty but a more advanced stage of civilisation. Bodies and clothing alike are coated with thick, impenetrable, primeval filth. . . . Haase poured himself out a glass of water and at once had twenty-seven flies in his mouth. . . . I had never before realised the true worth of the German worker. Neglected and betrayed by the State and by Society he has fought his own way to the standard of civilisation he has now attained. . . . Whether he is to be forced down again to the level of the Roumanian, or whether he will succeed in developing and establishing his inherent human worth—that is the battle that will soon shake Europe from end to end."

Bucharest was gaudy, ramshackle and stimulating. Their hotel was primitive and its sanitary arrangements appalling. But the Bucharest cabs were elegant and surprisingly cheap. Friedland was at once involved in negotiations for a Roumanian gas company. Lassalle himself saw possibilities of making money. "I want", he wrote, "my father to buy me some Jassy

Bank shares. I see no newspapers here, so cannot judge how political considerations may affect them: but otherwise they are a good investment and yield at least nine or ten per cent. . . . With us in Germany banking is camouflaged robbery, but here it is open robbery."

They were advised to pay a visit to a certain establishment. They did so, but were refused admittance. The *padrona* was full of excuses, but she had a party of boyars in the house and could admit no one else. Lassalle announced "*Je suis plus que Boyar chez moi, et je ne suis pas accoutumé à me laisser montrer la porte.*" He strode past her with his party and introduced himself to the young noblemen. Weitling sat down to the piano and a convivial evening followed.

From Bucharest they went on, via Galatz and Constanza, to Istanbul. Here Lassalle found a number of letters from the Countess.

"You are quite right to have bought a pistol. But I can't say how anxious I am that you have no proper clothes. Have you a rug and a fur coat? You *must* take care to keep warm, mornings and evenings, and don't lie on the ground. . . . Of course I will take care of your *Heraklitus* and all your books. . . .

"I am really worried by this terrible slump on the Bourse. It gets worse every day. French Rentes have dropped to 66 and the Geneva Bank shares to 87. . . . My heartfelt wishes go to you now and always. Write to me often in my loneliness—not long letters, just to say how you are and where you are going. You know how morbidly anxious I am. Think of me as one who, in spite of everything, will always be the truest friend you have. I won't go to your sister's in Prague. I am too ill and too dismal. I should be poor company. I may go to Berlin. I may just relapse into loneliness. Anyhow for the moment business will keep me here in Düsseldorf. The only person I would care to see, if he were to come, would be your father. But what would the poor man do, even on a short visit, with so dismal a creature as myself? So I won't suggest it. . . .

"As to our two selves, to give myself patience and calm I

ask myself: is it right that the healthy should be yoked to the sick and the living to the dead? . . ."

Lassalle telegraphed:

"*Arrivé heureusement trouvé lettre. S'il est nécessaire si vous désirez vivement je retourne directement. Télégraphiez.*"

The Countess wired back that he should not return, and he thereupon wrote to her:

"I can't tell you how I suffered when I read your letter of the 23rd. When I got to what you said about your lonely dreary house in Düsseldorf my tears began to flow. I sobbed like a child. . . . No, Countess. Yoking myself to you is not a yoke for me. It is my prerequisite for any real happiness. . . .

"Don't let yourself be worried by the fall in your securities, and, I repeat, do *not* sell. . . ."

It was in Istanbul that he had news of the death of Arnold Mendelssohn. Mendelssohn, to earn a living, had entered Turkish service as an army doctor and died during the Crimean War. Lassalle, though he had made no effort to keep in touch with him, was deeply moved.

"He had agreed to be transferred from his regiment at Kars to another unit, and had marched with them to Bajazid on the Persian frontier. Five miles short of Bajazid he contracted typhus. This was in April 1854, four months before I settled our case. . . .

"My God, could he but live again! Invulnerable myself, it is my hard fate that disaster always comes to those I love. Mine is the fate of the Wandering Jew. How far better if I had died! This is the due I had to pay for your victory, Countess. Now you have a debt to pay. My Arnold is dead. You must make good all the love and friendship I have lost in him."

His "open" letters—the day-to-day descriptions of his tour—are less dramatic. He liked his hotel and was delighted with the view from his bedroom window over the Bosphorus. His one complaint was the charge:

"My room, including English breakfast and dinner—here as in Switzerland they charge *en pension* terms—costs no less than 25 Swiss francs per day. Light and service are extras . . . the cost of living and especially of sight-seeing works out here at such enormous sums that I am frightened at the speed at which my purse gets lighter!"

He was assiduous in sight-seeing. He went to the bazaars. He visited a mosque where he was struck with the similarity of the chanting with that he had heard as a child in the synagogue in Breslau. He was taken to see the dervishes. But the outstanding experience was to watch the Sultan's procession to prayers. Not far from where he stood was a carriage with some of the Seraglio ladies:

"Their veils were so thin and transparent as to reduce the ordinance to a farce. And what eyes we saw, what features, and especially what dazzling complexions! It is not like flesh, it is sunshine itself on glowing marble! In Europe one can form no conception of what human beauty can attain. My pulse and breathing stopped! There was one, especially, in lemon-gold silk, with great dark gazelle's eyes. If I had only known a little Turkish and were ten years younger with the mad courage of my youth I would not have left Constantinople without her. As it was I left unto Cæsar the things that were Cæsar's."

From Istanbul the party went on to Smyrna. Here were more letters from the Countess.

"The slump on the stock exchange is getting worse and worse. . . . I have spent the last fortnight putting your books in order and drawing up a list. It was a tremendous piece of work as you had done nothing about it yourself. . . . I really must take you to task. In a country full of dirt and disease how could you drink out of anyone else's glass? The excellent custom of not drinking out of other people's glasses or eating with their forks is not just one of those social conventions you rail at. It is merely being sensible. . . ."

The Countess also dealt at some length with the question of the Klindworths:

"You tell me not to lend more money to the Klindworths. I had anticipated this advice. As soon as I got back here they asked for 300 thalers, which I very politely but very definitely refused. Since then I have not heard a word from them. They are like a bottomless pit. They could easily have got through this year with a little management. He has a thousand francs a month, free quarters, free travel and hotel bills paid. Then he has had 400 thalers from us I know—I believe you were mad enough to give them more; two hundred from Block. And they keep running up new debts. One has to be careful as this sort of friendship may lead anywhere. Weerth, whom I saw in Cologne, said they tried to get ten thousand francs out of him all at once. . . .

"From all I have seen and heard I feel we may have made a mistake about Agnes. She has a pleasant personality, and, I believe, a nice disposition; but has little character and takes the colour of whomever she happens to be with. She lacks a firm foundation, and, as I have noticed in certain small matters, she isn't always sincere. Don't think this is just silly jealousy. You know I'm not naturally jealous and you know too how pleased I should be at your liaison with her were she all I at first thought her to be. As it is my advice as a friend is that you should be careful. She is not a woman who can make you lastingly happy. . . . Do be careful. I have felt for some time you are being exploited and that she only ran after you because she saw you were generous. All sorts of little things have struck me—especially the way she talked about you in Wildbad. I was particularly annoyed at what she said to Paul. I may say nasty things about you, when I'm excited and upset, but I won't have anyone else doing so. I had a scene with Paul about it, and then I wrote to her demanding an explanation: but she didn't answer. . . ."

At Smyrna the party made an expedition on horseback with some local residents. They lost their way for some hours. Weitling's horse bolted and threw him: the unfortunate pianist lay where he fell and called to Lassalle that he had broken his arm and was ruined for life. There was excitement and alarm. Weitling was picked up and the runaway horse was caught. It was very late when the disconsolate party reached Smyrna, and there was more excitement and alarm when at first the only reliable doctor could not be found. At last he was located. He examined Weitling and pronounced that the arm was not broken; in fact there was no serious injury at all. All the company, including doctor and patient, sat down to a festive dinner. Afterwards Lassalle went off to the local casino and spent the night gambling. His luck was in, and next day he went round the bazaars and laid out his winnings on two Turkish carpets, one for himself and one for the Countess.

From Smyrna they took ship for Egypt. Lassalle's next letter home records his judgment on ocean travel:

"The view is so monotonous as to be tiring. The movement of the ship, being constant, is imperceptible. I cannot understand why the beauties of a sea voyage can ever be compared with those of a journey in the Alps. No doubt during a storm there is poetry and power in the spectacle. But one would not be in the mood for it, not because of the danger—that would not affect me—but because of seasickness."

There was no storm and the party duly arrived at Alexandria, to be fought over on the quay by a turbulent mob of porters, donkey-men, cab-drivers, guides, interpreters and touts. They drove through the streets, noting the first cab to be seen since Bucharest and the first omnibus since Pest. And "at last we arrived safely in the Hotel d'Orient, kept by a German, Herr Zeck, and with a German-speaking staff except for the Nubians and the Negroes. How pleasant to hear an honest German tongue in distant Africa!"

After a few days in Alexandria they went on to Cairo. Lassalle contemplated a trip up the Nile. But time was passing, and he wanted to return to finish his book. There were also the affairs of the Countess to attend to, as the persistent fall on the stock exchange was seriously affecting her fortune and, incidentally, his own. By the end of the year he was back in Germany.

Chapter 8

THE MAN OF LETTERS

I

February 1857 found Lassalle in the house at Düsseldorf, working on his *Heraklitus* and lobbying for permission to settle in Berlin. Early in the month the Countess went to the capital on family business. On the 8th Lassalle wrote to her: "Do everything possible to secure my move to Berlin. Send for my father if he could do any good. I shall have finished *Heraklitus* by mid-March and have a passionate urge to come to Berlin to arrange for its publication. . . . I am terribly impatient to get to Berlin. I can hardly force myself to be calm enough to finish the book."

Next day he wrote: "At last a letter from you so I needn't be anxious. But you don't seem to have done anything about my affair." On the 12th: "My letter shouldn't be taken as finding fault with you: it was only meant to spur you to greater effort." On the 18th: "You must give some time to my affairs even though it means less for your son and your sister." And on the 26th: "Why do you keep saying I'm always finding fault with you?"

There came a new complication. Lassalle had written to Agnes for an explanation of what the Countess had said about the scene between the two women at Wildbad the previous autumn. Agnes wrote back that she refused to start a long correspondence about this rubbish: all that had happened was that the Countess had told her she was grateful for what Lassalle had done, but she had to go back to her son and to society and would like Agnes's advice as to how to set about breaking with him.

This touched Lassalle on the raw. That same day, the 27th, he wrote to the Countess: "This morning there comes this letter from Agnes. Please tell me at once if there is any truth in it. . . . But how unnecessary to discuss it with Agnes and her father instead of just telling me! One word to me would have resolved all the difficulties. It never occurred to me that I might be a handicap to you. I had always assumed, in spite of our quarrels, that I was necessary for your happiness."

To his father, then also in Berlin, he wrote: "The Countess is letting herself become the victim of illusions. She thinks I am likely to provoke a scandal. I almost believe that because of her family she doesn't want me in Berlin." Meanwhile he instructs old Heymann to get an introduction to Manteuffel, the Minister of the Interior, so as to intervene in the matter of the permit. Or, better still, to telegraph to Friedland to come to Berlin and bring with him "letters of introduction from one of his Archdukes".

The Countess refuted what Agnes had written, but Lassalle was not satisfied and the wrangling correspondence went on. Friedland came to Berlin. But still nothing happened. "My God," Lassalle wrote to his father on 22nd March, "you must remember I am sitting here on a burning grill. I finished my book three days ago. . . . And you, you are getting nowhere, you don't write and you don't act."

His impatience was now directed more against his own relations than against the Countess, to whom he wrote a friendly letter on the same day: "If you are really worried about your Cologne shares you had better sell them to Wolff for 40,000 thalers." He discusses a project they had for visiting Egypt together and asks her to postpone it. "I have reached a time of life when I've got to do something about my immortality. I propose to bring off three big *coups* between now and next spring. First of all *Heraklitus*, then another thing I am just starting to write and am very excited about; thirdly my book on economics. . . ."

Three days later, 25 March, came the exasperating news that a Breslau professor was about to bring out a rival work on the philosopher of Ephesus. What was still graver was a report from Friedland that it was being said at the Prussian Court that the Queen did not wish Countess von Hatzfeldt and Lassalle to be seen in Berlin together.

However, Lassalle was nearer to his goal than he imagined. It may have been that the authorities wished to put an end to his permanent association with the Countess, whose normal domicile remained for the time being in Düsseldorf. It may have been that the police saw the force of the contention he advanced in one of his applications—that it would be easier for them to watch him in Berlin. In any case a final appeal, accompanied by a medical certificate, to be allowed to visit a Berlin eye specialist, produced the desired result. The Chief of the Berlin Police issued an order that "Ferdinand Lassalle, *Partikulier*, is to be accorded permission to reside in Berlin for a maximum period of six months on account of his need of medical treatment and in view of the publication of a work he has composed on Heraklitus".

Lassalle went off to Berlin.

2

IT WAS natural that on the eve of publication of his first major work Lassalle should turn to the one man whose opinion and judgment he profoundly respected. On his return from the East he had written to Marx. Marx had not answered. Now, in April, he wrote again.

"I have not heard from you for two years. Is it right to leave me all this time without a word? . . . How is your wife? And the children? And our friends—Freiligrath, Wolff, Engels, Dronke, etc.? It isn't you who are exiles, rather myself. There are so many of you old war comrades together in one town; but here I have been alone for years, cut off from my brothers in arms, the last of the Mohicans as I once sentimentally called myself. . . ." He goes on to the burning topic of his book—"a major work, half philosophical, half philological. I have finished it and am now about to bring it out. You may think I am being too academic, as it has so little connexion with the immediate or rather with the practical needs of the age." He counters this by maintaining that politics and intellectual science can never be independent. Finally "we Germans are a theoretical people —which I hope we shall not always be in one sense of the word.

It might be useful if I acquired a certain prestige among our theorists."

Marx sat on the letter. He asked Engels whether he should answer it. Engels thought he should, but Lassalle should be made to explain the Düsseldorf denunciation. Marx still hesitated. Finally he replied. He did not refer to Lewy's denunciation. But, on his side at any rate, the old confidence and friendship was never to be fully restored.

3

THE PUBLICATION of *Heraklitus* was undertaken by Franz Duncker, who besides his publishing business owned the *Volkszeitung* and had a large circle of friends in political, intellectual and business circles.

Lassalle, once in Berlin, made up his mind to stay there. There was, of course, the risk that the police might turn him out, but as he wrote to the Countess (back in Düsseldorf) "one cannot guarantee anything, not even life, so I have decided to have my furniture sent here. Please arrange this. I am surprised my books are not here already." The Countess had his furniture packed and recommended a servant. "Let me know", she wrote, "if you have taken him on. I would like to feel you had a good man. See that he gets into regular and economical ways from the start."

On the 12th May he announces in triumph: "I have taken a flat at 131 Potsdamer Strasse. A garden in front. The house is delightful. The upper ground floor (my flat) is too high to be damp. Two front rooms each with two windows—my study and my sitting-room. . . . But where is the servant to sleep? The kitchen (on the floor below) is damp; and the alternative, the alcove, leads out of my bedroom. It would be most disagreeable to have the man sleeping under my nose."

The furniture duly arrived and was installed, but before the end of the month there was more trouble. The Countess wished to pay another visit to Berlin, and Lassalle was afraid that if she came back so soon the police might cancel his own *permis de séjour*. The Countess suggested he should consult Paul. By this time Paul and Lassalle disliked each other heartily, and Lassalle wrote back (27th May): "I have neither time nor desire to consult your son. I am always ready to help him, but have not the slightest need of his advice. . . . I am perfectly prepared, if need be, to leave you to the exclusive cult of your family gods. . . ." On the 28th the Countess replied: "This is going too far. Only an idiot could put up with what I have had to endure from you in the last ten years." Lassalle retorts on the 30th that her letter was "a mesh of lies", and on the 31st the Countess refers to his as a tangle of "baseless and insulting reproaches and distorted facts".

The quarrel came to nothing. The Countess came to Berlin and left again for Wildbad. She was unhappy. She found herself cold-shouldered by her fellow cure-guests. "I am not old enough to be indifferent or young enough to laugh it off." Again, "I am very worried about my money matters—worried because I have had no benefit from the fortune we fought so bitterly to recover and so much of which has already been lost; worried because of Paul who is completely dependent on me; worried because I couldn't survive the shame of my enemies saying—as they always said—that any money I got would be lost."

Meanwhile Lassalle in Berlin was complaining of his health. "I am suffering from colic, although for a fortnight now I have eaten nothing but cold veal." Otherwise he was enjoying himself. Apart from seeing *Heraklitus* through the press he was working on his second bid for immortality. At the same time he was attaining his ambition of making his way into smart society. As regards this last we find a defensive note in his letters to the Countess, who knew much more about such matters than he did. On the 13th August he wrote:

"You maintain that no lady of good breeding in Berlin would visit a bachelor. Good. In the circle I move in here is: (1) a certain Countess Kalckreuth. She pretends to be an intellectual, but is really royalist, and religious into the bargain. Her brother has a high military post. She is a spinster, not quite forty; (2) Frau von Rappard, thirty-six years old, divorced

—her husband was a blackguard—but of unblemished reputation; (3) Frau von Dohm. These three with myself and two other men made an excursion to Tegel. We came back at midnight, all in very good spirits. I proposed a night-cap at my flat. None of the ladies even thought of objecting. We arrived at my flat at half-past twelve and drank champagne till two. . . . There is your answer. The Kalckreuth is a Countess and Frau von Rappard is also noble, and quite passably pretty, though very fat."

The Countess replied: "The women you mention are no criterion for my position. They can do what they like because nobody bothers about them. In my case it is quite different." In his next letter Lassalle takes a new line of approach. "What sanctions can 'Society' apply? There are none in law. The risk of the loss of an allowance or legacy does not apply to anyone financially independent like yourself. 'Society' can only employ sanctions against persons weak enough to pay attention to its dictates. True, twenty years ago a woman who cut herself off from society would be isolated. But that no longer applies. To-day there are dissident circles, who refuse to recognise Society's bonds and are now happy in ignoring them." He goes on to point out that the Countess's troubles are solely due to her persistence in clinging to her family connexions.

In September came news of the death of his daughter by Agnes Dennis-Street. On the 12th he wrote to the Countess: "My little Fernande is dead. I had a despairing letter from her mother. I am very sad about the child. I wanted to do wonders with her education. She was teething when she died." The Countess wrote back: "I am deeply moved that the poor little child is dead, both for your sake and mine. Later on, when I am old, she would have been an interest to me. . . . Perhaps this death of a little child whom you never even saw will make you realise what a parent's love can mean: think what it is when one has been with one's child for eighteen years."

The death of the child cannot have meant much to Lassalle. It further loosened his ties to Agnes, but for some time now these ties had been very slender. He had already had a liaison with Frau von Dohm, and was now turning his attentions to Lina Duncker, the wife of his publisher.

4

IN THE AUTUMN of 1857 there appeared the first volume of *Heraklitus the Obscure, the Philosopher of Ephesus.* It was a remarkable *tour de force.* By his ingenuity and research he added appreciably to the existing number of intelligible fragments; and he offered an elaborate and impressive reconstruction, on Hegelian lines, of the Ephesian's philosophic system. His work on the text has of course been superseded by the labour of subsequent and more exact philologians, and his reconstruction no longer appeals to an un-Hegelian minded generation. But it was a considerable achievement to have satisfied as he did the exacting standards of the academic world of the Berlin of his day.

The reception of both first and second volumes exceeded even Lassalle's expectations. Humboldt, Varnhagen and Lepsius, sent warm congratulatory letters or called in person. Brugsch, the Egyptologist, read the book and "got it into his head it is my mission to explain the Book of the Dead, which has been translated but not yet understood". Boeckh's letter was such that Lassalle made a copy and sent it to his parents, telling them, however, to send it back within twenty-four hours as he did not want it "to be hawked round to cousins and aunts". Karl Ludwig Michelet, the President of the Berlin Philosophical Society, arranged that Lassalle should be invited to become a member. Lassalle was radiant. He reported his triumphs in detail to the Countess, adding "I regard and value everything only in so far as it is connected with you. . . . I am doing all I can to win over the right people and prepare the ground for you." The Countess answered: "I can't tell you how glad I am at the way *Heraklitus* has been welcomed. Quite apart from my personal prospects from it I feel as if it was partly my own work, as if I had collaborated. I am just a little hurt that you did not dedicate your first book to me."

As was natural, Lassalle sent Marx a copy on publication, and followed it up with an account of its reception. "Philosophers and scholars go before me like the heralds of King Ahasueras before Mordechai and proclaim 'This is the man who has written *Heraklitus*.'" It was, perhaps, a tactless approach to Marx in the sordid obscurity of his Soho lodgings, and Marx did not answer. Weeks later, on 10th February 1858, Lassalle wrote again. Marx was at that time in desperate need of paid literary work and had failed to find a publisher for his *Zur Kritik der politischen Ökonomie*. He wrote back promising to give his considered opinion on *Heraklitus* when he had had the time to read it carefully. On 3rd March Lassalle announced that he was urging his cousin Max Friedland, editor of a Vienna daily, to appoint Marx London correspondent. On 26th March he reported that he had found a publisher for Marx's *Kritik*. Jenny Marx wrote back to thank him, her husband being ill. It was not till 31st May that Marx gave his opinion of *Heraklitus*. "Masterly . . ." but "I believe it could have been condensed without disadvantage. I would also have preferred a more critical attitude towards Hegel. While admittedly his dialectic is philosophy's last word it is essential to free it from Hegel's mystical nimbus."

In his letters to Engels Marx is more outspoken. "Heraklitus the Obscure, by Lassalle the Bright, is a feeble composition. There is an enormous display of erudition. But when one has time and money and, like Lassalle, can send to the Bonn University Library for any book one wants it is easy to compose this exhibition of quotations. . . . The book adds nothing to what Hegel wrote in his *History of Philosophy*: he merely goes into elaborate detail over what could have been easily contained in a small pamphlet. . . . One can see how important he feels himself. He is behaving just like a young man with his first smart suit." As to the book's reception in Berlin: "It seems a fact that the elderly professors were astonished to experience this posthumous flowering of a past age."

5

LASSALLE of course remained happily ignorant of what Marx wrote to Engels. Meanwhile his own letters show him in a cheerful mood. His father came to stay in the Potsdamer Strasse flat and he wrote to his mother: "What I've had to suffer from Father while he was here is unbelievable. He was bullying me the whole time. It would have been even worse if I hadn't threatened him with you. He still has some respect for you! Anyhow now you've got him back give me some revenge by taking it out of him."

He was extremely busy. He was writing one book and collecting the materials for two others. He was taking lessons in Egyptian hieroglyphics from Professor Brugsch. There were the sessions of the Berlin Philosophical Society. There was his voluminous correspondence. There was a great deal of talk. And there were his social activities. The Countess, who, after her stock exchange losses, was talking about having to give up her summer cures, grew anxious about the money he was spending. On 5th December 1857 Lassalle wrote back: "You know my heaviest expenses are incurred in view of the position I wish to create for you. . . . For this I have to go to a certain expense. If you think I am idiotic enough to try and impress people by spending money I can only laugh. A man of my personality and importance would have no need to do that. But since I am working for your social position I have to set about it in this way."

So he continued, keeping the Countess well posted: "I gave an extremely brilliant supper party" (there follows a list of the fourteen guests). "As one guest failed to arrive, and in order to reassure the superstitious, Madame Duncker was kind enough to send for her small daughter who had gone to bed" (the Dunckers lived across the street). "The thirteen of us—plus one child—drank five bottles of claret, four of hock and eight of champagne."

The Countess became a little restive at the increasingly frequent mention of Frau Duncker, and Lassalle had to write on the 1st March: "It would be most unjust to think that my friendship for you could be at all affected by my new friendships here. You yourself once realised that. You often used to laugh and say a love affair would make no difference, as I would always be ready to drop anyone else for your sake. Well, I am saying that to everyone here, women and all, and when you come I will prove it. I put on my dictatorial air—I am good at doing that—and announce 'Any one who fails to love, admire and respect the Countess will be regarded by me as an *être stupide* and will be struck off my list of lady friends.' . . ."

It was not only the Countess who took exception to Lassalle's growing intimacy with Lina Duncker. There is no record of Duncker himself making difficulties, but Frau Duncker's other admirers were exasperated to find themselves cut out by the self-satisfied Jew from the provinces. In particular there was a certain Fabrice, a senior official of the Commissariat. There had been a quarrel at the Dunckers' house early in the year: Lassalle was sarcastic, Fabrice felt insulted and sent him a challenge. Lassalle replied that duelling was against his principles. In late May Fabrice and a friend of his lay in wait for Lassalle in the Tiergarten and attacked him as he was going home. But they had not reckoned with their man. Lassalle had with him his ebony walking-stick with a gold knob in the shape of the Bastille. "Fabrice", he wrote to the Countess, "will long show the mark I made on him. The blow was so hard that the gold knob came off my stick. I hit him with all my force on the forehead and his face was a stream of blood."

He routed his assailants, but the incident got into the press and became the talk of Berlin. Lassalle was considerably embarrassed, and was tempted, in spite of his principles, himself to challenge Fabrice. He wrote to Marx for advice. "For the first time in thirteen years I need someone who can tell me what to do." It was true, he went on, he had always regarded duelling "not only as the fossilised relic of a vanished era but also as inconsistent with the principles of democracy". However if he took no action he would expose himself to the charge of cowardice, which "would be very painful to my vanity, which I find now I have quite a lot of".

Marx consulted Engels and Wolff and wrote out their joint decision on the 6th June. This was to the effect that, by their form of attack, Fabrice and his accomplices had proved themselves "*canaille*", with whom an honourable duel would be unthinkable. Duelling could only be justified when it was the only possible remedy for "a deep spiritual collision", which was not the case in this instance. Otherwise a duel "is a farce, and certainly so when it is merely the result of deference to public opinion". Further, as Lassalle had previously declared that duelling was against his principles the question of public opinion did not arise. Finally, fashionable duels were nothing more than the convention of a privileged class. To recognise the desirability of a duel would, in these circumstances, be a "counter-revolutionary act"

The Countess, an obvious authority on matters of good breeding, also advised strongly against a challenge and Lassalle let the idea drop. But the matter was not entirely closed. Lassalle's original permit to reside in Berlin had been for six months. It had been provisionally renewed but remained subject to cancellation at four weeks' notice. The police continued to suspect him. They had recently discovered that he was still giving money to the dependants of some of those sentenced in the Communist trial. The Fabrice affair gave them further ammunition. As Lassalle wrote to Marx on the 23rd July:

"This business has had another sequel. The swine Fabrice—I learned this myself from police headquarters—has made a denunciation about some alleged subversive remarks I am supposed to have made at the Dunckers'. To curry favour with the authorities he even says that this was the reason for his challenge. As a result the Chief of Police sent me an expulsion order. But I put up a *bonne resistance.* I set Boeckh and Humboldt in motion and they have both shown great energy. . . ."

When his first attempt failed to secure the withdrawal of the expulsion order Lassalle composed a petition which he presented, through Humboldt, to the Prince of Prussia. This document, extremely able like so many of Lassalle's compositions and rather too long, was primarily an appeal for royal favour on behalf of learning and the Arts. It represents the police as "arbitrarily and with threat of force preventing my labours in the sphere of philosophy . . . it is a question, Royal Highness, of my very existence in the learned world". This bid for royal favour on the part of a declared republican has provoked comment. Marx, it has been suggested, would never have taken such a step. It failed to have immediate effect and Lassalle left Berlin for his summer holiday with the threat of permanent banishment from the capital hanging over him.

Chapter 9

THE MAN OF LETTERS (CONTINUED)

I

Lassalle came back to Berlin in October to find a different political atmosphere. The old King was ill and dying, the Prince of Prussia had assumed the Regency and the reactionary Manteuffel cabinet had resigned. The German Liberals were hailing the dawn of the "New Era". The Berlin police fought a rearguard action over Lassalle's *permis de séjour* but they had no longer support from above. A few months later instructions were issued that "no further opposition should be made to the author Lassalle's application to settle in Berlin"

Lassalle resumed his former way of life. His mother wanted to give him a fur coat, and he wrote back (November 1858) explaining that "(1) A good one—i.e. the only sort I could wear—would cost at least 150 thalers. (2) I can manage with my present overcoat. (3) The Countess wants to give me one. (4) I have no time to go to a tailor to be measured. (5) I want a lot of expensive books for my work on economics, so I would rather you gave me the money to buy books with."

His relations with the Countess continued to be complicated by his jealousy of Paul and her jealousy of Lina Duncker. There had been trouble over the holidays which they had planned to spend together: the Countess suggested Wildbad (where Paul would be coming), and Lassalle Switzerland (with the Dunckers). As it was they went their separate ways. Lassalle wrote to her from Switzerland: "Believe it or not, beautiful things give only half their pleasure when you are not with me. I wander dreaming through this Paradise without the friend who would increase and create my happiness by sharing it." But soon after he returned to Berlin the Countess told him it was time he "transferred his allegiance to Frau Duncker"

Lassalle replied that he "must emphatically protest. I insist that you keep your office. I don't know how obedient I am to you, but it's a thousand times more so than I could or would be to anyone else."

The Countess was to have come to Berlin for Christmas, but she postponed her visit as, after her stock exchange losses, she did not think she could afford all the tips and presents that Christmas in Berlin would involve. Lassalle had also had losses, but his reaction was different. In January he wrote:

"I have just taken a new flat for—five hundred thalers! But what magnificence! Bellevuestrasse. *Haut parterre.* Four big reception rooms all adjoining. An immense drawing-room, *Bosserie* gilded ceilings, etc., dining-room where I can seat thirty people, magnificently decorated! A large library, then a smaller room, for a study, with windows looking on to a conservatory. . . . If I want to I can invite a hundred people. You may think I'm mad. I'm not. I just feel I only live once and I don't want to miss anything. Of course with a flat like this I shall entertain on a corresponding scale now and then. All this I can just manage with 2,800 thalers; perhaps not quite but certainly with 3,000—and, easily with 3,500. On an income of 4,000 there would be money over and I should have to think out how to spend it. If I had between 5 and 6,000 I should hardly know how to spend it all. Anyhow to make my income up to the 4,000 I need for a comfortable life and a good deal of hospitality I propose to make a new arrangement with my brother-in-law. If he doesn't agree I shall get it out of Geneva bank shares. But anyhow I can do it on 3,000 thalers and you make a fuss about an income of 6,000! . . . This winter, if you don't come, I shall not entertain on a large scale and will save money. Next winter I shall open my drawing-rooms and give three or four big parties—thirty persons. Each party will cost me from one to two hundred thalers. And an At-Home once a week for as many as can come—say sixty to seventy persons. These At-Homes would cost very little. . . ."

2

SOON after his return from Switzerland, in late October, Lassalle wrote to Marx: "I am working with the greatest concentration on my book on economics. . . . If your book covers the ground I intend to cover I shall not publish my own. But this does not prevent me from wishing your work to be happily launched as soon as possible." Marx replied that his own book "is the result of fifteen years' research, that is of the best period of my life. It is the first attempt to present an important aspect of sociology in a scientific manner. . . . As far as the question of rivalry goes the German public has no *embarras de richesse* in this particular field. In fact they will need a dozen writers, not just you and me."

Lassalle's work on economics was never completed, and the two books he published in the spring of 1859 were of a very different nature—a tragedy in blank verse and a pamphlet on foreign politics.

Franz von Sickingen, a drama in five acts, was the second bid for immortality of which he had written to the Countess two years before. He finished it in the early spring of 1858. He prepared a shortened version, designed for the stage, during the summer and sent it anonymously to the Berlin Hofbühne. It was declined, and the full version was published with his name a few months later.

The theme is taken from the Peasants War in Germany. Sickingen and his friend Ulrich von Hutten are the champions of freedom of conscience against the Papacy, and of German unity against the petty German princes. For Lassalle they represent the idea of Revolution. But, as the action proceeds, Sickingen fails to observe the Hegelian law that the strength of a revolutionary party lies in its passionate extremism, its refusal to rely on that realistic opportunism which is the natural strength of its opponents. He tried to outplay his princely opponents at their own game of deception and intrigue. Inevitably he failed, and died in a last heroic venture to redeem his failure.

"It is your cleverness that brought you low.
Great things you could have done but lesser things
Were not within your power."

The event was to show that the drama of von Sickingen was prophetic of Lassalle's career. But Lassalle, in writing it, identified himself not with Sickingen but with Hutten, whose advice if followed would have saved his friend from error. Indeed Hutten reveals many authentic marks of Lassalle:

"Had I a thousand tongues, then I to-day,
With every tongue would cry out to my country,
For I would rather drag my weary limbs
From field to field like some poor wounded beast
Than by my silence traitor be to truth."

And there are passages, no less authentic to Lassalle, which to-day sound curious as coming from a champion of democracy.

"It was the Sword, the Sword of Charlemagne
That brought the faith of God to German hearts,
It was the Sword struck Paganism low,
The Sword that freed the Holy Sepulchre,
The Sword that drove Tarquinius out of Rome
The Sword that pressed back Xerxes out of Greece
And freed the land for Learning and the Arts."

It would be rash to maintain that any blank verse drama of the mid-nineteenth century will have much appeal for the modern reader. No such claim can be entertained on behalf of *Sickingen*. Lassalle was neither a poet nor a playwright. The work is full of long monologues, Lassallean bombast and Hegelian argument. But it has ideas and it has vitality. *Sickingen* is an achievement which none, perhaps, of Lassalle's literary contemporaries could have equalled.

The work was well received by Lassalle's Berlin friends; and the Countess and his family were again filled with pride. On 6th March he sent copies to Marx and Engels with a ten-page letter ending with "the very natural request that you send me a thorough and absolutely sincere criticism."

The scene was set for friction and disappointment. Lassalle had no suspicion that the *émigrés* regarded him otherwise than as a close friend and colleague. In his thirst for praise and appreciation it never occurred to him that they had neither time nor inclination to read his blank verse drama or his interminable letters. Marx meanwhile was in the ignominious position of feeling unable to be openly rude to Lassalle. He was involved in yet another financial crisis, and could not afford to break with the one man likely to lend him money or find him a publisher. He was forced to smother his irritation as best he could.

On 4th March Engels acknowledged receipt of *Sickingen*. "In spite of your many-sidedness I never expected you to enter the field of drama." Neither Engels nor Marx had yet read the book, and the main object of Engels's letter was to find out the reasons for Duncker's delay in bringing out Marx's *Kritik*. Lassalle sent back an explanatory and reassuring letter. Then Marx wrote asking for a loan. Lassalle sent him a bill for £30 which Isidore Gerstenberg in London would discount, and complained rather wistfully that his (Marx's) letters were always so short and dry.

It was not till May that Marx read *Sickingen*, and his verdict was that the revolutionary idea was a fitting subject for a tragic drama but it had been a mistake to centre it round a member of a reactionary feudal class: the protagonists should have been the peasant leaders of the Peasant War. The letter containing this verdict crossed one from Lassalle announcing his political pamphlet. "I have been writing the whole night through, trying to forge out of fire and logic something that will influence the nation. It should appear within a week, anonymously of course, with the title '*The Italian War and Prussia's Duty: Democracy's Call*'."

Lassalle was so hurt by Marx's strictures on *Sickingen* that he replied at once in thirty pages of explanation and expostulation. "This is grotesque," Marx wrote to Engels. "It is incredible that at this moment in history anyone should not only have time to write such a letter, but should expect us to have time to read it." Of Lassalle's pamphlet, which reached him at about this time, he told Engels that "Lassalle, instead of running after his fire and logic, should try to get a grasp of what other people besides himself are thinking."

Marx's letter to Lassalle was curt. He would answer his explanations of *Sickingen* when he had time to read them. As to the pamphlet: "I and my associates completely disagree. We shall be publishing our views."

3

THE PUBLICATION of his pamphlet on the Italian war was Lassalle's first step back towards public affairs since his trial in 1849. The world had changed since that year. There had been the defeat of the revolution, the seizure of power by Napoleon III and the Crimean War with all its repercussions. Now Napoleon's attack on the Austrians in Italy seemed to leave Prussia with two alternatives. She could either come to the aid of her Austrian ally against the French; or she could exploit Austria's difficulties, in order to secure for herself the hegemony of the German states. This question split politically minded Germans regardless of party or group. On the extreme Right there were many who pressed for war against revolutionary France, while Bismarck favoured an ultimatum to Austria. On the Left opinion was similarly divided. But the leading Liberal papers of Berlin, the *Nationalzeitung* and the *Volkszeitung* were sharply anti-French, and it was largely their attitude that provoked Lassalle into writing his pamphlet.

He starts with the contention that the liberation of Italy remained a desirable cause even though a person of the stamp of Bonaparte had taken a hand in it. Further Bonaparte himself, a personal despot, was to be preferred to the permanent principle of reaction inherent in Austria. If Bonaparte intended to annex Lombardy and Venetia there might indeed be a pretext for Prussia to declare war on him. But that was not the case. Bonaparte's motive was to distract attention in France from his internal difficulties. But as it was impossible for one man to preach reaction in Paris and liberty in Rome his Italian adventure was bound, sooner or later, to involve his fall. Were Prussia to attack France, however, the French people would rally firmly behind their Emperor.

What then, Lassalle asks, was Prussia's task? Frederick the Great would recognise that the moment had come for the unification of Germany. He would march into Vienna, proclaim himself German Emperor, and leave it to the Habsburgs to see whether or not they could retain their non-German territories. But there was no Frederick the Great on the throne of Prussia and only little measures could be expected from little men. Accordingly Prussia should observe a strict neutrality, and, if and when Bonaparte altered the map of Southern Europe, Prussia should reincorporate the *Germania irridenta* of the North, the provinces of Schleswig-Holstein.

Marx took a different line. In his eyes France was the womb of revolution in Europe, and Napoleon, as the greatest enemy of the French proletariat, was the greatest enemy of the Cause. The second greatest was Napoleon's new ally, the Emperor of Russia. As a potential bulwark against these two even a Prusso-Austrian alliance was desirable. Engels accordingly wrote his pamphlet to establish the thesis that the Po and the Mincio were Germany's natural bastions.

It was through Lassalle that Engels arranged for the publication of his pamphlet in Germany. He had no one else to turn to for this purpose. Lassalle made the necessary arrangements with Duncker. He was unhappy over the disagreement with Marx, and wrote him long letters of self-justification. His pamphlet, he explained, should not be taken simply at its face value; what mattered was its "underground" argument. He had written knowing that his advice would not be taken. His real aim was to ensure that, if there was to be war between Prussia and France, that war should not be a popular one with the Prussian masses. A popular Prussian victory over France would be a "counter-revolutionary development *par excellence*". But an unpopular war and a French victory would finally discredit the Hohenzollerns and other ruling houses and open the door to the German people to work out their emancipation and unification along revolutionary lines.

The exchange with Marx was inconclusive. Both parties maintained their views. In any case Napoleon and the Austrians made peace in the early summer and the issue lost its immediate practical interest.

4

THERE WAS a further factor, destined to have more influence on the relations of Marx and Lassalle than their differences over the Italian war. Among the innumerable pamphlets published in the spring of 1859 was one by a Dr. Karl Vogt, a former Left-wing leader in Frankfurt and now a professor in Switzerland. Vogt had so vigorously supported the idea of Prussian neutrality that he was suspected of being on Napoleon III's payroll. Information to that effect reached Marx and was passed on by him to his fellow exile Liebknecht. Liebknecht made it into an article for the *Augsburger Allgemeine Zeitung*, of which he was correspondent. Twelve years later confidential archives were discovered and published by the Paris Commune, which showed that the allegations were true: Vogt had received a secret subsidy of 40,000 francs. But for the moment there was no tangible proof. Vogt sued the newspaper for libel, lost his case on a technical point but scored a moral victory. He then went over to the counter-attack and published another pamphlet in which Marx was accused of living on blackmail and the proceeds of police denunciation. Marx was furious. Not only was his pride outraged, but he felt that these allegations would irrevocably impair the influence of his work: he owed it to himself, his family, his associates and to the future of humanity to wipe out the slur. The heat of his subsequent campaign against Vogt brought him as near as he ever got to losing his sense of proportion.

Marx turned to his former associate and disciple for sympathy and help. Lassalle did not refuse. "You wish, my dear Marx, to have copies of all local papers which printed your statement or commented on the Vogt affair. There are certain ladies with whom I am on friendly terms—all most conscientious and capable—and I have asked them to go through the press and bring me any relevant passages." But Lassalle was no longer the obscure youth of 1848. He was a man of means and position. In view of his literary reputation he could not afford to become involved in other people's polemics unless he was sure of his facts. "I conclude", he wrote to Marx, "from what you say that you have documentary evidence. If so please send me copies. . . ."

There was always the money question. Marx asked Lassalle to back a bill for £40 at a moment when one of Lassalle's speculations had turned out badly. "You could certainly have reckoned", he replied, "on £40 from me, as I would always do all in my power to save you from embarrassment. But this forces me to tell you at once that this time it is quite impossible. Through a combination of various and most unfortunate circumstances I shall myself be forced—*horribile dictu*—to live on credit until July of next year." Marx wrote back: "I am not asking for money but for permission to put your name on a bill. May I draw on you at three months?" Lassalle replied: "Very well, draw on me. But on your responsibility. I shall not have the money." To which Marx wrote: "Thank you for your letter. Probably I shall be able to raise the money here in London on some extortionate terms."

There were many little matters that added up to make trouble. Lassalle was tactless enough to contribute to periodicals in which articles by Vogt were appearing. Duncker was slow in bringing out Marx's book and Marx suspected that Lassalle was responsible. The Hatzfeldt case had given Lassalle a good working knowledge of law and he was free with his legal advice. The advice was often sound, but not of a kind to be welcome to Marx. Lassalle's tone grew increasingly superior. In January 1860 he wrote: "You cannot deny that your case is not very good. You were wrong to accept as facts unconfirmed statements by so pitiful a liar. . . ." He went on to criticise Marx's choice of associates: "A second point, even more disagreeable for yourself and for the party, is your connexion with Liebknecht. How in the world can a man with such strict ideas as yourself consort with someone who writes for the *Augsburger Allgemeine Zeitung*?"

And so it went on until, in late February, Lassalle was finishing a long and complacent letter when he received a note from Marx dated the 23rd: "You have no reason to complain that I am suspicious. Enclosed is what I have had privately from America. The official accusations against you—including statements from a deputation of Düsseldorf workers—are not in my possession." The enclosures to this note included the denunciations already quoted on page 83.

The sting went home. There was enough truth in the accusations to hurt; that they should have come through Marx and that Marx should have preserved them carefully for years made the incident all the more bitter. Lassalle was ill and run down and the wound rankled in his mind. At once he added a long postscript to his letter indignantly refuting the charges; on the following day an even longer postscript, and on the day after that yet another. "And now for yourself," he wrote. "Why do you send me this stuff with so triumphant a mien and superb a gesture? To prove you mistrust me a little? Or not at all? Heaven help us, surely it is an elementary duty not to believe such mud slung behind a man's back. . . . To me it seems evidence of your aptness to believe anything bad against anybody that you bring it up to prove that in this case you have not done so. . . . I get the impression these notes were in reply to a request for a confidential report on me. So you have been holding enquiries on me. *Merci pour la découverte*. . . .

"Among our Düsseldorf collaborators was a little man called Lewy who once went to see you in London . . . he wanted the Countess to lend him 2,000 thalers. . . . That is how it all started. Isn't it? I would be prepared to bet. . . .

"PPS. . . . And now *adieu les amis*. I am weaker and worse in health even than yesterday. I shall have to go back to bed. Don't forget to give me the names of your informants in Baltimore. I insist. And the more you can tell me of that very confidential 'secret official accusation' against me the better pleased I shall be."

Marx wrote back: "The 'superb gesture' only exists in your imagination. I sent you the stuff to give a practical demonstration of how you would start to roar at a piece of dirt which has not been published and which is far less outrageous than that put out by Vogt."

5

THERE WERE more letters of expostulation from Lassalle to Marx. Marx's replies were short and dealt with his pending law suits, arising out of the Vogt affair, with the *Nationalzeitung* and the *Daily Telegraph*. ("The *Telegraph* is the most vulgar of the London papers, which is saying a lot, but it is not a small paper.") Lassalle endeavoured to interest Marx in his own personal plans: "The book I am now engaged on (*The System of Acquired Rights*) is a big one. Then will come my work on economics, and three others, already complete in outline in my mind. What I lack is time to finish them. Very possibly, even if my health does not break down, much of this work will never be completed because the time for action and battle is becoming imminent. It is all the harder for me because my creative effort lies not in one but in four or five branches of science. This puts an unbelievable strain on me. Ah, if only I could start a paper here together with my associates, could hope to exercise a direct influence on revolutionary developments, I would willingly drop everything else."

Marx showed no interest and Lassalle complained: "This correspondence is just a monologue. I write, and you send back two words saying you will write later, and so on for ever."

The spring and summer of 1860 was an unhappy period. The freshness of Berlin life had worn off. The strain of writing his new book brought with it staleness, and, as he had hinted to Marx, a feeling of the futility of purely academic work. There were irritations in his private life. Varnhagen's niece, Ludmilla Assing, conceived a violent passion for him; and it made him feel ridiculous to be so openly pursued by an unattractive spinster of forty. His speculations continued to go wrong. He bickered with the Countess. "Even though", he wrote to her, "you were peevish in the past you had your cheerful moods. These you used to share with me and that was my recompense. Now you keep these good moods for Paul and the Nostitz. All you have left for me are whines and complaints and reproaches." He and the Countess were perpetually quarrelling over Lina Duncker.

All this time his health was deteriorating. He suffered from gout, from nervous exhaustion and from some complaint which his doctors seem to have been unable to diagnose. In one of his letters he once referred to an "infection caught from a servant in 1847"; and it has been suggested that the real trouble was tertiary syphilis. In any case throughout his adult life, for all his great output of energy, he was never in perfect health for long at a time; and after his death one of his doctors admitted he never expected him to live to fifty. By July 1860 he was seriously ill and went for treatment to the *Kuranstalt* at Aachen.

He was not, at first, very happy there. "I had hoped", he wrote to his family, "at least to be able to save money here. But though I live like a dog I have never had to pay so much. One thaler and two groschen for every steam bath; one thaler five groschen for table d'hôte dinner without wine . . . *petit déjeuner* after the bath 12 groschen, plus a beefsteak (on doctor's orders) 10 groschen, and 3 groschen for three potatoes to go with it! Washing: 4 groschen for a shirt. . . ." The one economy he could make was to engage a servant locally at one thaler a day. Had he brought his own it would have cost at least as much to feed him, and then there would have been the man's railway fare.

To the Countess he wrote:

"Here the usual boredom. I have not yet seen your Russian. The only interesting (and very interesting) person here is a Countess Zichy. She is at my table for meals, but unfortunately not next to me. The poor woman is as bored as I am: she has her mother, child and governess with her, but no husband and she doesn't know any of the men. So she must be bored. And I am bored too, though we could amuse each other very satisfactorily. But we have no means of getting introduced. If I hadn't my work I would find some means—even if unconventional—of getting to know her. As it is I have no time for these adventures. None the less it is a true saying, *A bas les aristocrats, vivent leurs femmes!* A little while ago we had a French Marquis de Paroy here—legitimist and reactionary—who talked politics with me and used to lose his temper. So to show him there was some good in his class I told him this saying. Far from reconciling him it made him lose his temper again. He is anti-Napoleon III, but when one sees him and his like one feels there is some justification for Napoleon."

And a few days later:

"Not much news of my health. Apart from some easing of the pain I don't make any progress. . . . Without a body on which one can make any demands and treat with tyrannical ruthlessness, people just can't become what I am. And without such a body they can't stay so."

He was keenly interested in the news of Garibaldi's triumphant progress in South Italy. He wrote again to Marx who replied: "I was sorry to have no better news of your health. I have my same old liver trouble—not so painful as gout, nor, according to English ideas, so fashionable. Though perhaps even more of a handicap to brain work." Lassalle wrote back by return asking Marx to find out through Freiligrath (who had a minor post in a bank in London) whether it was a good time to sell out his Geneva bank shares. Marx passed on the request without comment, and in due course a cautious and non-committal report came back from Freiligrath.

It is almost certainly to this period that belongs the draft (undated) of a very long letter to Lina Duncker. It contains a manifesto of his relationship to the Countess. "She is my own re-embodied Ego. She is part of all my triumphs and perils, fears and toil, sorrows, strains and victories, part of all the emotions I have ever had. She is the first and essential condition of my happiness. . . ." It goes on to explain that, while he demands complete devotion and subservience from any other woman that loved him, there would always be part of his life in which this other woman could never hope to play a role.

This draft letter reads like an ultimatum. It did in fact entail his break with Frau Duncker and was almost certainly intended to do so. The liaison had lost its freshness. Lassalle was increasingly conscious that sooner or later he would break with her husband and her husband's political friends. He wanted a girl to whom he would be everything, and yet who would play second fiddle to the Countess when required. He was beginning to hope he had found such a girl.

Chapter 10

SONIA SONTSEV

I

On the 9th September Lassalle wrote to the Countess:

"I have made the acquaintance of a Russian Governor, M. de Sontsev, who is here with his daughter. I find them exceptionally interesting. The daughter is charming. Nineteen years old. I am continually astonished at finding how cultured and intelligent they are. And quite revolutionary—even the father! . . .

"Yesterday it rained, and I had myself taken over to their quarters in a little handcart they have here for paralysis cases. Daughter and father could not have been nicer to me. I very nearly fell in love with the daughter. She is certainly worthy of it. But, I don't know. My heart is consumed with past fires and cannot flame up for any new passion. And I have too much respect for her to run after her just for physical reasons. . . ."

Four days later he wrote to the Countess again telling her she was "the only one I have really loved as I realised in 1848 in Cologne", but nevertheless asking her to come to Aachen as soon as possible. He wanted not so much her advice as her approval: he already knew his own mind with regard to Mlle. Sontsev.

2

SONIA SONTSEV (whose father, incidentally, was not a Governor but the sub-Governor of Vitebsk) later wrote an account of her relationship with Lassalle, whom she describes as "a young man, erect and rather above medium height, whom one would take to be proud, arrogant even, were it not for the cast of concentrated thought on his pale, intelligent and handsome face."

When Lassalle left Aachen it was arranged that they should meet again in Berlin. A change in their plans made Sonia write to explain that she and her father had first to visit Dresden. Two days later, to her surprise, Lassalle turned up again in Aachen.

"His joy on seeing me was such as to confirm my suspicions of his feelings towards me. But I could not help thinking that just an ordinary friendship between a man like Lassalle and a girl of an age to be his pupil was quite enough. I hid my suspicions and tried to be as open, friendly and natural with him as before. Two days later we left for Dresden. Lassalle and the Countess came with us as far as Cologne. . . . On the way he was talkative and cheerful—excited even. But all this completely changed in Cologne where we stopped for two days. He hardly spoke, was very pale, distrait and preoccupied. Now and then I heard him sigh. Sometimes I found him looking at me with a curious expression. . . .

"He came to the window where I was standing and suddenly declared his unbounded and passionate love. He said his whole heart belonged to me, he could not live without me, I was not just an ordinary pretty girl, I was something higher, endowed by God with feeling for all that was noble and holy. All this came out in a flow of passionate words. He begged me eagerly and importunately to return his love. Every muscle of his face seemed to reflect what he was saying. I stood there spellbound. Then my father came in. . . .

"That evening we took tea with the Countess. She took my father aside—no doubt as prearranged with Lassalle. He at once begged for my answer. He was very pale and looked very tired. There was so much love in his glance, so much anxiety in his voice, that I was sorry for him and told him that perhaps some day I would love him. But I said it so calmly and coldly that I felt that I never would love him. As he was speaking he had taken my hand. He let go when I answered; his face grew even paler and was hard and cold. I saw he did not like my answer, but he had no time to say more as my father came back.

"All that evening he was very excited. I was too young to appreciate the depth of his feeling. As I sat there at the tea table I was merely annoyed that all this had happened. Up till then I had been so happy with him. I recognised and appreciated his brains, his energy, his genius. I felt myself his pupil, at most a younger comrade, and that I enjoyed. His presence made me happy, I felt akin to him. And now suddenly it was all changed. He was like a stranger."

It is probable that Sonia's lack of response came as a shock to Lassalle after the easy conquests of his Berlin circle. But his next step was a characteristic one. On his return to Berlin he wrote her a sixty-page letter.

3

THIS REMARKABLE DOCUMENT is an *Apologia pro vita sua*, a portrait of the writer at the age of thirty-five, and an assessment of the trials and triumphs awaiting his future wife. It has been compared to the schoolboy's diary of twenty years before. But Lassalle was no longer the Ferdinand of 1840. He had hardened, his egoism, armed with Hegelian dialectic, had taken firmer hold of him, his sense of humour had dwindled. Furthermore he was no longer writing a diary for himself alone; he was trying to influence someone else on a matter which was then of burning importance to him. The letter is the work of Lassalle the special pleader, not of Lassalle the analyst. Nevertheless it is, consciously and unconsciously, an interesting piece of self-revelation.

"I have told you already I am a very proud man. I could never bring myself to take a woman by storm. I could never try to make her feel for me what she did not feel of her own accord. A woman must love me of her own free will, freely and utterly. . . .

"This letter will serve as a memorial to your power of attraction; for sooner or later you will realise that it is no small achievement to have inspired a man of my stamp with feelings of love and thoughts of marriage.

"Thoughts of marriage! Up to now my love was just a devouring flame for women who threw themselves at me. I know of no woman who would not do all in her power to attach me, should she believe, even for a moment, that I would tolerate such a relationship. That is why I have always avoided young girls. Only twice have I made love to unmarried young women. Both loved me passionately, and both aroused in me the desire to possess them. In each case I began with the frank avowal that marriage was not my intention. Apart from these two cases I confined myself to married women. I was, as you yourself once said, 'their spoilt child'. You know that women always ask questions when they are in love, and to each one of them I replied, with my usual frankness, that even if she were free I would not want to marry her. In spite of, or perhaps because of that, they were always falling in love with me. . . ."

After telling Sonia that she should not make her decision until his health was restored, he goes on to warn her of the difficulties she would have to expect as his wife:

"I am a man who has devoted his whole existence to a holy cause, the cause of the People, absolutely and uncompromisingly. That cause will triumph before the close of the century, but meanwhile its adherents must face the risk of dangers and defeats. My fortune, my freedom, my life, may well be in constant jeopardy. For me and mine there is no such thing as security. In marrying me you will be building your house, your whole existence, upon a volcano. . . .

"Will you be able to bear the second blow I have for you? Sophie, I am a Jew. My father and mother are Jews, and though inwardly I am no more a Jew than you are—less so if that were possible—I have so far not renounced my religion as I did not wish to adopt another one. I can say truthfully I am no longer a Jew, but it would be false to pretend I had become a Christian.

"With us it makes no difference being a Jew. In Germany, France and England that is merely a religion, not a nationality. Being a Jew is like being a Protestant or Catholic. Especially here in Germany, a man, like myself, with a reputation for talent and intelligence, suffers from no discrimination. If I cared to come to terms with our present Government I could aspire to any position. But it is all very different with you in Russia. . . . It is true I could make you the sacrifice of becoming a

Christian, although in our laws there is no bar to marriages between Christians and Jews. But if it were absolutely necessary I would do it. All the same it would be hard for me, Sophie. I will tell you why. I do not like Jews. On the whole I dislike them. I regard them as degenerate sons of a great but long-vanished past. During their centuries of servitude they have assumed servile traits and that I find repellent. I have no contact with them. There is scarcely a single Jew in the society I frequent. But, Sophie, I am a politician. What is more, I am head of a party. And it is a fundamental principle of my party never to give way to prejudice. That would be cowardice."

He goes on to explain the social position that his wife might expect, with half the world hating him and all the women jealous of her. He tells her his income, and how it was derived. There follows, at great length, the history of the Countess and of his relations with her. The Countess, he continues, possesses "a depth of character and a warmth of feeling which I have never met elsewhere except in you. Yes, I know no other woman who is like her. But you are very like her. You are both cut from the same block, you have the same mentality, the same enthusiasm for all that is high and holy. How lucky I am to have found the same type of woman for my mother and my wife. . . . I hope to persuade her to share our home so that the three of us may live happy and united."

He concludes:

"If then you were to decide to become my wife, what would you gain in return for all your sacrifices? Two things only: a man and a heart. But at least a man in the true sense of the word and a heart which, if once given, is given for always.

"What, Sophie, can I say more? However you may decide, I tremble when I think of it, I shall never cease to bless you and your memory. I shall never cease to be your best and truest friend. I bless you once again with tears in my eyes."

4

SONIA had not yet made her mind up when she and her father arrived in Berlin. Lassalle met them at the station and took them to their hotel. Sonia writes:

"That evening one could feel a trace of sadness in him, but true sadness without any of the theatrical pose he so often assumed. I felt drawn towards him, particularly as his attitude to me was just one of friendship. He stayed till quite late; then he saw my father was tired and hurried away.

"Next morning he arrived in a cab and took us to his home in the Bellevuestrasse. His flat was a mixture of the luxurious, the artistic and the austerely academic: the last was represented by his study. . . . Leading out of it was a room in the oriental style, with low Turkish divans covered with Eastern embroideries, cabinets, stools, little inlaid tables, hookahs, Turkish pipes with huge amber mouthpieces. . . . The big drawing-room had its windows looking on the street. There were expensive carpets, heavy velvet hangings, a mass of great mirrors, bronzes, Japanese and Chinese vases. I did not like this room; it was overdone and ostentatious.

"Lassalle treated us as if we were part of the family. His father arrived—a sturdy, healthy old man, not tall, with thick grey hair. His blue eyes lovingly followed his son. One could see how proud he was of him. His honest, kindly intelligent face inspired confidence. . . . Then Countess Hatzfeldt came. Old Lassalle went out to get tickets for the opera and brought his wife back for lunch. She was the opposite of her husband; as fragile and weak as he was fresh and strong. A small, ailing, deaf old woman who sat with loving eyes watching her son and her husband. She would nod her head, smiling, as if to say 'I don't understand a word of what you are saying, but I'm glad you are enjoying yourselves'. Now and then she pulled her husband's sleeve and made him explain what was going on."

In the evening the whole party went to the opera, where Wagner himself was conducting *Lohengrin*.

"Lassalle had explained the action to us beforehand. He sat just behind me and throughout the whole opera recited the libretto, which he knew by heart. It was hard to tell which was the better, his declamation or the acting on the stage. He had a remarkable control of voice and range of intonation. . . . I have never heard an opera with such eagerness, I have never understood one, down to the slightest nuance, as I did on this occasion. Lassalle himself seemed quite carried away. In the intervals he explained the ideas portrayed and the feeling behind them. He spoke with enthusiasm, without a break. His eyes flashed; he seemed not so much speaking as intoning, like a Nordic bard. The whole evening made an enormous impression on me. I was under a spell. Then, more than at any other time, I was bound to him. I felt that next day I would promise to be his wife.

"Next morning he arrived almost before we had finished breakfast. He was pale as marble. He had hardly said good morning to us when he took me to the window and tried to force me into accepting him. He spoke passionately, tenderly, his voice quivered. He said he could not live without me. His heat and violence frightened me; and brought about a complete reaction. All that I had felt the previous evening vanished. My hero and master had turned into an ordinary mortal, arbitrarily demanding from me a feeling I did not possess. From that moment I knew my own mind.

" 'Lassalle, I am not in the least in love with you,' I said. 'Let us stop. I'm sorry but all I can offer you is friendship.'

"There were tears in my eyes.

" 'That is not true,' he shouted. 'Marry me and you will come to love me. You will find yourself loving me.' . . ."

It was an unsatisfactory day, relieved only by a visit to von Bülow, the pianist, who, after a pompous opening, thawed and gave them a first-class musical evening. Lassalle escorted Sonia and her father back to their hotel, where there was a scene.

"Lassalle took my father's hand and began excitedly impressing on him that I was bound to fall in love with him, that he would make me eternally happy.

" 'Make her love me,' he said, 'give her to me. Just now she is annoyed with me and thinks she does not love me. You have to realise I can not live without her!'

"He fell on my father's neck and began to sob. I felt weak: I could bear it no longer.... My father put his arms round him and said 'Good-bye, Lassalle. You are a strong man. You must not lose heart. Do not be angry with my daughter. I know what she went through before she gave you her final answer. Let us consider the whole story as finished. Good-bye. We leave by the early train to-morrow. I would not like to part with you like this.'

" 'No. You cannot take her away so suddenly. Leave by the evening train. Bring her to spend one more day with me.' "

There was a long argument at the end of which the Sontsevs were forced to agree to stay. The day passed as might have been expected. In the morning they went once more to Lassalle's flat:

"Lassalle's attitude to me was tenderness itself. He kept repeating that the only decision he could accept was one I should make when I got back to Russia; he hoped that parting would awake my feelings for him. I begged him with tears in my eyes not to torment me, but he went on and on in this style. The whole atmosphere was so depressing one would imagine there was a corpse in the house.

"There was one short interlude caused by the arrival of Lassalle's brother-in-law [Ferdinand Friedland]. He was the typical Jewish *nouveau-riche*, quite untouched by European culture. He had a very smart suit, heavy gold watch-chain and a number of flashing rings: but one felt he had very recently stood behind a counter. He at once began to attack Lassalle's political and social views. A curious quarrel started. Friedland grew hot and excited; reproached Lassalle for his luxurious flat; said he ought to make over his property to the workers and become a workman himself. Lassalle was cool, sarcastic and contemptuous. He said Friedland's ideas were beside the point; it was just because of his position and background that he was able to work effectively. He hoped the workers would soon realise how they were being exploited by people like his brother-in-law. This went on for some time and then Friedland, seeing perhaps where our sympathies lay, got up in a huff and went out, without saying good-bye to Lassalle.

"After the midday meal we said good-bye to the Countess and went back to our hotel to prepare for our journey. Lassalle followed us and remained with us till the train left. Every quarter of an hour he repeated: 'I shall expect your answer from Russia. Don't hurry. Make sure of yourself.' I looked at his pale unhappy face and promised I would write. As we sat in the waiting-room Lassalle was in a state of nervous excitement. He sat next to me but could say nothing. He tried to speak but the words would not come and he sobbed. I was near to crying myself, felt stifled, ready to faint, but forced myself to keep a calm appearance so as not to raise false hopes in him. I thought how nice it would be if we could only part as friends as in the past.

"He put us in our compartment and then stood leaning against a pillar, his arms crossed, white and miserable. I shall never forget this last glimpse of him. Our train started; he made a sudden move as if to follow it. Then he stopped, waved his hand and leant against the pillar again. The train moved on and he passed out of sight."

Sonia's decision was of course already made, and her only problem, back in Russia, was to find a form of words that would cause the least pain. In the end she wrote:

"I assure you, Lassalle, that if it were for my head to decide, I would marry you at once. But what can I do with this heart of mine that will not listen to orders and yet controls my life and all that I do? I assure you I am thinking just as much of your happiness as of mine."

Chapter 11

JOURNEY TO CAPRERA

I

In the months immediately following Sonia Sontsev's return to Russia Lassalle completed his second major academic work, *The System of Acquired Rights*. The first volume sets out Lassalle's conception of Law, and contains an important section giving his philosophy of history. This section emphasises the progressive limitation of the rights of private property, which, according to the author, has led to a corresponding increase in man's real freedom. The second volume compares, with great ingenuity and much parade of learning, the Germanic and the Roman laws of heritage, and is designed as an appendix to and illustration of the first.

Lassalle was insistent on the revolutionary tendency of his book. "I have endeavoured", he wrote to Duncker, "to build up for socialism and for revolution a scientific system of law. This will be a strong fortress on which we can base our further operations. Past experience shows that this is badly needed. I think I have succeeded in raising a tower of steel."

Lassalle, as a good Hegelian, presents "natural law" not as something static and eternal, but as an organism developing with the evolution of popular consciousness (*Volksbewusstsein*). What is right or legal in one age is not necessarily so in the next. Written laws tend to lag behind the march of popular consciousness; and therefore cases arise when new laws may and should be made retrospective. This of course will simplify the task of revolutionary legislatures and courts, especially in issues involving expropriation and compensation.

The book was first offered to Duncker, but Duncker refused it. It was finally published by the firm of Brockhaus. The reception was somewhat tepid. It was a difficult book to place;

there was too much law in it for the philosophers, too much philosophy for the jurists and too much speculation for practical revolutionaries. Marx refused to read it right through, a hard blow to Lassalle's feelings. Engels spoke of the author's "superstitious belief in 'absolute law'". Even friends and admirers like the economist Rodbertus asked difficult questions. How, Rodbertus inquired, is one to discover what are the demands of the popular consciousness of any particular age? Lassalle could only reply: "This question cannot be answered in terms of law. Only philosophy can give an answer to it. You are quite right in maintaining that a majority vote or even a unanimous vote cannot establish the requirements of the age. How can I then discover it? My answer is simple—what you can prove to yourself and to an age by reason, logic and science. That is the requirement of the age."

2

THE ABSENCE of any chorus of applause such as had greeted *Heraklitus* may well have increased his distaste for purely academic work. We have seen that already in the summer, in spite of the pain Marx had caused him, he was hoping they might start a newspaper together. In January 1862 the new King Wilhelm I proclaimed an amnesty for political refugees. This appeared to open the way for Marx's return to Germany, and Lassalle at once wrote to him: "Once more I ask you (1) How much capital would we want to start a newspaper here? (2) Which of the old *Neue Rheinische Zeitung* people could come back to work on it?" At the same time he wrote to his father to look round Breslau for possible financial participants.

But it turned out that Marx's return was not so easy. The amnesty was conditional: Marx, in view of his ten years' absence, was deemed to have lost his Prussian nationality and would have to be renaturalised. An application for his renaturalisation was submitted but was opposed by the police. Lassalle took up the challenge. He called on the Chief of Police and the Minister of the Interior, drafted memoranda and petitions, inspired press articles and generally conducted the campaign with all his pertinacity and resource. The issue was still undecided when Marx arrived on a visit: he had to go and see an uncle in Holland in connexion with family money matters, and, thanks largely to Lassalle's intervention with the authorities, was able to spend a few days in Berlin.

He arrived on 1st April and spent ten days with Lassalle in the Bellevuestrasse flat. Lassalle and the Countess made much of him. "Marx is here," Lassalle wrote to his father, "which takes up a lot of my time." They went on an expedition to Potsdam; they attended a debate in the Landtag; they went to the opera where Marx's republican humour was tickled to find himself placed directly opposite the Royal Box. During this visit Jenny Marx wrote to Lassalle: "I thank you from my heart for your nice letter and for your friendship to my lord and master, which you have proved once more during his stay in Berlin. I have always thought of you as one of our oldest and truest and best of friends, and have never doubted the sincerity of your sympathy and kindness. Only once was I really angry with you—when that loathsome campaign started against my husband. I counted on your impulsiveness; I thought you would rush on the wretched crew with fire and sword—the one live voice in a silent world. But you too were silent. Only later did I understand that you had no hand in the filthy campaign and only kept silent because you had no arena. Now it's all over, I must forget that little old grievance and offer you my hand in friendship. You offer glowing prospects of my early return to the Fatherland. I don't want to show myself to my old friends as I am now—I have got so ugly and so different. But my pretty little daughter. . . . Don't keep the Moor [i.e. Marx] too long. I would let you keep anything else but not him. That is the one point on which I am really selfish and jealous."

There is no full record of their conversations in Berlin. Lassalle's proposal for a newspaper was discussed at length. Lassalle's idea was a board composed of Marx, Engels and himself, himself retaining two votes as he would otherwise always be outvoted by his colleagues. How far Lassalle was serious in putting this forward we cannot tell; but in any case it is significant. We can be sure that the ten days' discussion made it clear to both that their differences of opinion and temperament would never allow them to work closely together. When Marx left, with a loan of £40 and a parcel of gowns as a gift from Lassalle to Jenny and the children, it was morally certain that the proposed newspaper would never be inaugurated.

On the 5th May Jenny Marx wrote again:

"I have always to thank you for something—sometimes for friendship and sympathy, sometimes as now for all those presents. How I wish you could see how blooming and happy the girls look in them. Even I look quite well in mine. When I first put it on and paraded up and down the room little Eleanor shouted 'Just like a peacock.' If it wasn't so bitterly cold here I should have gone out already. A coat like that impresses our philistine neighbours and gives us prestige and credit. . . .

"PS. I do wish one day we could have you here as our guest. But you would find everything so small and higgledy-piggledy."

Marx started his letter of thanks "Dear Lazarus," and returned £30 of the loan, promising to send the remaining £10 as soon as he could. He went on:

"It is quite possible I shall come and spend six months or so in Berlin—always supposing my renaturalisation goes through. But I can't deny that London has a remarkable attraction for me. . . . And now, *mon cher*, I must close with my heartiest thanks for all your kindness in taking me in and looking after me and bearing with all my tiresome ways. You know I had a head full of troubles as well as my liver. The great thing was we found a lot to laugh at."

But to Engels Marx wrote:

"Lassalle is so dazzled by the reception of his *Heraklitus* and the attention of certain people who like his dinners that he does not realise his bad reputation in the world at large. Then there is his continuous pose as a know-all, his speculative ideas—he even wants to write a new Hegelian philosophical system—his infection with superannuated French liberalism, his itch to write about everything, his pushingness, tactlessness, etc. He might be of use as one among other editors. Otherwise merely an embarrassment."

Shortly afterwards the Prussian authorities rejected Marx's application for renaturalisation, on the grounds that "his convictions were republican, or at any rate not royalist."

3

LASSALLE planned an autumn tour to Switzerland and Italy. He wrote to ask Marx for an introduction to Garibaldi. In September he arrived in Zürich with a fairly large party, including the Countess and Ludmilla Assing. They drank a good deal of champagne, and we hear of a *fracas* at a restaurant, involving Gottfried Keller the poet. Another poet whom Lassalle met in Switzerland was Georg Herwegh, who, after a somewhat inglorious revolutionary career, was now living in Geneva on his wife's income. A more impressive figure was Wilhelm Rüstow, ex-regular officer in the Prussian Army and also a veteran of 1849. After ten dreary years as a political émigré and journalist Rüstow had volunteered for the Sicilian campaign and served with distinction as a Colonel on Garibaldi's staff.

When Lassalle and the Countess left Switzerland for Italy they took Rüstow with them. After a few days in Venice they arrived in Genoa in early November. Here they met members of the extreme Left wing of the Italian national liberation movement. On the 14th Lassalle went over to Caprera and spent four days with Garibaldi in his island retreat. Then he returned to Genoa.

We have no record of his conversations, either in Genoa or on Caprera. But as a result of them he wrote, in complete seriousness, to his father: "The revolt is to start in Greece in early spring and to spread to the Slav populations of the neighbouring areas This will hamstring Austria. Austria has always drawn her strength from her Slavs and used them against Hungarian, German and Italian revolutionaries. But she will not be able to do this once the Slavs and Roumanians are in revolt. So it is now to start in Greece, and as it spreads Italy will join in." And later he wrote: "Revolution in Budapest is revolution in Vienna. Revolution in Vienna is revolution in Berlin."

Rüstow, after the intoxicating experience of the Garibaldi campaigns, was eager to believe that something of the sort might happen in Germany. He drew Lassalle's attention to the sports and physical-training clubs that the Liberal *Nationalverein* were sponsoring in a number of German towns: and the two conspirators thought out means of providing arms so that these clubs might form the core of the democratic army of the unification of Germany. Marx, when he came to hear of the scheme, was sardonic. "They will finish it all in six weeks," he wrote. "The driving force will be Lassalle's political influence or his pamphleteering in Berlin. Rüstow will lead an army of German guerillas in alliance with Garibaldi. Bonaparte will be completely paralysed by this Lassallean *coup d'éclat*."

Lassalle's Italian tour ended in personal quarrels. Rüstow conceived a romantic devotion for the Countess. It was natural for a woman of fifty-five to be flattered by such feelings in a man twelve years her junior. No doubt her dread of loneliness in her old age had become accentuated since Lassalle's attempt to marry Sonia Sontsev. She and Rüstow were soon inseparable. Lassalle became jealous and started to make scenes. In December he left them in a huff and went back to Germany alone. He kept up a correspondence with Rüstow but it was months before he would write to the Countess.

Back in Berlin his mind remained full of the coming European revolution. He established touch with *Nationalverein* leaders, reporting to Rüstow on his progress. He took other steps. In mid January he wrote to his father to sell short, on his behalf, 4,000 Upper Silesian Railway shares and 6,000 thalers' worth of Cöln-Mindener, for delivery in mid-March. "I can tell you", he wrote, "with absolute certainty that securities will fall in the course of February, or, at latest, by mid-March. The certainty is such that I could sell five times as much. But I don't want to get rich all at once. It will be enough if I make 30 per cent." Old Heymann wrote back, expressing misgivings. Lassalle replied angrily, pointing out the number of times they would both have made their fortunes if his advice had been followed. His father made the arrangements. February came. There was no indication of either a slump or a revolution.

Lassalle became nervy, frustrated and depressed. He wrote to Rüstow:

"I eat and drink and have all that a man needs. And yet as far as satisfaction goes I'm worse off than a dog. I've been like this for years, progressively getting worse. All I can do about it is to plunge into work, three times as much work as I can do in the time I allot for it. Once embarked on this new torment my other troubles are overlaid. I work and toil, strain towards the unattainable goal, press the red-hot goad ever deeper into my side, tear my flesh, fight and struggle, day after day, with this all-devouring nerve-shaking passion, letting it pervade my soul and take possession of my mind, till at last I am satiate and accomplish the impossible. But as soon as the work is finished and done and the goad is pulled out of my entrails I become once more a sort of Faust. No dog would want to live such a life."

By March there was still no sign of trouble in South-Eastern Europe. There was a minor boom on the stock exchanges: Upper Silesian Railways and Cöln-Minderer rose appreciably. On settlement day Lassalle had lost 2,600 thalers. He put a bold face on it. "Why", he wrote to his father, "should I bother about the loss of the money? As far as I remember I made 4,000 thalers on the Geneva Bank shares and I can therefore risk at least that sum."

We have few significant letters dating from this period. Marx, as ever, was a grudging correspondent. He wrote at last in late April after a long silence: "You will be angry with me, old boy, and justifiably so. But also unjustly. I have kept putting off writing till I could repay your £10." The excuse was unconvincing, and Lassalle in his turn did not reply for some weeks.

Bülow lent him a copy of Richard Wagner's *Nibelungen* trilogy, and this was a real emotional experience. He wrote: "If only you knew how grateful I am for that book, and, at the same time what torment you thereby caused me! I am still tossed and torn by continual excitement, like a foaming sea. It will be days and weeks before I am in a state to concentrate on the dry statistics and economics which I have planned for my immediate study. . . . Wagner is one of the very few, in these sad days, who stands as a living proof that if the German genius will only arise in its untarnished greatness the Germans have something that all others lack. . . ." Bülow, at Lassalle's request, persuaded Wagner to give him a copy. He was eager to meet the composer, though when he did so two years later the latter did not take to him. "An important type of the future", was Wagner's verdict. "A type I can only describe as Germano-Judaic."

Outwardly his Berlin life followed its usual course. But among the intellectuals and the slightly equivocal smart world that came to eat his dinners were three new friends destined to play a part in his political future. There was Ziegler, the Radical ex-Mayor of Brandenburg, dismissed from his office in 1849 and now, an ageing man, making his way as an industrialist. There was Ludwig Löwe, like Lassalle of a provincial Jewish family, an ex-commercial traveller, now partner in a growing business, keenly interested in political speculation and dazzled by Lassalle's intellectual fireworks. And there was Lothar Bucher, a former deputy of 1848–9, forced into exile under the reaction, and now, thanks to the recent amnesty, back in Berlin and earning a meagre living as a clerk in the Wolff Telegraph Bureau. Bucher was not of the stuff that heroes are made of; but he had a keen intellect and a good political sense. He collaborated with Lassalle in a skit—*Herr Julian Schmidt, the Literary Historian*, a pungent attack on one of the more pretentious of the Liberal intellectuals. A copy went to the Countess in Switzerland who was delighted with it and her warm letter of praise to Lassalle did much to bring about their reconciliation.

But Bucher's great service to Lassalle was in being an adequate sparring partner in a series of all-night discussions. It was due more to Bucher than any one else that Lassalle was able to clear his mind of much of his Garibaldian fantasy and to appreciate the potentialities of the Prussian political scene of 1862; and thus to compose the two lectures which were to be the foundation of his political career and which remain to-day as masterpieces of their kind.

Chapter 12

THE WORKERS' PROGRAMME

I

Towards the end of 1861 there were unmistakable signs of impending conflict between the two main political forces of Prussia—on the one side the Crown together with the Army and the bureaucracy, and on the other the bourgeois Liberal groups, headed by the recently formed Progressive Party. The immediate issue was Army Reform, or rather the right to allot funds for that purpose.

The Crown, at the instance of von Roon, the Minister of War, pressed for extension of the period of service to three years, extension of the period of service in the reserve, subordination of the Landwehr or Militia to the regular army, and increase in the number of regular officers. The Liberals in the Diet urged a two-year period of service and safeguards against the "creation of an instrument for absolutism". Elections were held in December, resulting in a large Progressive majority. In March the crisis came to a head, and a Right-wing Government was appointed to conduct new elections. In April when the electoral campaign was in full swing, Lassalle addressed a suburban audience on "The Working Class and its Significance in the Present Age". Four days later he spoke in another suburban hall on "The Nature of Constitutions". With an eye to the susceptibilities of the Prussian police he was at pains, on each occasion, to impress upon his hearers that he was approaching the problem from a strictly academic and scientific angle.

It will perhaps be more convenient to deal first with his address on the constitutional issue. He began by asking a question: what is a constitution? What is it in actual fact, quite apart from any juridical definition? What is it that, in any age and in any country, inevitably determines the scope and nature of the laws passed in that country? The answer is "the factual power relationship in any given society". The procedure for making a constitution, he goes on, is to "write down, on a piece of paper, the actual existing power ratio. When that is done it is no longer merely a power ratio, it has become law, a set of legally binding enactments, and whoever goes against it is punished." The resultant facts are not stated thus crudely. It is not, for instance, explicitly laid down in the Prussian Constitution that a millionaire like Herr Borsig should have more power than an ordinary citizen. But under the Prussian Three Class electoral system Class I contains 153,808 voters and Class III 2,691,950; and this is as good as saying that in Prussia a rich man has seventeen times as much voting power as a poor one. Again it is to be noted that under Article 47 of the Prussian Constitution it is the King who makes all military appointments, and that under Article 108 the Army's oath is to the King and not to the Constitution: the Constitution thus ensures to the King an enormous preponderance of organised disciplined power.

Lassalle goes on to give a historical survey of the ever-changing power ratio within the country. In 1819 the strength of the Prussian Army was 137,639 and the population of Berlin was 192,646. In 1846 Berlin had grown to 389,308 while the Prussian Army still numbered only 138,810. The power ratio had correspondingly altered and Prussia was therefore ripe for the revolution of 1848, when the "unorganised power of the people showed itself greater than the organised power of the Crown". But in 1848 the people had not pressed home this advantage. They had not brought the Army under their control. They accordingly forfeited their position and allowed the Crown to proclaim the Constitution of 1848. Or rather what was called the Constitution. "If you have an apple tree you may put a ticket on it to say it is a fig tree. But it still produces apples, not figs." The first fruit of that Constitution was the Three Class Electoral System of 1849. By 1862 the Constitution had become "more torn and rent than any flag that had been through a hundred battles". And yet there was now the curious spectacle of the Progressives gathering round this rump and calling upon the world to save it. "Now Gentlemen, when you hear an anxious cry to rally round the Constitution, what conclusion can you draw? . . . You can affirm, with complete certainty, that the Constitution in question is at its last gasp. It is as good as dead. We do not hear this cry when a Constitution corresponds to the factual power-ratio. . . . That this cry should be uttered at all is a sign of alarm, a sign that the written Constitution is in contradiction to the real Constitution, that is, the internal balance of power. Once that contradiction is present, then no God and no appeal can help. The written Constitution is dead. . . . It can be modified towards the Right or towards the Left. But it cannot stay as it is. It can be modified to the Right by a Government taking steps to adjust it to the organised forces of the community. Or the unorganised forces of community will arise and make clear that they are stronger than the organised forces. In that case the Constitution will be modified towards the Left. But in any case, as it now is, it is lost. . . . Think over what I have said and when once more you are in the position to give yourselves a Constitution you will know how to set about it. You will know that achievement consists not in writing out a sheet of paper, but in the alteration of the actual power-ratio. Meanwhile, although I have not discussed the matter, my lecture will enable you to think out for yourselves the motives lying behind the increase in the armed forces which you are now being asked to approve. . . . The Crown, Gentlemen, has practical-minded servants, not mere pretty speakers, but practical-minded men such as one would like to see serving your cause."

2

THE OTHER ADDRESS was delivered four days previously to members of the local Handworkers Association in a hall in Oranienburg. The original elaborate title, chosen presumably to emphasise the academic nature of the speech, was changed, when it appeared in pamphlet form, to *The Workers' Programme*.

Lassalle starts with a historical survey, designed to emphasise the social and political significance of control of the means of production.

In the Middle Ages the means of production were tied up with the land. The big landowners, nobles and ecclesiastics, formed the dominant class. Individuals and classes dependent on other means of livelihood were despised. Further, "it is a characteristic and ever-recurring phenomenon, Gentlemen, that any privileged or dominant class will always attempt, openly or covertly, directly or indirectly, to place the burden of the maintenance of the State upon the shoulders of the oppressed and non-possessing classes. When Richelieu in 1641 asked the clergy for a special tax the Archbishop of Sens replied: 'The tradition of the Church is that the commons should contribute their goods, the nobility their blood and the clergy their prayers to the needs of the State.'"

After a digression designed to prove that the Peasant War of the sixteenth century could not be taken as "revolutionary" —an echo of his controversy with Marx over *Sickingen*— Lassalle goes on to explain that the real revolution consisted in the economic developments of the period between the Renaissance and 1789. "Revolution was there, in the factual circumstances of society, before ever it broke out in France. All that was necessary was outwardly to recognise this transformation —to give it legal sanction. That, Gentlemen, is the case with all revolutions. It is impossible to 'create' a revolution. It is only possible to recognise and establish in all its implications a change that has already taken place in the factual circumstances of society. To attempt to create revolution is the foolish and immature act of one without knowledge of the law of history. It is equally immature and childish to obstruct or refuse to recognise a revolution that has already taken place in the womb of society; or to reproach as revolutionaries those who play the role of midwife."

Lassalle points out that in the Prussia of 1862 there were still a number of restrictions and privileges dating back from medieval days. "You will see from this, Gentlemen, that however great the advantage of reform by legal means, this course has the disadvantage of century-long ineffectiveness. On the other hand the revolutionary course, with its undeniable disadvantages, has at least the one merit of leading quickly and energetically to a practical end."

He then reverts to the French Revolution. The Abbé Sieyés had remarked in 1788. "*Qu'est-ce-que c'est que le tiers état? Rien. Qu'est-ce qu'il doit être? Tout.*" This apothegm might more properly be put: "What is the Third Estate in fact? Everything. What is it in law? Nothing." The French Revolution established and legalised the position and rights of the Third Estate. No distinction was made then between the Third Estate, or bourgeoisie, and the Fourth Estate or proletariat. But the way things were shaping became apparent as early as 1791 when suffrage was made subject to a property qualification.

Lassalle lays down the attitude to be maintained regarding persons of birth or wealth. "No commoner can or should object to a nobleman being proud of his ancestors or enjoying his estate. But should he make use of his ancestors and his estate to attain privilege and domination, then the commoner becomes angry and talks of feudalism." Similarly, "that a rich bourgeois should enjoy the comfort and luxury that comes from his wealth is natural and reasonable. . . . The workers must not and will not forget that lawfully acquired property is proper and untouchable." [This is hardly consistent with the argument of *The System of Acquired Rights*: but Lassalle knew that representatives of the secret police were present.] However, the bourgeois, in the ideological and technical sense of the word, goes further. He uses his wealth to exercise privilege and domination. In Prussia under the Three Class Electoral System a rich man has the voting power of seventeen. And of the Prussian State income only some thirteen million thalers are derived from direct taxation of the rich, whereas indirect taxes, borne largely by the poor, amount to ninety-seven million.

Such are the results of the domination of the bourgeoisie. But their day is passing. Universal suffrage will enable the working class to establish its ascendancy, to abolish all privilege and thus to open the way to freedom and unity. "On 24th February 1848 [the Paris revolution] came the first dawn of the new age."

Finally, Lassalle develops his theory of the role of the State. According to bourgeois ideas of *laissez-faire* the State's function is merely to allow the individual to do what he likes. "Were we all equally strong, equally clever, equally educated and equally rich this conception might be acceptable. But as we are not, this conception is inadequate and leads to immorality and exploitation." For the bourgeois the State, at best, is nothing more than a night-watchman. But for the worker the State is something "that will achieve for each one of us what none of us could achieve for himself". It is the mission of the working class to ensure that the State will work actively for the utmost well-being of every member of the community. The Fourth Estate is the "rock on which the Church of the present age will be built".

3

THE EXTREME Right-wing newspapers showed considerable interest in these speeches, which they rightly interpreted as indicating a rift in the ranks of the opposition. The speech on the constitutional issue aroused particular attention. "Dr. Lassalle," wrote the *Kreuzzeitung*, "a Jewish revolutionary who was once very much in the news, has hit the nail on the head though he has not yet told us all he has on his mind. Supreme contempt for the written Constitution; a clear perception that power factors—including troops and guns—form the only real Constitution. Arising out of which is the conclusion that the primary task is to alter the existing power-ratio, and then, in particular, to disarm the conquered. . . ."

The Liberal press, as Lassalle foretold in a letter to the Countess, "proceeded to scream death and murder". The implication of the two speeches was only too apparent: the working class must form their own political party, as the Liberals were unwilling to look after working-class interests and unable successfully to oppose the extreme Right. To the Progressives, in the heat of their electoral campaign Lassalle appeared a deserter, if not a renegade. Many who had been his personal friends broke off relations with him, and the trouble even spread to the Philosophical Society. Heymann Lassal, now sick and ageing, wrote from his cure at Wildbad to protest to his turbulent son: "I have just read in the *Augsburger Zeitung* that you have been expelled from the Philosophical Society. . . . I am very unhappy. My poor heart which as you know is ailing in any case will break with all this grief. I can say like Father Jacob that in sorrow I go down to the grave. I am ashamed to go out. Everyone stares at me because every day there is something new in the paper about you. If only I were in another continent where I knew nobody and where nobody knew me. . . ."

The speeches made one unexpected convert—Gustav Lewy, the former associate in Düsseldorf, who had been the main instigator of the denunciation to Marx. Lassalle still kept up with one of the working-class friends of his Rhineland days, a certain Kichniawy, and it was through Kichniawy that Lewy made his approach. "Lewy", Kichniawy wrote on the 30th May, "has always shown the greatest interest in your literary and political work. . . . I brought up the former affair with him, and he said the breach had not been due to any fault of his. He had completely forgotten the matter." Lassalle, for all his pugnacity, was never vindictive, and he did not refuse the proffered reconciliation.

But Lewy was an isolated case. There was no response from the German working class to whom the speeches had been primarily addressed. The prospects of launching a new movement seemed as distant as ever. For the time there was nothing for it but to return to the long-projected work on economics and to the Berlin social round of which disquieting reports reached the Countess and Rüstow in Switzerland. On the 11th June the Countess wrote: "Rüstow tells me Hiersemenzel has been behaving himself badly again. I am not surprised. You know I often said he was no friend of yours. I never liked any of that Berlin crowd except Scherenberg and your cousin. They eat your dinners and flatter you, just in order to abuse you behind your back."

Lassalle wrote back:

"It would take too long to tell you of Hiersemenzel's dirty

behaviour. . . . As to these people eating my dinners and then abusing me behind my back, my answer is that is all I expected of them. In many cases I am glad they do. Anyhow I have changed my set of friends here, you only know very few of them. . . . I still find the world astonishingly wearisome. If I had not the urge to do something practical, which in my case means politics, I would withdraw and go back to my books."

Both the speeches, meanwhile, were being printed and were issued as pamphlets during June. The Prussian authorities took action. The police confiscated all copies of the *Workers' Programme* they could lay their hands on, and a charge was laid against Lassalle, under Article 100 of the Criminal Code, of "endangering public order by stirring up hatred and contempt among subjects of the State".

4

MARX, in his last letter, had excused his long silence on grounds of inability to repay the £10 outstanding. It was not till 9th June that Lassalle replied: "I do not accept your excuse about the £10, as it would bear out Polonius on a loan entailing loss of both friend and money. We must not let this apply to us, old boy." He was still unable to give a considered verdict on Marx's book. "Other matters have kept me so busy for the last three years that all the economic material in my mind has fossilised: I must liquify it which will take four months' reading. Until then there is no point in my reading your book again as I will not be at the height of my critical powers." Then there were his own recent achievements. "Meanwhile I have written my *Julian*; the Fichte centenary address, various articles, my speech on the Constitution. Also a certain amount of political agitation—I repeated the Constitution speech on four subsequent occasions. Also I have composed and delivered a long lecture on the working class which I have decided to print."

He concludes by announcing his impending visit to London to see the International Exhibition, adding "Among my motives in coming is the wish to see your daughter, reputed to be so beautiful."

Marx wrote back: "We shall be very glad to see you. Apart from myself I shall be glad for my family's sake. All our friends —English, German and French—now live out of town so they never see anybody."

In July Lassalle duly arrived and took rooms at No. 19 Brompton Crescent. With him was Lothar Bucher who had lived in London as an émigré and thus was qualified to act as cicerone. Lassalle's chief motive in coming was to clarify his relations with Marx. He envisaged the prospect of active political work in Germany. He wished to find out whether and how far he could count on the active collaboration or the sympathetic interest of the man whose intellectual pre-eminence he recognised and whom he still hoped he could regard as a personal friend. But it is not to be excluded that in his heart of hearts he was also playing with the possibility of becoming Marx's son-in-law.

Soon after his arrival he wrote to his friend von Bülow:

"It is quite nice here, and interesting; but not particularly amusing. It is *not* Paris. I don't know that I shall leave with any great regret. . . . Are you also having such appalling weather? How is Wagner? What new vast work is he engaged on? I cannot imagine him doing anything else. On Tuesday I am going to Covent Garden. A seat costs a guinea; if you reckon cab fare there and back, gloves, etc., all at London prices, it works out at a small fortune. . . ."

Lassalle's stock exchange losses earlier in the year had made him sensitive to prices. But they made no difference to his luxurious style of living; and the contrast between this and the bitter penury of the Marx household may well have clouded the atmosphere of their talks. Marx, in the throes of yet another crisis, had just written to Engels: "To keep up appearances while Lassalle is here my wife pawned everything not actually nailed to the walls." The position was a difficult one for both parties. In any case Lassalle with his diamond rings, his rather too elegant clothes and his expensive perfume was unlikely to be attracted to a girl brought up with so dingy a background. His attitude to Miss Marx was patronising. She might, he suggested, go as companion to the Countess; or he would ask his friend Isidore Gerstenberg—now a very rich man—to employ her as a governess. He quite certainly did not fall in love with her.

We have few details of this London stay. There is a note of Lassalle's referring to a visit to Westminster Abbey with the Marx family. Also a proposal for an expedition to Windsor, unless the Queen was there; in which case Kew or Richmond, always provided that it did not rain. We hear of Lassalle, with Bucher's help, spending £20 on Blue Books, "so that", Marx wrote to Engels, "we shall not be able to quote Blue Books at him". And again "If my own affairs were not quite so bad he would have given me a lot to laugh at." As it was "the creature took up a lot of my time. He seemed to think that as I had no trade or business and was only engaged in theoretical work I might just as well devote all my time to him." The tone becomes even more bitter. "He turns out to be not only the greatest of scholars and deepest of thinkers but also a Don Juan and a revolutionary Cardinal Richelieu."

It is only from Marx's caustic notes that we have any knowledge of the details of their political talks. There was never any likelihood of their coming to a real understanding. Marx dismissed the *Workers' Programme* as merely "a vulgarisation of what we have so often said in the *Communist Manifesto* and our other papers". Lassalle's report on his talks with Garibaldi caused derision. "He got angry with me and my wife for laughing at his plans and calling him a Bonapartist. He shouted and gesticulated. Finally, he convinced himself I was too 'abstract' to understand politics." As to Rüstow, "the joke is that Rüstow wants to use the sports clubs, etc., so that when the day dawns there will be, at any rate in the small German States, a volunteer force under Rüstow to oppose the Army. The idea is damned silly, and I doubt whether Lassalle believes in it." Marx's one proposal to Lassalle was that the latter should act as Berlin correspondent for a German daily appearing in the States. But, "Lassalle maintains America is of no interest: Americans have no ideas."

The visit dragged to its inconclusive end. Engels remained in Manchester, and his suggestion that Lassalle should go there to see him did not appeal to Lassalle. The only result of the London talks was a promise from Marx to write, if adequately paid, for any newspaper Lassalle might establish in Germany. But this, Marx stipulated, was to be "without incurring any responsibility or partnership, as, in the political field, we agree in nothing except in a few ultimate aims".

Lassalle went back to Berlin and on to Wildbad. Here he got a letter from Marx who was in great distress and wished him to accept a bill for £60. Lassalle replied asking that Engels should undertake to provide cover. This was a reasonable request, but Marx misunderstood it and an acrimonious correspondence ensued. Finally, in November, Marx wrote:

"You do not realise what made me annoyed: it was the idea I conceived—wrongly, as a second reading of your letter convinced me—that you imagined I might be acting without Engels's agreement. I admit I said nothing of this in my letter to you. Still, it appeared so to me at the moment I wrote. I further admit my actual grievance was not expressed or even implied in my letter. You were therefore wrong in what you read into my letter and I was wrong because I wrote it and provided the *materia peccans*. Shall we let this estrange us? I think our friendship is substantial enough to survive this shock. . . . I admit that I, sitting as I was on a powder barrel, allowed circumstances to rob me of my self-control to an extent improper for a rational animal. But it was not generous of you to take the line of a prosecuting lawyer at a time when I was in mood of wanting to put a bullet through my head. So I hope our old relationship will go on, in spite of everything. . . ." Marx went on to analyse "the sophism of passion". Coming from a man as proud, bitter and unhappy as Marx was then, it was a generous letter. But for Lassalle, smarting under his real and imagined slights, it was not enough. He did not answer; and the break with his former friend and leader was now final and complete. From now on he stood, politically, alone.

Chapter 13

WHAT NOW?

I

Lassalle's correspondence, on his return to Germany from London, shows his sense of isolation. But he was determined to go ahead, without Marx, without the Prussian Progressives, without the *Nationalverein*. "If Rüstow", he wrote to the Countess, "has time for these people [of the *Nationalverein*] he must have a stronger stomach than I have. For all eternity I will have nothing more to do with them. And if my present idea succeeds, which is very doubtful and must be kept most secret—to found a workers' union for all Germany and put myself at its head—I will start off with a campaign against the *Nationalverein*." The Countess was more concerned with Lassalle the man than Lassalle the politician. "I miss you very much," she writes, "and it makes me sad when you talk about your complete emotional isolation. I doubt if you really miss me; but whatever and whomever else I have I shall always miss you."

On 21st October, old Heymann died, a very real blow, for Lassalle was devoted to his father. He went to Breslau for the funeral and on his return wrote to the Countess: "You are the only person now to whom I can show myself as I am. . . . I would like you to come to Berlin as soon as you can. But not just for my sake. That would make me unhappy. You have not had so much happiness that you can afford to give it away, and if you meant to stay with Rüstow in Zürich I would not be able to make a return for such a sacrifice."

To his mother he wrote: "Three words of love so that you will not be too long without a letter. And please do not cry all day. One mustn't cut oneself off entirely from the world even though our dear ones die and it is hard for us not to want to do so." He tried to make her come to Berlin, but there was the question of Jewish cooking. "We have no Jewish restaurant near here. One can have food sent in from Franks, but it isn't very good." In the end Frau Lassal, anxious about money matters, about Ferdinand's political adventures, about everything and not least about being a burden to her son, could not face the plunge that the move to Berlin would entail. Lassalle was tireless in his attempts to reassure her. "You are not old and not a burden, but my own and dearly loved mother."

Then there was the arduous task of settling the family money matters, complicated by the facts that Ferdinand Friedland played so large a role in them and that the Friedland ménage was now finally breaking up. Lassalle had no longer any illusions about his brother-in-law. He wrote to his Breslau lawyer "I beg and implore you, send that scoundrel to the gallows, strangle him in an iron mesh of law suits and I will be eternally in your debt." But it seems clear that in the final settlement it was Friedland who profited most. Lassalle made his report to the Countess in mid-December: "I have settled with my brother-in-law and my sister's position is now satisfactory. I only had to give way over small points. On the other hand I myself had to make sacrifices—i.e. I have renounced all personal claims against the Prague Company. That means a lot, for I could have had 40,000 thalers. But this was the only way I could make him agree to my sister's settlement; I was alone, I wanted the thing settled so that I could get on with my work. So I did it. Probably I wouldn't have if you had been there. But you had to be away and I was alone and out of sorts and wanted to be left in peace. The devil take it. . . . Look out in Italy for a good-looking woman for me; that is probably the only thing that could cheer me up."

The Countess was disturbed to hear of the settlement and keenly hurt at the suggestion of having deserted Lassalle. It would have been very different, she wrote back, if he had handled her more sympathetically. As to Rüstow, "the injustice of fate, the lack of recognition, money troubles, a sense of failure and an unhappy marriage have made him bitter against the world, against himself, against everything. It is a tragedy not to be able to do more for so good and capable a man. He is devoted to me and thinks I am absolutely necessary to him. But cheer him up I cannot."

And so the correspondence goes on, sentimental, rather sad, with an undercurrent of reproach. Lassalle was now keeping one Marie, a salesgirl from Gerson's Stores, but on Christmas Eve he wrote that he was very unhappy. "I who have never wept am weeping like a tear box." He wistfully recalled the cheerful festivities of the Düsseldorf days. The Countess wrote that she found her "lonely glass of champagne with Rüstow" a poor apology for a Christmas tree. There was truth in what she told Lassalle—"however much we may have quarrelled at least we have spoilt each other for any one else." It was cold and wet in Italy and she was homesick for Germany. "It is true that when in Germany one gets annoyed at German stupidity and tactlessness. But when one comes abroad and compares Germans with foreigners one learns to appreciate them. A day will come when it will be a proud thing to be a German."

The New Year found Lassalle still in a mood of self-pity. "My dearest," he wrote to the Countess, "has anyone else been as morose and peevish as you were? That sort of thing is much harder for a man to bear with than a woman. . . . And then you went off towards a new friend, happy and triumphant as one always is after making a new conquest." But the old relationship would never come back. It would not be fair to Rüstow. "So in future I can only have half or a quarter of your time, and in my loneliness I must look for a woman companion. This you have made difficult if not impossible. How and where can I find a woman who could take your place? And who knows how many years may not pass before I have a real political success? My father is dead. Before I have a triumph you may be dead too. Then what point would it have? Who would care for it? . . . My sister has been with me since the third and sends her love. I don't much like having her here as her conversation etc. isn't interesting."

He did not tell the Countess he had already met a prospective candidate for the role of woman companion. She was not yet twenty and thus unlikely to be peevish or morose.

2

WHEN Crown Prince Max of Bavaria visited Berlin on the occasion of his betrothal to a Prussian Princess he inquired for someone to go back to Munich with him and help him with his studies. The choice fell on a certain Dönniges. Relations between the two were happy; and when the Crown Prince ascended the throne as King Maximilian II, von Dönniges had become a person of some influence in the Bavarian capital. He married a vivacious and attractive woman of Jewish blood, and their house was a centre of smart and artistic society, in which Helene their daughter began to play a part at a very early age. Her education was haphazard; and at the age of twelve she was engaged.

"My parents", writes Helene in her memoirs, "went on a tour to Sardinia, and there among the wild and semi-wild inhabitants they met a man who seemed relatively tame. By some means or other, perhaps by his cooking (which was the only thing he was good at) he so fascinated my parents that they promised to make their twelve-year-old daughter his wife. How far any definite arrangements were made for the marriage remains obscure. The point was that it amused my mother—young, lively and attractive—to play at being mother-in-law to a man she liked."

No objection was raised by the precocious and romantic heroine herself when the news reached her in Munich. "It was a real thrill to receive the ardent love-letters of my fiery Italian, to show them to my little friends and to have them all envying me. It is true I had not yet seen my intended husband. He was an officer stationed at Alessandria and had some difficulty in getting leave. . . . My future was painted in the rosiest colours. I found myself enormously interesting. I conceived a high idea of my irresistible beauty, which had enslaved the wild Italian by a mere photograph. I acquired the greatest contempt for my governesses, who, although much older than I was, were still spinsters."

Eventually the fiancé arrived and the spell was broken. "I

thought he was horrible. This great, gross, dark-faced, hairy man seemed so repulsive to me, that, knowing I would get no sympathy from my parents, I took refuge with Thérèse the housemaid who comforted me with these words: 'We (it went without saying that Thérèse and I would remain together) will have to marry him because we have to. Your mama has the idea so fixed in her head that it's no good talking. But anyhow the good God and the Blessed Virgin will take pity and soon send us another one we like better, and can run off with. Or if one doesn't turn up soon the Lord Jesus and the dear Saints wouldn't take it as a sin if we did in this horrible man. One way or another we shall get rid of him. But we have a hard time to go through first.'"

The upshot however was that Helene was sent off to her grandmother in Berlin. The old lady spoiled her and her life was a round of parties and gaieties. "Thanks to the artists and writers who used to come to my father's house I was not only used to intellectual discussions but had none of the inhibitions of conventional society. . . . I was always ready for anything and took the line that I was an exceptional person and therefore at liberty to do what was forbidden to others. So it naturally happened that I was sought after and courted by all the young gentlemen and by not a few of the older ones."

It was in Berlin that Helene met Yanko von Rakowitza, a young Roumanian nobleman "of about the same age as myself but in everything else my complete opposite. To picture his character and appearance one should think of Othello as a boy; his dark skin and curly hair, the black silken gleam of his eyes as can only come from Africa, it all made me give him the nickname of 'my Moorish page': he was still a boy and I, his chosen queen, thought of him only as a page. But already he possessed the noble qualities of Shakespeare's Moor; and also his weakness. It was not his intelligence that was remarkable, it was his heart, where love soon reigned supreme until that heart ceased to beat."

Helene first heard of Lassalle from a Baron Korff, a cavalry officer with a taste for smart Bohemian society, whom she met at a ball. A fortnight later she sat next at dinner to a Dr.

Oldenberg who remarked: "You are something completely out of the ordinary. You are the only woman I can imagine as Lassalle's wife." He described Lassalle as a man of brilliant intellect and so interesting "that any one who had once been to an evening of his in the Bellevuestrasse would break any engagement in order to go there again—in spite of the Countess." Helene asked about the Countess and was told she was "an old friend of Lassalle's. About sixty. Painted up to the eyes. False eyebrows. A neck like yellow parchment: a continuous succession of two-foot Havana cigars between her false teeth. But in mind a woman of extreme importance, who has as good a grasp of economics and Roman law as any expert."

Helene records:

"All this made me picture Lassalle as just a Brain, a Brain with the Countess in the background. Good-looking young men are proverbially stupid, so I thought vaguely of a short, if not hunchbacked, awkward, black, crooked little Jew. I did not even ask what he looked like. I felt I knew. Next day I asked my grandmother about Lassalle. She would only say he was a loathsome demagogue who had been involved in a charge of theft. In any case he was not a man that one could afford to know."

Helene made Yanko von Rakowitza hunt round for more information, but he was unable to find out much. Before long, however, she got to know the Hiersemenzels, and was invited to a party at their house which Lassalle was due to attend. Helene took care to arrive late. Lassalle, she discovered, was in the study with the host and another man. She herself was shown into the adjoining drawing-room, a room "fitted out in the ornamental style of furniture recently become so fashionable, chairs with high carved Gothic backs and soft padding, combining beauty with comfort". Helene installed herself and waited. In due course the study doors opened and there appeared "three gentlemen in animated conversation—Hiersemenzel, an ugly little Jew and a tall slim handsome man with a head like a Roman Emperor and flashing eyes. The thought came to me, if only this one were *he*. Then I looked at the Jew. But only for an instant. The Roman Emperor sat down on the sofa behind which I was hiding and began to talk. In a few seconds I had forgotten all else. I left off wondering which could be Lassalle. I just listened, listened with every nerve in my body. But my nature did not allow me merely to sit and listen. He said something I thought was wrong—I forget what it was—and I jumped up and said 'No, I don't agree.' And there we were, for the first time, looking into each other's eyes. That moment decided our fate. . . . He laid his hand on my arm and said: 'But we know each other. You are Brünhilde, Adrienne Cardorville, the little golden fox that Korff was telling me about. You are Helene.'

"I laughed and a flood of golden sunshine broke into my heart. 'This is he! How wonderful that he should be like this and not as I had imagined!' I was happy, carefree, light as air and a feeling came over me that I had never known before. Everything else in the world had vanished and this man and I—we—were all that mattered."

When the party was over he walked home with Helene and her companions.

"He took my arm. 'We must talk seriously,' he said after a short pause. 'When are we going to see each other again? And when can I come and call on your grandmother to put everything on a proper footing?' Suddenly I remembered what they said about him at home and felt frightened. . . .

" 'No,' I whispered. 'Don't come. It won't do. Later perhaps, but not now. There are all sorts of difficulties. And then my grandmother is ill.'

"It all comes back to me as clearly as if it was yesterday. A full clear moon was in the sky. It was a fresh transparent night. A breeze stirred the bare branches of the trees. The Tiergarten lay dark and lonely. All was still except, from some way off, the regular footsteps of our companions along the pavement. Lassalle stopped and made me look into his eyes. 'You child,' he said softly, almost reproachfully, 'why make it so difficult? Why hold back what is bound to happen? Don't you know it is dangerous to play with fate?' I did not answer. And for the first time I had the feeling that afterwards always came to me when he was there, a yearning anxiety, a tightening of the heart, an obscure fear that I must do whatever he told me, as if I were hypnotised. He knew what I was feeling. 'No,' he said softly. 'You must not be unhappy. It is a pity that we are losing time, but it is no tragedy. We have our lives in front of us.' . . .

"I hardly slept that night. I told no one at home of my experience. But in the evening when Yanko came I said: 'Yanko, I met a man last night and if he wants me I shall leave you and everyone else and go wherever he wants to take me.' The great dark eyes of my Moorish page were filled with tears as he answered 'So long as you are happy.'"

However, the story of the evening leaked out. Helene's grandmother held a family council. The Hiersemenzels were cut out of the von Dönniges visiting list and Helene was forbidden to go to any house where Lassalle might be invited. Enterprising match-makers tried to arrange a meeting, but the watch over Helene was too strict. It was months before they saw each other again.

3

MEANWHILE the constitutional struggle was taking its course. During the summer of 1862 various attempts had been made and had failed to find some settlement. On the 23rd September Parliament refused by a large majority to sanction the cost of the Army reorganisation. The Government resigned and Bismarck became Prime Minister. Three weeks later Parliament was adjourned.

The first mention of the new Prime Minister in Lassalle's correspondence comes in a letter to the Countess, the rest of which was concerned with an abortive attempt to have *Sickingen* produced at Weimar.

"Everybody here of course is furious with Bismarck Fine-Trousers (*Schönhosen* for *Schönhausen*). He is and remains a reactionary Junker from whom one can only expect reactionary measures. He differs from the *Kreuzzeitung* crowd in that he has not their doctrinaire rigidity. He is baroque—a baroque

Kreuzzeitung man! He will either rattle his sword to get through the military budget on the pretence that war is imminent (though people will not swallow that), or else try and cook up some reactionary recipe for German unity. But German unity cannot be obtained on reactionary soil. That is the most ridiculous and baroque idea of all."

On the 19th November Lassalle followed up his earlier address on the Constitution by a further speech *What Now?* It was read by Ludwig Löwe as Lassalle on that day was too ill to speak, though he recovered in time to repeat it himself a few days later in another hall. He was quick to quote Bismarck's recent speeches in the Chamber as tending to admit that the Constitutional question was a power question. "I can, Gentlemen, draw your attention—in particular the attention of the Police representatives here with us—to the fact that my attitude is shared by the highest authorities of the State."

He proceeded to give his advice to the Parliamentary majority: "I propose that immediately on reassembling the Chamber should pass a resolution in the following terms: 'In view of the fact that the Chamber has refused to approve the monies for the new military organisation; in view of the fact that none the less the Government has continued to pay out these monies; in view of the fact that so long as this takes place the Prussian Constitution is a lie; in view of the fact that as long as this situation lasts it would be unworthy of the representatives of the people—and would indeed entail their complicity in the Government's breach of the Constitution—to continue their sessions and help the Government to keep alive the semblance of a Constitutional régime—

" 'In view of the above the Chamber decides to adjourn indefinitely, that is to say until such time as the Government produces evidence of the discontinuance of these payments for which approval has been refused.' "

Once, he continued, the Chamber passed this resolution the Government had lost the battle. Absolutism was no longer possible in Central or Western Europe in 1862. In the end the Government must give way: "And then, Gentlemen, you will be in a position to impose your conditions. You will be able to demand and attain Parliamentary rule, without which Constitutionalism is an illusion. There is no conciliation panacea. You have collected enough experience to know what the old Absolutism is. So no fresh compromise with the other party! Your knees on his chest and your thumbs in his eyes."

Chapter 14

THE FIRST APPROACH

I

There were, in the autumn of 1862, signs of restlessness among the German workers. The American Civil War and the cotton blockade were affecting the textile industry. The slump was spreading and there were wage cuts and unemployment. For the politically minded there was the excitement over the constitutional crisis. The more far-sighted of the Progressive leaders were well aware that it would be a political blunder to neglect the workers. Schulze-Delitzsch was busy with his schemes for co-operatives, and Max Wirth took a party to visit the London Exhibition. But there was no attempt by the Progressives to sponsor a working-class political movement.

In late October there came a spontaneous step from a small group of workers. A self-constituted committee published in the Press a proposal for a Workers' Congress in Berlin:

"Workers! German Brothers!

"The sun of a new life has dawned on our Fatherland, and under its warming rays all classes are awakening to fresh deeds and fresh aspirations. Only we, the workers, have rested in the drowsy belief that others are looking after us and that there is no point in our active participation in questions of the highest interest to us. . . ."

The proposed agenda was very anodyne—the removal of certain superannuated guild restrictions, the formation of benevolent societies and the organisation of a world exhibition in Berlin. Nevertheless the Liberal Press took fright. The *Volkszeitung* declared that the proposed Congress was most ill-timed. "Everything else must wait till the present crisis has been overcome. Enemies of the pro-Constitutional Party ascribe to it all sorts of motives, subversive revolutionary activities, etc. They try to frighten its more timid adherents with the bogey of a

Red Republic, of a Socialist Workers' Movement, in order to drive them in panic into the ranks of reaction. Nothing could be more propitious for the enemies of freedom in their secret machinations as this most untimely workers' movement. . . ."

In the event a joint mass meeting of working men and Progressive Party members was held in Berlin on the 2nd November. Schulze-Delitzsch spoke. One of the workers, Karl Eichler, made the remarkable statement that he knew Bismarck was about to do something for the workers. The meeting was stormy and confused. In the end it adopted a motion by the Leipzig delegates that the proposed Workers' Congress should be held at Leipzig at a date to be fixed later. There was considerable haziness as to what this Congress should accomplish, and some doubt as to whether it would be held at all. The workers lacked leaders. Eichler, who at one time seemed making a bid for leadership, was later discovered to be on the pay roll of the Prussian police.

2

IN LEIPZIG, however, there were men who meant business, and one of them was a friend of Lassalle's friend Ludwig Löwe. This was Dr. Otto Dammer who earned a small income as editor of the *Illustrierte Gewerbezeitung* but whose main interest was a local working-man's club. Löwe sent a copy of the *Workers' Programme* to Dammer, and Dammer showed it to Vahlteich and Fritsche, his two chief associates in the club. Vahlteich afterwards recorded: "It made a tremendous impression. We had never heard anything like it. It was very different from the milk-and-watery stuff hitherto served up to the workers."

In early November Löwe wanted the three to come to Berlin to meet Lassalle, but the latter was at Breslau for his father's funeral. Later in the month the Leipzigers invited Lassalle to Leipzig, but he wished to avoid any appearance of being too eager and therefore refused. Dammer and his associates then put out feelers to the Progressive Party and

Nationalverein leaders: they asked the Progressives to make universal suffrage a plank in their programme, and they asked for facilities for working men to become active members of the *Nationalverein.* The Progressives were unwilling to commit themselves to universal suffrage, and the only reply from the *Nationalverein* was that working men "might consider themselves as honorary members". It became increasingly evident to Dammer, Vahlteich and Fritsche that Lassalle was the leader they were seeking. On the 4th December they wrote to him in their capacity of members of the Leipzig committee set up to make arrangements for the German Workers' Congress:

"The workers' movement requires strong and intelligent leadership. . . . We the undersigned committee members have considered the matter with the greatest care. We find that in all Germany there is one man only whom we wish at the head of the movement, one man only whom we feel capable of the task, one man only in whom our confidence is such that we would place ourselves under his orders. You are that man. Your pamphlet has won you the right to the position we wish to see you occupy. It has also laid upon you the duty to devote yourself loyally and completely to the cause of the workers. We request and require of you to fulfil this duty. . . ."

A fortnight later they wrote again:

"We do not wish to undertake any step without your approval. If you agree with our suggestion please say when one of us can come and see you. We must add that unfortunately we cannot afford all the travelling expenses, and therefore ask you if you would bear half of them. The sooner a meeting takes place the better." They arrived in Berlin in mid-January, and were present in court when Lassalle conducted his defence against the charge arising out of his *Workers' Programme*, the charge of "inciting to hatred and contempt".

3

THE COURT was crowded. Lassalle was sufficiently a public character to make any case in which he appeared a *cause célèbre.*

The Public Prosecutor who had drawn up the charge was son of the philosopher Schelling; and current rumour offered the piquant possibility of Lassalle citing Schelling the father to confute Schelling the son. Members of the public who managed to get seats were not disappointed. Lassalle, stimulated by the recent approach from the Leipzig workers, was at his provocative best.

His speech, which he later printed with the title *Science and the Worker*, puts up a double defence. In the first place *The Workers' Programme* must be regarded as a scientific work. As such it cannot be made the ground of a criminal charge in view of Article 20 of the Prussian Constitution which lays down: "Science (*Wissenschaft*) and its teaching are free." Secondly, the whole tendency of the work is to promote harmony and reconciliation rather than incite hatred and contempt.

"Five branches of learning have contributed to my pamphlet, have had to be mastered before I could compose it—History, Law, Economics, Statistics and Philosophy. The Public Prosecutor must indeed be a prodigy of learning, if he finds this insufficient to qualify my pamphlet as a scientific work. . . . It is stated in the charge that 'a condition of science is that it should have no practical tendency'. I wish to ask the Prosecution—the charge is signed Schelling—where did he learn that? From his father? Certainly not. Schelling the father laid down for philosophy no less a mission than to transform the age we live in."

And later:

"How can I be called to answer for the limitations of the Prosecutor's education, for his ignorance of the range and scope of modern scientific thought? Am I his intellectual whipping boy?"

There were heated and indignant protests from the Prosecution, sharp and frequent exchanges with the Bench. But Lassalle's audacity was guided by his intimate knowledge of Court procedure and reinforced by his ability to turn every interruption to his own advantage. A newspaper report of the proceedings—which he afterwards quoted with great satisfaction—spoke of his establishing an "intellectual supremacy".

The second part of his defence contains some striking passages:

"How is it that the middle classes have come to be so frightened of the common people? Look back to March and April of 1848. Have you forgotten how things were then? The police force impotent. The common people swarming along the streets. The streets and the people themselves under the sway of unthinking agitators like Karbe and Lindenmüller, rough ignorant men thrown up by the storm. The middle classes trembling behind their doors, trembling for their lives and their property, patently in the power of these ignorant agitators who were too good-natured to use that power. The middle classes ardently praying for the return of despotism and government by gendarme, shuddering with a fear they have not yet forgotten. Where were the intellectuals then? Where were you, Gentlemen?

"Berlin is not a city of cowards.

"But you said: 'These people would not understand us. They do not speak our language. There is a gulf between us and the masses. They would not understand us.' So you were silent. But, Gentlemen, are you so sure there will never again be a political earthquake? Are you convinced that the march of history has come to an end?

"If it has not, then you should thank those who are working to bridge the gulf between the thinkers and the masses, who are pulling down the barriers between the bourgeoisie and the people. . . ."

Finally he concluded:

"Middle class and workers, we are members of one nation and stand united against our oppressors. I have now finished. To one who has dedicated his life to the cause of science and the working class, conviction and sentence will mean no more than, to a chemist, the breaking of a test tube in his laboratory. With a slight frown at the momentary inconvenience he will continue at his work."

The Court found him guilty and sentenced him to four months' imprisonment. Lassalle gave notice of appeal.

4

LASSALLE could justifiably regard the case as a resounding success. All Berlin were talking of it. The papers were full of his name. The Berlin correspondent of the *Kölnische Zeitung* made history by being the first German journalist ever to telegraph to his paper the result of a trial. Lassalle's new friends from Leipzig were tremendously impressed by what they had seen and heard and he himself looked forward to his appeal with supreme confidence. Nevertheless in his private correspondence we find the familiar note of petulance. "It was better", he wrote to the Countess, "when I fought court cases for you. You at least realised what I was doing for you. But the working class does not know and does not understand."

The Countess showed the letter to Rüstow and Rüstow wrote to Lassalle:

"My trouble is just the opposite of yours. You complain you have nobody to care about. I have to care for many more than my position allows, in spite of all my efforts. I have to cope with just those prosaic miseries of day-to-day existence which you in your cavalier manner ignore. And yet I am simple enough to aspire to be engaged in higher things."

This was no comfort to Lassalle and in his next letter to the Countess he wrote:

"Rüstow did me a great wrong in taking you away from me. Just now I am in the mood of Faust: I would give all my intellect for any naïve Gretchen that turned up. I would not be like that if you were here. I wish I could fall in love, never mind with whom."

It was in this state of mind that he again met Helene von Dönniges. Holthoff, who had been his lawyer in the Hatzfeldt case, was now in Berlin and it was Frau Holthoff who arranged the meeting. It took place at a public ball and Helene in her memoirs has left a remarkable but probably not unauthentic account of their conversation. "Lassalle said: 'Supposing you were my wife, what would you do if I was sentenced to death and you saw me ascend the scaffold?'

"It was an odd question to ask at a ball and after so long an interval. But I felt it was right he should ask it. 'I would wait', I said, 'till they cut off your proud head so that up to the very end my Eagle could see something that he loved. Then I would take poison, which we would have prepared together.'

"My answer pleased him. 'The poison is ready,' he said, 'but it will not come to that. I have a lucky star.' "

They were interrupted by Yanko von Rakowitza who took Helene off to dance. When she came back to him Lassalle said:

" 'I must know about your parents. How does one manage your mother? Make love to her? Or talk about clergymen? Or play whist and hold her wool?'

"I had to laugh at all this about my lively and attractive mother. 'Better make love to her,' I said. 'She's more used to that. Or talk about books and art.' 'And your father?' I had little to say about my father but Lassalle saw no difficulty there. 'One can manage men,' he said, 'that is, intelligent men. But the one unsurmountable obstacle is a stupid woman.' "

There were other brief meetings in the ensuing weeks and Helene met Riekchen—"a Madame von Friedland, a short, plump, lively, intelligent-looking lady, no longer in her first youth."

And then:

"A few days later Holthoff called and asked me: 'Would you marry a man who was a commoner and a Jew?' 'Yes,' I said, 'if his name was Lassalle.' Then I asked: 'Did Lassalle send you to put this question formally on his behalf?' Holthoff became embarrassed. 'Not exactly,' he said. 'He just asked me to see how the land lay.' I stood up and said: 'In that case there is no point in going on with this conversation.'

"Nothing happened for a fortnight during which Holthoff seemed to be taking care that I did not meet Lassalle. Then my grandmother came into my room with a letter. 'I wrote to your father,' she said, 'about your marriage with Lassalle. He will not hear of it.' I felt hot and angry. 'Did I or Lassalle ask you to write to my father?' 'No,' she said, 'but Holthoff came——' 'Then you and Holthoff can settle it,' I said. 'It is not of the slightest interest to Lassalle or to me.' I got up and went out.

And I had trained my poor grandmother so well she never mentioned the subject again."

Lassalle's version of the affair, which does not square up with Helene's, is given in a letter to the Countess of the 3rd March:

"My sister wants to marry me off. The girl is pretty, of good family, lively and cheerful, can keep her end up in society—but I don't know how deep her education goes. It's a funny story. We met some time ago at an evening party, liked each other and let each other know that we did. Thereupon her family put up an impenetrable wall all round her, and I haven't been able to see her or get to know her. I put out a feeler through third parties, might I call on her? The answer came: only if I brought a formal proposal of marriage. Otherwise not. They would agree to a marriage; but they knew all about me, I just wanted another little romance, they were not going to have the girl being talked about etc., etc. The girl herself told the intermediary she wished to accept me, would do all I wanted, but could not go against her family's orders. I answered: damn it, marriage isn't the first step, it's the last. But if I liked her self as much as I liked her looks I would certainly take her. That I could only find out by getting to know her within the limits set by usage and propriety. I couldn't marry a cat in a sack (i.e. a pig in a poke) for the sake of her *beaux yeux*. An answer came back that perhaps I was right but there it was. That is how things stand, and, as far as I'm concerned, that is how they will stay. After all, much as I admit I'm taken with her, I can't let myself be forced into marriage. One doesn't jump in off the deep end like that. What chiefly keeps me back is the money side. If, as is likely, my money from the Gas Company comes to an end my income in 1870 will be only about 1,500 thalers, or 2,500 or so if my mother dies. I can't keep a wife and children on that without gruesome economies. It would be a big sacrifice. And if she isn't the *âme d'élite* that I want, what is the point of the sacrifice? Up to 1870 I can live comfortably, even if married: but by then I would have got used to her beauty and the sacrifice would begin—and unless she can, in herself, compensate me for it I shall have done something very silly. On the other hand, as things are now, it would be most pleasant and desirable to be married. I am very taken with her. She has a lovely body. She is witty and amusing: is quite (not wildly) in love with me. And finally it is quite possible that my income will go on after 1870 and that then I won't be able to find a wife."

5

MEANWHILE the negotiations with Dammer, Vahlteich and Fritsche were making definite progress. Before the end of January they asked him to give his considered views on the policy to be adopted by a working-class movement. He replied that he would only do so on the official request of their committee. This official request was sent to him on the 11th February. He spent the next fortnight composing his *Open Answer*. He discussed his draft with Lothar Bucher and Ziegler. Both advised against publication: the time, they maintained, was not yet ripe. Lassalle went ahead and published it; and thereby entered on that phase of his life which won him his place in history.

Chapter 15

'THE OPEN ANSWER'

I

On the 9th March while *The Open Answer* was at the printers, Lassalle wrote a long letter to Gustav Lewy of Düsseldorf, with whom he was by now completely reconciled. He begins with his analysis of the world situation:

"1. The internal development in France, England and America shows that the bourgeoisie has lost its vocation for political leadership. It can no longer lead a revolution. Its time is past.

"2. National revolutions, as in Italy, Poland and Hungary are not to be confused with political revolutions.

"3. The German bourgeoisie is even less fitted than any other to conduct a political revolution. This is proved by the existence of a party like the Progressives, fifteen years after 1848.

"4. There remains the possibility of a national revolution in Germany (unification); but this will be much more political in its nature than the national revolution in Italy, Poland and Hungary. Therefore the German bourgeoisie will never carry it through. Their motto is: above all, no revolution from below; better despotism from above.

"5. Nevertheless it is still possible that external factors, e.g. war, will bring about a national-political revolution. I hope and believe that this will be the case. But such a revolution will only be effective if driven on by a solid and class-conscious workers' party."

He goes on to explain what he himself was undertaking. ". . . I am standing on the eve (as the newspapers say) of a very important event. I mean my reply to the Leipzig workers.

It is now at the printers; I expect the proofs to-morrow and it should appear next week. The workers asked me a straight question and I had to give them a straight answer. The difficulties were enormous. One cannot expect the workers to have any grasp of economics; nor that I could compress my work on economics into a small pamphlet. But my labour would be futile if I did not give the workers a clear conception of their economic position and thus arm them against all the lies, deceptions and illusions to which they will be exposed. The whole pamphlet must be clearly intelligible to all. When I set myself this task I felt the difficulties were insuperable; but to my own surprise I have solved them all. The whole is so easy to read that the worker will feel he has known it all for years. He will henceforth be proof against lies and sophisms. As the paper is addressed to an actual existing movement it will have much the same effect as Luther's thesis of 1517 on the door of Wittenberg church. It must have that effect if our working class possess energy and stamina. . . ."

He proceeds to tell Lewy of the objections and misgivings of Ziegler and Bucher.

"I answered them as Luther did. 'Here I stand. I cannot do else. God help me. Amen.' And if I were indeed struck morally dead on the spot, and physically torn into seventy-seven pieces, I still could not have done otherwise. A workers' movement is there. It is necessary, even if one had to die thirty deaths, to give the people a theoretical exposé and a practical slogan. . . . But perhaps the working class as a whole is not ripe for it. In that case I am a dead man and the Progressives can rejoice at my fall. But even that would not disturb me. I would merely retire to my studies having proved that the times are ripe only for humbug. I could turn my back on politics with a clear conscience and live like a dead man with the dead. The seed I have planted with my manifesto will grow. It does not matter when. . . . The comic side is that in my manifesto I have said nothing that is not strictly 'conservative' in the good sense of the word. It sets out the most conservative, most legal and most peaceful way of emancipating the workers. But its effect can only be revolutionary, decisively so. For the ruling classes do not want labour to be emancipated. They not only want their property to be respected—as is done in my manifesto—they want the continuance of their privileges."

2

The Open Answer starts off by refuting the convenient bourgeois theory that the working class should not meddle in politics. Equally untenable was the idea that the workers should regard themselves "as the appendage of the Prussian Progressive Party and act as its chorus and sounding-board". The impotence of the Progressives had been revealed in the constitutional conflict. Accordingly "The working class must establish itself as an independent political party, and make its slogan and banner—Universal, Equal and Direct Suffrage. The legitimate interests of the working class can only be satisfied by representation in the German legislative assemblies. . . .

"This party's attitude towards the Progressives is obvious. It must feel itself, and be, an independent and separate party. It must support the Progressives where common interests so demand. Where interests do not coincide it must desert and oppose the Progressives—must either force them forward, or leave them to sink even deeper in their present morass of insignificance and helplessness."

Lassalle then turns to the question: how can the working man better his living conditions? He dismisses as inadequate or irrelevant the palliatives proposed by the Berlin workers' committee. He attacks the idea of workers' co-operatives as propounded by Schulze-Delitzsch; manufacturing co-operatives, such as the meagre savings of the workers could set up, would be unable to compete with large capitalist concerns, and consumer co-operatives afford only local and temporary help. He then proceeds to expound "the iron law of wages". This law, according to Lassalle, entails that in a world of free competition the average worker's wage cannot exceed the bare minimum of subsistence for himself and a limited family. Increase above this minimum would result in larger workers' families entailing an increase of available manpower, and, by the law of supply and demand, a decrease in wages. On the other hand, should wages drop below this level, families would shrink and a shortage of manpower would force wages up again.

Lassalle then goes on to propound his remedy—i.e. co-operatives, not circumscribed, as those sponsored by Schulze-Delitzsch, by the narrow limits of the workers' own resources, but financed and promoted by the State.

"To make the working class its own employer, that is the way, the only way by which this cruel and iron law can be set aside. Once the working class is its own employer, the contrast between wages and profit disappears. . . . It is therefore the task of the State to facilitate the great cause . . . and to offer you the means and possibility of self-organisation—and self-association. Do not be led astray by screams that this intervention of the State does away with the principle of self-help. It is not true that I keep any one from climbing a tower by his own effort if I give him a rope or a ladder. It is not true that the State prevents young people from developing their own powers when it provides them with teachers, schools and libraries. . . . Do not be led astray by cheap references to 'Socialism' and 'Communism.' . . ."

After pointing out that there was never an outcry against State aid for the rich—for instance Government guarantees of railroad dividends—Lassalle proceeds to quote statistics showing that 96 per cent. of the population of Prussia possessed incomes of less than 400 thalers per annum. It follows that, "the State, Gentlemen, belongs to you, the needy classes, not to us well-to-do, for you *are* the State".

But the State as at present constituted was unlikely to take the steps required for the well-being of the great majority of its members. In order to force the State to action it would be necessary to introduce universal suffrage.

". . . When that comes, you can depend upon it, there will be at your side men who understand your position and are devoted to your cause—men, armed with the shining sword of science, who know how to defend your interests. And then you, the unpropertied classes, will only have yourselves and your bad voting to blame if the representatives of your cause remain in a minority....

"But how can one bring about universal direct suffrage?...

"Organise yourselves as a General German Workers' Association, with the object of legal and peaceful but uninterrupted and untiring agitation for universal direct suffrage in all German States. From the moment when this association contains even 100,000 workers it will be a power to be reckoned with.... Collect funds—a penny a week from 100,000 workers means 160,000 thalers a year.... Start newspapers, collect funds, employ paid agents, compensate workers dismissed for propaganda work for the Association.... The art of practical success consists solely in this—concentrate all your strength on one point—on the most important point....

"Government and bourgeoisie can haggle and squabble over political rights. With their inherent trickery they can deny your political rights—even universal suffrage. But as soon as 89 to 96 per cent. of the population conceives universal suffrage as a need like food and drink and the demand spreads hot and strong throughout the whole nation—then, Gentlemen, you need not worry. There is no power that can long resist that. It is for this that you must strive. It is by this that you will triumph. For you there is no other way."

3

OF INTEREST are Lassalle's letters of this period to Rodbertus the economist. Rodbertus had long retired from active politics to his Pomeranian estate. But his prestige was such that Lassalle was anxious to secure his open support for the new movement; and the two men were on sufficiently friendly terms for Lassalle to write frankly.

On the 22nd April he replied to an inquiry from Rodbertus on his proposed State-aided co-operatives:

"I am quite willing to support any alternative and equally effective measure that you may suggest. I proposed, provisionally, the idea of co-operatives, because, for the time being, I see no other so easy and effective step. The worker must have something definite and tangible put before him if he is to take any interest."

Six days later he wrote:

"That private ownership of land and capital is to be abolished, that has been the inner kernel of my conviction ever since I began to think about economic matters. . . . True one cannot tell the mob that now, and that is why I avoided mention of it in my pamphlet. But I believe that State credit for co-operatives is the first little step."

On 30th April he wrote:

"Without universal suffrage, i.e. a practical instrument with which to enforce our demands, we might grow into a philosophical school or a religious sect. But never into a political party."

4

MARX, on receiving a copy of *The Open Answer* wrote to Engels:

"Itzig [i.e. Lassalle] . . . flings about phrases borrowed from us. His attitude is that of the future workers' dictator. He resolves the question between labour and capital as easily as play. The workers are to agitate for universal suffrage and then send people like himself armed with the shining sword of science into Parliament. They will establish workers' factories, for which the State will put up capital, and by and by these institutions will embrace the whole country."

Two months later, on receiving Lassalle's pamphlet on indirect taxation, he wrote:

"There are some good points in it but it is written in a self-assertive verbose manner with ridiculous pompous airs. It is essentially the compilation of a schoolboy in a desperate hurry to pose as a learned man engaged on original research. It abounds in errors of fact and theory. . . . I have not been able to bring myself to write to the fellow since the beginning of the year. To criticise his stuff would be waste of time; to afford him any recognition in his tactlessness and boasting would not do either. He would at once make use of it."

An exhaustive examination of Lassalle's political and economic theories is not within the scope of this book; and it is not intended to go into the question of his obvious debt to Marx, or his debts to von Stein, Bucher and other now forgotten theorists. Marx himself demolished much of Lassalle's elaborate argument. The "iron law of wages" had been called in question by responsible economists before ever Lassalle propounded it; and the experience of France under Napoleon III should have prevented illusions as to the worth of universal suffrage as a social panacea. But all this touches only one side of the issue as between Marx and Lassalle. Marx was addressing a small, select, highly educated, international audience. He was preparing a scientific and philosophical basis for a movement to become practically effective only in the distant future. Lassalle was addressing the backward, uneducated mass of the German working class of the 'sixties and was aiming to mould that unpromising material into an immediately effective political force. Further Marx enjoyed the freedom of utterance provided by English law and practice, and reinforced by the unawareness of any British authority that anything he said or wrote could be of any importance. Lassalle had to launch his movement within the framework of Prussian law and under the vigilant and hostile eye of the Prussian police.

It was not without justification that Lassalle could claim, as he did the following August: "Without decrying the services of Marx and the *Neue Rheinische Zeitung*, it is now, for the first time in Germany, that a Socialist party exists with political importance and with power behind it."

5

LASSALLE had 12,000 copies of *The Open Answer* printed to be sold at one groschen a copy. The pamphlet created a considerable stir. The reaction of the Liberal press was violent. The *Volkszeitung* and *Nationalzeitung* proclaimed him ignorant of economics; the *Tribune* branded him as a renegade endeavouring to curry favour with the authorities in the hope of a remission of his sentence of imprisonment. Schulze-Delitzsch gave a series of polemical addresses; and in Berlin and other areas where the Progressives' influence was strong workingmen's associations and clubs passed resolutions condemning Lassalle's proposals. But Leipzig remained loyal. On the 24th March, a mass meeting was held at which *The Open Answer* was approved by 1,350 votes against 2, and a new committee was set up to organise the formation of a General German Workers' Association. Promises of adhesion came from workers' committees in Hamburg and the Rhineland.

All this entailed a real physical strain, as Lassalle soon discovered. "I'm half dead with a chill," he wrote to the Countess, "and as hoarse as a corpse, and I have to make a speech in Leipzig. I must get Frerich's prescription made up at a chemist's." To Rodbertus in Pomerania he wrote: "How fortunate you are. This correspondence with workers in every town will be the death of me. I have to write fifteen letters every day."

Rodbertus composed a letter cautiously supporting *The Open Answer* but no newspaper would print it. Lassalle approached his ex-friend Duncker, of the *Volkszeitung*: "In view of the vulgar abuse daily heaped upon me by your newspaper I feel it would be fitting, from every point of view, if you would arrange for the publication in full of the attached letter from our leading German economist Rodbertus. . . . The length of the letter entails a certain financial sacrifice on the paper publishing it. In view of the former relations between us I feel, rightly or wrongly, that I am justified in asking this sacrifice from you."

Duncker replied:

"In your letter of yesterday you made a request to me personally that in view of our former relations I should make the financial sacrifice of printing Rodbertus's letter in full in the *Volkszeitung*. Apart from the fact that your own behaviour has shown no sign of consideration for our former relations I am convinced that, as a matter of principle, you would never allow personal considerations to play a part in purely political affairs."

Ludwig Löwe, who had first brought Lassalle and the Leipzig workers together, began to hedge. His association with a man whose views were anathema to Berlin big business was bringing him difficulties with his partner (though "I admit he would be more reasonable if he were not piqued over my relations with his wife") and, more important, with his bankers; and in the end he warned Lassalle that his business ties left him no leisure for political work.

Loyal friends also had their difficulties. Gustav Lewy who was energetically distributing the *Open Answer* throughout the Rhineland had to report:

"What I told you before is now getting more and more obvious—I mean our handicap through lack of money. If funds had been available Kichniawy would have made his tour in the Maingau and I mine to Westphalia. I myself cannot leave my business if it means all that I have. If I were to go bankrupt I should lose all influence and effectiveness. The bourgeoisie who hate me because I am the only one openly to oppose them would dance in triumph—'Yes, he wants communism because he's nothing more to lose!' " . . .

6

MEANWHILE a workers' association in Frankfurt invited both Lassalle and Schulze-Delitzsch to come to Frankfurt in May and hold a public debate. Schulze-Delitzsch hesitated and finally refused on the score of his Parliamentary duties. Lassalle accepted. A debate, he wrote to Rodbertus, would never decide the issue, but "in view of the line the Berlin Press is taking and of the fact that we have no newspaper ourselves, I must make some big stir and thus force the bourgeois papers to serve our cause. Therefore I must go to Frankfurt and win the battle. I must. The people there are all against me. But I must go and throw in all the force I have. I will shake my old revolutionary mane."

Rodbertus had little sympathy with this shaking of the revolutionary mane. To his cautious and ordered view another five hundred years would have to pass before the coming of the Socialist State that was both his and Lassalle's ultimate aim. "Earnestly, I beg you this," he wrote to his friend. "Jealously concentrate on the social issue and do not let yourself be deflected along a political revolutionary path. . . . I fear you misread the signs of the times if you think to reach your aim along that path. It leads to Cæsarism. . . ."

Recent developments in European history emphasise the significance of this warning. But to Lassalle it meant the loss of an ally, at a time when he was most in need of allies. However a greater blow was in store for him—the defection of Lothar Bucher. Bucher had arranged to come to Leipzig at the end of April and give a public address in support of Lassalle. His superiors in the Wolff Telegraph Bureau heard of the project and threatened to dismiss him if he carried it out. Bucher, after his long years of exile and unemployment, was not of the stuff that martyrs are made of. He wrote to Lassalle:

"I must give up my connexion with you. If I go on with it sooner or later you will involve me in complications—or I shall involve myself in complications. Instead of giving my reasons—which must in any case be clear to you after our recent arguments—let me just say it is instinct that leads me to this step. I need not tell you what it costs me. . . . Now I can part from you as a friend, as if setting out on a journey. Whether I could still do so in a few days' time I do not know. I leave it entirely to you when and how you reveal my decision to the others. It will be long before I shall need to do so. And when I must, I shall simply say I drew back, knowing my own weakness."

Lassalle seems fully to have understood his friend's position. A few months later Bucher asked von Bülow to arrange a reconciliation, and the former personal intimacy was restored and lasted to Lassalle's death. But Bucher's defection, at this decisive moment in Lassalle's career, meant the loss of his one remaining associate of real intellectual distinction. In a mood of self-pity Lassalle wrote a despondent letter to Rüstow which

Rüstow answered on 5th May: "I myself have had to live from hand to mouth, trying to keep my family from starving. This you know very well. But have I given up? No. It is only natural there should have been moments of despair, but they have never appreciably stopped my continuing to work for others. And you, what is your attitude? 'If I don't secure a triumph within a fortnight I shall retire to my studies, live on my investments, take a trip to Syria and write a learned book.' . . . The Countess told me you were being attacked and now you tell me so. Don't be too proud that in the excitement of the moment you have the strength to fight. Who hasn't? What is needed is persistence. . . ."

Lassalle wrote back angrily:

"It is ridiculous to suppose that because I wrote as I did I could really be capable of losing heart in a fortnight and giving up politics. Don't you understand that passionate natures have to give vent to passionate complaints? Retire from politics? My God!"

If, as seems likely, this letter was written on the 11th or 12th May Lassalle was in a mood in which nothing could have induced him to retire from politics. He had just received a direct approach from Bismarck.

Chapter 16

THE GENERAL GERMAN WORKERS' ASSOCIATION

I

The Bismarck-Lassalle correspondence (discovered in Berlin in 1927) starts with the original invitation, with corrections in Bismarck's own hand, dated the 11th May 1863: "In connexion with current deliberations on working-class conditions and problems I wish to obtain considered opinions from independent quarters. I would therefore be glad to have your views on these issues."

This note was brought personally by Zitelmann, one of Bismarck's staff, who was charged to arrange an early meeting. Lassalle acknowledged the note the same day, and the first meeting took place within forty-eight hours.

Fifteen years later (September 1878) Bismarck was pressed by Bebel in the Reichstag to give an account of his relations with Lassalle. The Chancellor made the following statement:

"I saw him, and since my first conversation I have never regretted doing so. I did not see him three or four times in that first week: I saw him perhaps three or four times altogether. There was never the possibility of our talks taking the form of political negotiations. What could Lassalle have offered me? He had nothing behind him. In political negotiations the principle of *do ut des* is always present, though politeness may prevent it being voiced. He, as a minister, could have given me nothing. But he attracted me as an individual. He was one of the most intelligent and likeable men I had ever come across. He was very ambitious and by no means a republican. He was very much a nationalist and a monarchist. His ideal was the German Empire, and here was our point of contact. As I have said he was ambitious, on a large scale, and there is perhaps room for doubt as to whether, in his eyes, the German Empire ultimately entailed the Hohenzollern or the Lassalle dynasty. . . . Our talks lasted for hours and I was always sorry when they came to an end. It is wrong to, suppose there was any personal rupture. He apparently had the impression that I regarded him as a man of genius whose society I appreciated, and the no less agreeable impression that I was an intelligent and interested listener. There could be no question of negotiations for the simple reason that in our conversations I had but little chance to speak. He assumed the burden of the conversation—in a pleasant and attractive manner. Every one who knew him will agree with my description. He was not a man with whom concrete agreements on a basis of *do ut des* could be concluded. I am sorry that our positions did not allow a more extended intercourse. I would have been glad to have as a neighbour a man of such intellect and talent."

Bismarck was careful not to disclose that it was he who made the first approach; and he was not, in consequence, called on to explain his motives. But it was natural that he should be interested in the new movement that was threatening to disrupt the Opposition. In any case the material well-being of the workers was a cause that was near to his heart. For Lassalle the approach must have been the cause of considerable gratification. It came at a time when he was conscious of the difficulties in the way of his creating an effective working-class party in opposition to the Progressives: Bismarck's note was welcome evidence that a highly qualified observer considered that he was likely to succeed.

We have no record of their conversations beyond occasional references in the correspondence, which will be noted later. It is certain that the atmosphere was cordial, particularly at the earlier meetings. The personality of the Iron Chancellor could not fail to appeal to the author of *Sickingen* and of the speech on the Constitution. Besides both were good Germans. Lassalle had once written to Marx "Do not forget you are a German socialist and should and must work for Germany." He looked forward to the day, "when the heritage of Turkey will fall to

Germany and when regiments of German soldiers and workers will stand on the shores of the Bosphorus." And he had said: "I allow the right of being a nation only to the great civilised peoples: to be assimilated by these is the only right I allow to the others."

2

IT WAS with the stimulus of his first meeting with Bismarck that Lascalle went to Frankfurt to shake his revolutionary mane. Schulze-Delitzsch was not present; but the Rüdelheim hall was packed with his supporters. The spirit of the meeting was hostile, and Lassalle met it in a combative mood. He would, he declared, accept the challenge. "My confidence in the power of truth is such that, although you may have determined to vote unanimously against me, I would not be surprised to find a unanimous vote in my favour before leaving the hall." He would, he warned his audience, speak at great length and with a ruthless elaboration of statistics, facts and argument. He demanded complete silence and the utmost attention.

The speech was indeed long. The two parts of it took seven hours to deliver, and made up a sizable pamphlet, when later printed as *The Worker's Reader*. After speaking for four hours, with frequent sharp exchanges with hecklers in all parts of the house, he arrived at the consideration of the sum required to launch his State-sponsored co-operatives. He put forward the figure of one hundred million thalers, and derided the idea that the State could not afford this sum. "Has there ever been a war that did not cost twice as much? And what was it that started these wars? In the last century it was the whim of a prince's mistress. And in this present century any prince's itch for conquest. Or one or other of the markets that the bourgeoisie may happen to covet. England's opium war against China in the 'forties cost at least twice as much. That was only fought to force opium down Chinese throats—just for one special bourgeois interest. This hundred million are doubly there for the trading interests of the possessing classes or for the whim of a monarch. When the redemption of humanity is in question is it then and then only that the money is not to be found?"

There were cries of "stop" and cries of "go on". Lassalle threatened: "If there are further cries of stop I shall sit down." The shouting was renewed. Part of the audience surged towards the platform. The Chairman had a hurried consultation with his committee and with the speaker and then announced that Herr Lassalle would continue his speech the day after next in the Hall of Harmony in Frankfurt.

To have provoked the adjournment was an astute tactical move on the part of Lassalle. Few men want to listen for more than four hours to opinions they disagree with; and few opponents or hecklers turned up to the meeting in the Hall of Harmony. Lassalle spoke for a further three hours with very little interruption and then put his motion to the vote.

Forty persons left the hall, cheering for Schultze-Delitzsch. The remainder accepted Lassalle's motion by over 400 votes to 1. The following day Lassalle spoke in Mainz, and carried his motion by 800 votes to 2. The degree of success was such that he could return in good heart to Leipzig to take part in the formal inauguration of the General German Workers' Association.

3

THE ASSOCIATION was formally founded on the 23rd May at a meeting at which eleven towns were represented—Leipzig, Dresden, Hamburg, Harburg, Cologne, Elberfeld, Düsseldorf, Barmen, Solingen, Frankfurt and Mainz. The five north Rhineland towns were represented by Gustav Lewy and one other. It was a small and manageable gathering, and Lassalle had little difficulty in securing acceptance for the statutes which he and his friend Ziegler had worked out some weeks before. The statutes are remarkable chiefly for the wide powers assigned to the President. Lassalle made no attempt to gloss this over. "Whoever is President," he remarked some days before the meeting, "his powers must be dictatorial. Otherwise, nothing will get done. We can leave mass talking to the bourgeois."

The statutes were approved, Lewy became Treasurer, Vahlteich Secretary and Lassalle President.

It was a modest beginning—at a rival Workers' Congress held a fortnight later under Progressive auspices no less than fifty-four towns were represented. But at least the new party had come into being; and it was with an obvious sense of achievement that Lassalle sent a copy of the statutes to Bismarck on the 8th June, together with his latest pamphlet—*Indirect Taxation and the Working Class.* The statutes he describes in his covering letter as "... the constitution of my kingdom which perhaps you will envy me! But this miniature will be enough to show how true it is that the working class is instinctively inclined to dictatorship if it feels that such will be exercised in working-class interests; and therefore, as I explained to you, the workers in spite of, or perhaps, because of, any republican tendencies would be prepared to see in the Crown the natural bearer of a social dictatorship in contradiction to the egoism of bourgeois society, if the Crown for its part (and this is most unlikely) could make up its mind to adopt a really revolutionary and national attitude; and become a social, revolutionary and popular monarchy instead of a monarchy of the privileged classes."

He goes on to comment on the restrictions on the freedom of the Press that Bismarck had recently introduced. "If anyone is to profit by these measures it will be my revolutionary party. To be frank, if it is really your intention to move the Crown one day to proclaim universal suffrage and to form an alliance with the people, measures like this will make such an alliance very difficult to attain. ... That would indeed lead to the victory of the ideas represented by myself. But it would not be a victory by the peaceful means which your Excellency gave me reason to hope for."

He finishes by urging the Prime Minister to ensure that their meetings and correspondence be kept strictly secret. He would, not, he said, be averse to publicity. But half-publicity was another matter.

The statutes empowered the President of the General German Workers' Association to appoint a Vice-President to act for him in his absence. On 27th June Lassalle issued his first official notice in his new capacity:

"Workers,

"In view of my departure to-morrow to Swiss health resorts I hereby nominate Dr. Otto Dammer of Leipzig as Vice-President of the Association till my return."

4

IN THE SUMMER of 1863 Marx was still working on volume one of his *Capital*. Engels was still tied to his business in Manchester. The stir that Lassalle was making in Germany filled them with mixed feelings.

Marx wrote to Engels: "As I am busy on economics, *ex officio*, for ten hours a day, I cannot be asked to devote my leisure to reading this puerile stuff (i.e. *The Workers' Reader*) . . . When I look at this work of mine (i.e. *Capital*) and see how I have had to turn everything round, how even the historical part is based on material some of which was quite unknown, Itzig and his economic system already in the making seem rather funny . . . though so far he has been hawking round as his latest discovery things that we were giving out (ten times better) as small change to our adherents twenty years ago."

Engels was obviously anxious. "This Lassalle business", he wrote Marx, "is getting unpleasant. It is high time you finished your book."

5

THE URGENT NEED of the General German Workers' Association was rapid recruitment. But the reports to reach Lassalle in his health resort were not encouraging. With the prevailing unemployment, workmen were unwilling to join a body of which their employers so strongly disapproved. Again, recruiting meetings could only be held in cafés and beer gardens, and the proprietors were unco-operative. "If we announce a meeting," Lewy wrote on the 25th June, "we risk the landlord refusing to have us." Landlords were afraid of "more beer spilt and glasses broken than beer drunk and paid for. Landlords have no feeling for the cause."

A month later Lewy wrote: "It will be autumn before we can mobilise and muster our full strength. This is impossible in the summer when the workers like to spend their scanty leisure out of doors. There is still a lot of unemployment, and this means the workers haven't even got the money to go to a café. In Düsseldorf we have now about eighty members, the same in Solingen and about a hundred in Elberfeld. But only forty in Cologne. . . ." On the 25th August he sent in another depressing report: "On the first of August Elberfeld had 223 members, Solingen 75, Düsseldorf 80, Cologne 29, Hamburg 220, Frankfurt 75, Leipzig 182. As to money I have had 22 thalers from Hamburg, 10½ from Solingen and 2½ from Cologne. No payments have come in from the others. At Hildburghausen, Harburg and Elberfeld the expenses have equalled the receipts. It is impossible to send you complete accounts, as I don't know how many members there are in the small centres, and I can't tell what the receipts have been in centres which have sent in no returns."

Lassalle in Switzerland could only rail. He wrote to Vahlteich, the Secretary: "This apathy drives one to despair. Will these dunderheads never shake off their lethargy?"

There were other irritations. A young Frankfurt lawyer of good family, Dr. J. B. von Schweitzer, had made the flattering request to be allowed to dedicate to Lassalle his ideological novel—*Lucinde, or Capital and Labour*. In the summer of 1863 he joined the Frankfurt branch of the Association. A few weeks later he announced his intention to speak at a meeting. But his private life was the subject of talk: a year previously he had been in prison for an offence against a boy in a Mannheim park. And Strauss, head of the local branch, wrote to Lassalle that if he did not prevent Schweitzer from speaking he (Strauss) and a number of other members would resign.

Lassalle replied:

"I am doing as you ask but will not conceal that the letter

you wrote me at the instance of a number of your members has caused me much displeasure. . . . The abnormality attributed to Dr. von Schweitzer has nothing whatever to do with his political character. I need only remind you that, however incomprehensible such unnatural tastes appear to us, the tendency of which Dr. von Schweitzer is accused was the general rule among the ancient Greeks, their statesmen and their philosophers. Ancient Greece saw nothing wrong in it, and I consider the great Greek philosophers and the Greek people knew the meaning of morality. . . . I could understand your not wishing Dr. von Schweitzer to marry your daughter. But why not think, work and struggle in his company? What has any department of political activity to do with sexual abnormality?"

To Schweitzer Lassalle expressed his personal regrets. "We did not establish our Association in order to give way to prejudice. . . . But to prevent a split in the local branch which, in view of its small numbers, it could ill afford, I would be grateful if you could make the sacrifice of keeping away from the meeting."

Shortly afterwards Lassalle arranged for Schweitzer to be transferred to the Leipzig branch.

6

LASSALLE finished his summer holiday with four weeks at Ostend. In late September he returned to Germany and launched his autumn campaign with a series of speeches at Barmen, Solingen and Düsseldorf.

A picture of Lassalle at the time of his political tours has been left us by Paul Lindau the young editor of a Düsseldorf newspaper. He first met Lassalle after one of his meetings.

"We walked back together. We talked of everything under the sun and had not nearly finished by the time we reached his hotel. We walked round the square four or five times in lively conversation; on his side, that is. It was really a monologue. . . . He gesticulated in the manner of a Southerner. Every now and then he would come to a halt. He would start his sentences in a high tone and then sink to a pleasant baritone. One could see he had practised public speaking. He tried perceptibly, though not always successfully, to avoid a Silesian accent. We shook hands warmly on parting and arranged to lunch together next day.

"When I called for him next day I found him in that uncomfortable posture so dear to the Americans—lying on a sofa with his feet on the table. He had a blue pencil and a pile of manuscript. It was the draft of his next speech which he was correcting and memorising. He rose to greet me and I was struck by the remarkable elegance of his suit: except on the stage I had seen nothing like it. I had realised the previous day the great importance he attached to his appearance. . . .

"He did not disguise the fact that his political campaign had its disagreeable side for him. 'Believe me,' he said, 'a man of my way of life and my social inclinations . . . speaking to packed houses in an unbreathable atmosphere. . . . I have a real horror of workers' deputations where I always hear the same speeches and have to shake hard, hot and moist hands. I hate to be touched. But there it is. One must go through with it. But I think that in the not too distant future I shall be able to devote myself to the direction of the movement, without the need for taking the field in person. . . .'

"As on the previous evening I myself said next to nothing—merely brought up points on which I wanted to hear him discourse. Two o'clock came. Lassalle went on talking and was so interesting that I could not interrupt. Twice I got up, so as to remind him we had arranged to have lunch, but he did not notice. On he went, till about half-past three. I blurted out 'What about lunch? I am getting hungry.' He reproached me for not having said so before and changed quickly into another suit. We went down to the floor below and knocked at the Countess's door.

"The Countess was in her early sixties. Lassalle did me the honour of introducing me; she put aside her cigar and offered me her well-cared for, well-formed hand. I knew she had been a famous beauty; but from seeing her I would not have realised it. She seemed to me older than she really was. But there was something kindly and pleasant about her personality. And I was touched to see her relations with Lassalle: on his side respect and gratitude, on hers a warm and sympathetic interest in all that concerned her young friend and a keen understanding of every word that he spoke. Our meal together was gay and delightful."

7

THE SPEECH that he made in Barmen and again in Solingen—by the time he reached Düsseldorf his throat was so bad that he could not finish it—marks the beginning of Lassalle's final phase as a politician. It is the work of Lassalle the demagogue and tactician rather than Lassalle the constructive socialist. "Friends," he began, "I have come not so much to hold long speeches as to review an Army!" He referred to his activities in the Rhineland in 1848 and after. "Those were glorious days—glorious because of the speed, determination and loyalty with which you rallied to my side. I have been away from you for seven years. You might well have forgotten me. A new generation of workers has grown up. I did not come to you before because I wished to see whether without me you could remain loyal to your principles. You have done so. You have remained as true to me as I to you. The young generation has grown up in the tradition of its fathers."

Otherwise the speech is a violent attack on the "Saturnalia of the German bourgeoisie", on the flirtation of the Progressives with the smaller German princes, on the cowardice, ineffectiveness and bad faith of the German Liberals generally. He exploited an ill-timed admission of Schulze-Delitzsch that it was middle-class fear of working-class aspirations that had hamstrung the revolution of 1848. One striking passage is concerned with the Press. Lassalle had the full support only of the obscure and insolvent *Nordstern* of Hamburg. Otherwise the whole German Press, especially the Liberal Press, was consistently and bitterly hostile. Lassalle now passed to the counter-attack:

"When the restrictive Press measures were issued, instead

of offering intensive resistance to this act of compulsion, the whole Liberal Press threw itself flat on its stomach.... 'How,' cried the *Rheinische Zeitung* as even the ranks of the Progressive Party began to murmur over such cowardice—'how could one suggest to the publishers that they should risk the capital they put into the paper?' ... Just as if a soldier—and newspapers should be soldiers, front-line fighters for freedom—as if a soldier made it his first duty to make sure that he never comes within range of a bullet...."

The papers, Lassalle maintained, should have formed a united front: if one received a warning from the authorities the others should all publish the article which gave rise to the warning. This, however, was unlikely in an age when newspapers "while still pretending to be the champions of intellectual and moral values" were primarily concerned with the sale of advertising space and with circulation. Newspaper work had become "not merely business but fraudulent business, because conducted under the banner of high ideals and the common good." Such a state of affairs would continue until complete freedom of expression was granted and all paid advertisements in privately owned newspapers forbidden. Advertisements should be confined to State or municipal newspapers.

Such was the Barmen speech. "I wrote it," Lassalle told Lewy when he sent him the manuscript to be printed, "with an eye to one or two people in Berlin." It was primarily groundbait for Bismarck. But it was too good a fighting speech not to be a welcome event in the dreary lives of the Ruhr factory workers. It was warmly received in Barmen and even more warmly in Solingen. In the latter town enthusiasm reached such a pitch that the authorites became alarmed and the Mayor arrived at the head of a squad of policemen and broke up the meeting. Some of the workers resisted. There were broken heads and a number of arrests. Lassalle, with the crowd surging after him, went straight to the post office and sent off a telegram:

"Prime Minister von Bismarck, Berlin. Progressive Mayor at head of gendarmes with bayonets and police with drawn swords has without legal justification dispersed workers' meeting called by me. Have with difficulty restrained crowd numbering five thousand inside hall and many thousand outside. Was accompanied to telegraph office by gendarmes and by crowd of many thousands who believed I was under arrest. Banner belonging to Elberfeld workers confiscated. Request full immediate satisfaction—Lassalle."

Chapter 17

THE LAST WINTER

I

From the Rhineland Lassalle returned to Berlin, where on the 12th October was heard his appeal against the sentence arising out of *The Workers' Programme*. The speech he made on this occasion had already been printed, forming part of his pamphlet *Indirect Taxation and the Working Class*. The verdict of the Court below had been largely based on the Prosecutor's contention that his indictment of indirect taxation had been an "incitement to hatred and contempt" under the relevant paragraph of the Criminal Code. Lassalle proceeded to refute the prosecution's argument with a mass of statistics and considerable scorn. "I did not see fit to make use of my obvious superiority in a branch of learning with which I had long been familiar to cause pain to the Prosecutor by bringing home to him how inadequate was the little knowledge he had been able to acquire for the purpose of framing his charge." And again "I ask you. Here am I, one who like Faust has striven doggedly and stubbornly with Greek philosophy and Roman law, through all the various branches of historical study up to modern political economy and statistics—can you seriously believe that such a man is to crown this long pursuit of learning by inciting a mob to arson?"

The Court of Appeal commuted the sentence of imprisonment to a fine of 100 thalers, having doubtless in mind that an acquittal would automatically raise the ban on the *Workers' Programme* pamphlet. As it was Lassalle was justified in claiming the decision as a triumph. "Once more", he announced to the Countess, "I have been right and all my timid friends have been wrong."

2

HE WAS now free to launch his movement in the capital and set to work with supreme confidence. On the 15th October he wrote to Rodbertus: "I cannot describe how well things are going in the Rhineland—seven times better than my boldest dreams. Rapid progress also in Saxony, Hamburg and Frankfurt. Now I shall concentrate on Berlin. The Progressives still dominate the place, but it will be mine within six months."

On the 19th he wrote to the Countess: "I came here proclaiming that within three months we should have Berlin—and laughed at my friends who laughed at me. When I arrived we had ten members. Two days ago we had twenty-five. . . . Unless I am very wrong we shall have three to five hundred members within four weeks, and then the battle is won. The Berlin workers are moving in my direction. Who was right? Who? Who was it that when things looked black kept up his morale and maintained 'I will have Berlin as I have the Rhine?' "

He composed an address *To the Workers of Berlin*, and had sixteen thousand copies printed. But the Berlin police and the Public Prosecutor's Department, no doubt piqued by the recent decision of the Court of Appeal, remained implacable. As many copies of the pamphlet as the Police could find were confiscated and Lassalle was indicted for high treason. Pending the hearing (which took place the following March) he continued his campaign.

He held a relatively uneventful meeting on the 27th October. At the next meeting, on 2nd November, Lassalle tried to read the poem which Herwegh had composed in honour of the Association but was interrupted by cat-calls and hisses. The hall had been packed with Schulze-Delitzsch supporters and the meeting broke up in disorder. A third meeting, on the 22nd November, ended in disaster. Once again the majority of the audience were hostile. A force of police arrived while Lassalle was speaking, arrested him amid terrific applause and took him off to the cells. The event was a first-class sensation.

The Liberal Press was jubilant. Timid friends were panic-stricken, and Ludwig Löwe, now on the way to making a large fortune, became frantically eager to recover the letters he had written to Lassalle in his mood of ardent discipleship a year before.

Lassalle was a difficult man to keep in custody. On 25th November he was at liberty again; and the same day he wrote to his mother: "The good Countess showed all her old courage and energy, and played a large part in securing my early release. She is worth a dozen men."

He continued his campaign. The publicity of his arrest and his consequent aura of martyrdom attracted a few new recruits. Berlin membership rose to 200 in early December. But this was a flash in the pan: the newcomers drifted away again, and before the end of February the numbers had dwindled to thirty-five. The Progressives were too strongly entrenched in the working-class suburbs of Berlin. Try as he might (and did) to hide the fact, Lassalle's assault upon the capital was a complete failure.

3

ALL THAT WINTER he was a very busy man. He had postponed his long-planned scheme for an authoritative work on economics, but was working up the material into a polemic against Schulze-Delitzsch. There was a voluminous correspondence with Gustav Lewy and with the Branch representatives of the General German Workers' Association. There was trouble with the Secretary, of which more later. There was von Bülow to be cajoled and pressed into composing a tune for Herwegh's poem. And he made a point himself of answering such letters as one which came in early December from Eduard Willms, an out-of-work sword-maker in Solingen:

"For some time I have been making a living by framing prints of your portrait and selling them to members of our Association. Unfortunately, this source of income is unlikely to last much longer, and there is little chance of employment in any of the factories here. . . ."

He had Countess Hatzfeldt's financial affairs to look after, as well as those of his mother and sister. He played with a scheme of buying a site in the Hohenzollernstrasse and putting up a new block of flats; and invited his mother to invest in a mortgage on this venture, but the old lady could not make her mind up.

His social life went on at the accustomed tempo. We have a menu, written in his own hand, of one of the dinner parties he gave that winter: Soup, Lobster Mayonnaise, Ham, Salmon, Sauerkraut with Larks, Venison, *Entremets Nesselrode* and finally Cheese. With it went two kinds of claret, two kinds of hock, burgundy and champagne.

Through it all we find the familiar restlessness and sense of frustration. And although the Countess was now back in Germany and their friendship as close as it ever had been, and although Marie of Gerson's was still in residence, he was still searching for the woman who was to give him emotional satisfaction. At one time he seems to have had hopes of his old flame Agnes Denis-Street. In the autumn he wrote from Ostend to von Bülow for her address. Von Bülow sent it to him—Agnes was a friend of Bülow's wife—but we do not know whether he went to see her. If he did nothing came of it. He was reaching a stage where he was only interested in girls of twenty or under.

There was another meeting with Helene von Dönniges, almost certainly during the winter though Helene in her memoirs is vague about dates. Lassalle was busy with plans for the decoration of his dining-room. He wanted a fresco round the walls, and had not yet decided if it was to depict the Edda Saga or the Siege of Troy. But in any case the heroine—whether Helen or Brünhilde—was to be modelled on Fräulein von Dönniges. Helene claims that they parted with the understanding that Lassalle should, as opportunity arose, make the acquaintance of her parents and "exert his unique gift of winning over people." Not long afterwards her grandmother died. There was a deathbed scene in which the old lady called for Yanko Rakowitza and solemnly bequeathed Helene to him. Yanko was still at the university, so there could be no question of an early marriage. Helene accordingly went to live in Switzerland where her father was Bavarian Minister.

It is hard to say how far Lassalle was really attracted by Helene at this time. In any case she was completely supplanted in his interest by Minna von Lilienthal who was only seventeen and a music pupil of Bülow's. Her father was a wealthy banker and she herself was already prominent in the smart young set of Berlin. Besides Lassalle, Baron Korff and half a dozen others were in love with her, and she seems to have played them off with considerable skill. At times she assured Lassalle she had no interest in anyone without a title. At others she posed, in company, as "Lady President of the General German Workers' Association". Lassalle's friends were disconcerted to find him liking her doing so.

4

ON THE 23rd October, ten days after the hearing of his appeal, Lassalle wrote to ask Bismarck if he might call to report to him on the Solingen affair. A meeting almost certainly took place, and was followed by two or three further meetings in the course of the winter.

The relationship between the two men was not quite what it had been in the early summer, when Lassalle was hoping that his movement would sweep the country. The General German Workers' Association had created a good deal of sound and fury; but Bismarck knew, and Lassalle knew that Bismarck knew, how meagre was the actual membership. As the winter wore on the failure of the Berlin campaign became apparent. Lassalle's great hope was to induce the Prime Minister to introduce direct universal suffrage, which he might claim to his followers as having been the result of his pressure, and which would facilitate the formation of a Lassallean Parliamentary Party. But he had nothing to offer to Bismarck except the embarrassment he was causing to the Progressives; and he had, in any case, broken with the Progressives beyond hope of reconciliation.

Soon after the October meeting he wrote to Bismarck,

complaining of police confiscation of his pamphlets. On 17 November he wrote complaining of the failure of the police to keep order at his Berlin meetings, and implying that the Berlin police and the Progressives were hand in glove. Two days later he wrote again, this time complaining of Schelling the Public Prosecutor who was laying charges solely for motives of private pique. "It is all the same to me", he wrote, "how many prosecutions the man initiates. But to be arrested is quite another matter. I know from experience how long it takes to get out of the hands of Justice. My time is too precious. It would be fatal to the interests I represent if, just in order to give pleasure to Herr Schelling, I were to spend a number of months in prison. . . . If your Excellency wishes to take action not an hour must be lost. . . . I shall have no peace in Berlin until Schelling is transferred."

This appeal seems to have been not without effect. In any case Schelling was shortly afterwards transferred to Glogau.

Early in the New Year there were rumours of an imminent dissolution of the Chamber and of the promulgation of universal suffrage for the consequent elections. On the 9th January Lassalle wrote to ask for an interview. This took place on the 12th. The next day Lassalle wrote that he had spent the whole night in thought and had now worked out a "magic solution" for whatever problem it was they had discussed. "I am therefore now waiting for your Excellency to fix an evening. I would, however, earnestly request you to choose a date and time when we shall not be disturbed. I have a great deal to tell you about the technique of electioneering and other matters." Bismarck did not answer. On the 16th Lassalle wrote again: "I do not wish to be insistent, but circumstances are insistent and I must therefore ask you to excuse my insistency. I wrote last Wednesday to inform you that I had found the magic solution. . . . I propose to call to-morrow (Sunday) evening at eight o'clock. If that is inconvenient please suggest as early an occasion as possible. . . ."

The "insistent circumstance" to which he referred was the Schleswig-Holstein question. On the 14th January Prussia and Austria declared that they would act independently of the

German Confederation. War with Denmark appeared inevitable, and once the country was at war the political aspirations of the General German Workers' Association would fade into the background.

It was at this moment that Lassalle was summoned to appear before the Examining Magistrate at Düsseldorf to answer a charge arising out of his Rhineland speech. He did not obey the summons, and the police arrested him with the intention of taking him to Düsseldorf in custody. Lassalle resisted by every means at his disposal, including a confidential appeal to Bismarck, and it may have been in consequence of a hint from Bismarck that the authorities released him. As soon as he was at liberty he drew up and sent to Bismarck a long exposé, with copies of the documents concerned, setting out the official persecution of which he was the victim.

It was at this time, either late January or early February, that the last interview between the two men took place. It is clear that Lassalle used it to make an urgent appeal for the immediate introduction of universal suffrage; it is clear too from the letter he wrote Bismarck that same night that he realised his arguments had not carried conviction. "... A warning from the depths of my soul. You *must* bring in direct universal suffrage before war breaks out, because during or after the war you cannot do it." He amplifies his point. To bring in such a measure during war would be taken as a sign of weakness. The war, if it lasted for any length of time, would bring with it discontent, disorders, perhaps even revolt, and these in their turn would induce a post-war atmosphere which would make electoral reform impossible. Bismarck himself might be dismissed. The King might reject any idea of universal suffrage. The temper of the people might be such that they would refuse to co-operate with either King or Government. "Why", Lassalle asks, "can you do anything you like in peace time? Why did I admit to you last May that the country would acquiesce in the strictest absolutism so long as no external conflict arose? ... In peace time the interests of private life are supreme, and, whatever conditions may be, the popular mood is one of indifference...."

Bismarck did not answer.

A very few days later Lassalle made an approach in another connexion. His economic book against Schulze-Delitzsch (entitled *Herr Bastiat-Schulze*, from the French originator of Schulze's ideas) was soon due to appear; and on the 5th February he wrote to Bismarck that there was "something very important (and in this case easy to arrange) which I wish to intrude upon a moment of your time, busy though you are. In eight to ten days' time my *Bastiat-Schulze* will be published. I would not like you to suspect me of harbouring an author's vanity but I must inform Your Excellency that this work will bring about the utter destruction of Liberals and the whole Progressive bourgeoisie." He goes on to ask that Bismarck should arrange for the Ministry of Justice to instruct the Public Prosecutor's Department that no proceedings are to be taken against the book. There is a postscript:

"I have had notice from the authorities that I am to be charged with 'treachery' and with 'inciting to hatred and contempt' in connexion with my address to the workers of Berlin. ... I shall be able to deal with these charges; but, if Your Excellency does not protect my new book against persecution, I propose to lay down my arms and let events take their course."

Four days after this ultimatum Lassalle returned to the charge, this time in a letter to Zitelmann: "Last October, when we were discussing the confiscation of my Rhineland speech, Herr von Bismarck offered to issue—unless I felt that the risk of leakage might entail undesirable publicity—a circular to all Public Prosecutors telling them to leave my writings alone." Lassalle goes on to say he had refused this offer and all that he now has in mind in the case of *Bastiat-Schulze* is a verbal hint to the authorities concerned.

Bastiat-Schulze duly appeared and Lassalle sent an advance copy to Bismarck. He also asked for an interview. But the Schleswig-Holstein war had broken out and Bismarck had other preoccupations. On the 20th February a short note came back signed by von Keudell of Bismarck's staff to the effect that the Prime Minister regretted that he was too busy to fix an appointment. Lassalle's answer was addressed to Bismarck.

He was he said, "surprised to receive a letter from a complete stranger. I sent you my book in a personal, not official capacity; and you might have written me a couple of lines or else sent Herr Zitelmann whom I have accepted as Your Excellency's personal assistant. I will, of course, await Your Excellency's initiative before bothering Your Excellency again."

The initiative never came.

Six months later Helene von Dönniges asked Lassalle what truth there was in rumours of his having seen Bismarck. He replied: "Yes, I was with Bismarck. The Man of Iron wanted to win me over. . . . Nothing happened. Nothing could have happened. We were both too clever. Each saw the cleverness of the other. The matter—politically—could only have ended by our laughing in each other's faces. We were too well bred for that, so it stopped short at visits and intellectual conversation."

It was not in Lassalle's nature to admit defeat.

Chapter 18

THE LAST CAMPAIGN

I

Bismarck having refused, for the time, to introduce measures for which Lassalle could claim the credit, Lassalle proceeded to claim in advance credit for measures which he considered Bismarck would soon be forced to introduce. It was a bold move, and Bucher, now once more on terms of close friendship, considered it ill-judged. Lassalle, however, did not listen to these counsels of caution. In his speech at his treason trial, on the 12th March, he declared: "Not only do I intend to overthrow the Constitution—within a year I may perhaps already have done so. . . . I solemnly declare that within one year we may well find Herr von Bismarck assuming the role of a Peel and introducing direct universal suffrage."

On this occasion he spoke, as he wrote to his sister "for four hours, at times with the fury of a Hyreanian tiger; on three or four occasions the judges rose from their seats with a veritable howl of rage." He was acquitted of the charge of high treason, and the subsidiary charges, again of incitement to hatred and contempt, were passed on to the competent Courts, thus adding to the tangle of litigation in which he was enmeshed.

His economic work *Herr Bastiat Schulze von Delitzsch, the Economic Julian, Or Capital and Labour*, was not confiscated by the authorities and created a certain stir. As a polemic it was not ineffective. Schulze-Delitzsch had no claim to be a theorist. "The individual", he had naïvely remarked, "exchanges that much of his own produce which he does not himself require for the produce of other individuals." Lassalle retorts: "Herr Schulze, what period of the Middle Ages do you come from? Do you not realise that the present economic structure is bound up with people producing what they cannot consume themselves?" He goes through the list of the great industrial magnates. "In your view Herr Reichenheim manufactures his own requirements in cotton thread. His daughter knits him his stockings and makes him a night shirt; and what is left over he exchanges. Herr Borsig makes machines for his family. If any are left over he sells them. Undertakers are primarily concerned with family funerals, but should their families take a long time to die they accumulate a surplus of funeral equipment which they exchange. Herr Wolff of the Telegraph Agency has his agents' report for his own education, and if they send him more reports than he can do with he passes them to newspaper proprietors and stock brokers in exchange for superfluous shares and letters to the editor."

The constructive, as opposed to the purely polemical, chapters owe more to Marx than was acknowledged in Lassalle's respectful reference to the older man's *Critique of Political Economy*. Marx was highly indignant to find that chapter 4, on capital, had been lifted, "with embellishments in the Lassallean manner," from a series of articles of his in the *Neue Rheinische Zeitung* of 1849. This was a chapter to which Lassalle attached particular importance. In a circular to his Branch representatives he laid down that it was to be regarded as an essential part of the "theoretical codex" of the General German Workers' Association, and as such to be read aloud as part of the proceedings at the next Branch meeting. In addition every member was to buy a copy of the book and read it at home.

2

MEANWHILE the movement was growing in those areas of Germany where it had a hold, but it was growing slowly. Lassalle had hoped for 100,000 paying members. The total number in his lifetime never exceeded 4,600. More than half (2,669) came from the Rhineland, the largest branches being at Barmen (529), Ronsdorf (523), Solingen (500), Düsseldorf (259), Duisburg (239) and Cologne (161). Saxony provided 670 members (Leipzig 349), and Hamburg and district 675.

There were 208 in Silesia. A further 270 were spread over the rest of Germany, including Berlin. Across the Austrian frontier there were 112 at Asch, in Bohemia. These were textile workers hard hit by the American Civil War, simple-minded men and pious Protestants, who had written to Lassalle: "what Huss, Luther, Zwingli and Calvin have done for the Church your writings will do for the State."

Further recruitment was and remained an urgent problem. Vahlteich the Secretary considered that greater local autonomy would enable branches to increase their numbers. Lassalle feared that decentralisation would lead to a loosening of his control. Vahlteich favoured co-operation with the Left wing of the Progressives. This ran completely counter to Lassalle's plans. Apart from these administrative and tactical differences there was the personal factor. Lassalle demanded complete subservience; Vahlteich was aggressively independent. Friction between President and Secretary became more and more pronounced until finally Vahlteich resigned, and Willms, the unemployed sword-maker of Solingen, was brought to Berlin to take his place.

Vahlteich became Branch Representative in Dresden, but he remained a source of some anxiety to Lassalle. At about this time Liebknecht returned to Germany after years of exile in London, and at once established close touch with Vahlteich. It was true he joined the General German Workers' Association, but he was still to be counted as Marx's man. He was sure to know, and to remember, what Lassalle had written about him at the time of the trouble over Vogt. Lassalle's position arising out of his relationship with Bismarck was highly delicate and somewhat equivocal. He had now to face the prospect of informed but unfriendly reports on what he was doing going back to Marx in London.

3

THERE WAS the case of the Solingen workers. These were three men who had been involved in the disturbances at Lassalle's September meeting there, and charged with assaulting the police. They came up for trial in March and were sentenced to three months' hard labour. While they were awaiting the commencement of their sentence Lassalle conceived the idea (in tenor with his talks with Bismarck) of a royal pardon. He wrote to Klings, the Solingen Branch Representative, suggesting that the men should petition the Crown: on 20th March Klings wrote back "... I have discussed your proposal with the men concerned and also with our leading members here. They were all against it, and I too think the idea should be dropped. The men convicted are very resolute Workers' Party members. Even if it were a sentence of four years they could not be persuaded to put in a plea for pardon, because it is against their principles to put themselves under an obligation to the King. ..."

Lassalle replied:

"Your news of the workers refusing to submit a plea for pardon has made me very proud of them. One cannot demand that every worker should be a hero: and I would not have thought ill of them if they had made that plea. But since they are heroes on their own initiative, so much the better. It is a proud thing to lead men like that. ..." But he was unwilling to give up the idea of a royal pardon, and suggested that perhaps a petition could be organised on the men's behalf, without their own participation. But this idea too was rejected by the Branch.

One of the men went to prison; the other two escaped into Belgium. They went on to London, and Lassalle received news that they had seen Marx. He was anxious to know what took place at their interview, and wrote to Willms: "There is no need for you to ask Liebknecht; it would be out of place for you to do so and might be misunderstood. But there is no harm, if an opportunity arises, of your finding out from Klings if the men have let him know what Marx said to them."

What Marx said to the men was, however, never revealed.

In due course the charges arising out of Lassalle's Rhineland speeches of the autumn came up before the Düsseldorf Court, and he was sentenced in his absence to twelve months' imprisonment. He lodged an appeal.

4

THESE ANXIETIES and difficulties affected his health, and his health affected his spirits. In one of his private letters he confesses: "I am engaged in a *métier de dupe* and am worried to death. It is all the worse because I cannot give vent to it—I have to keep my worries to myself and proclaim to the world the opposite of what I am thinking. But I will not give up so long as there is the slightest flicker of hope on the political horizon. What makes it all the worse is to realise how splendid everything would be, if only the working class had done its duty. We should already have had direct universal suffrage." And again: "We cannot deny that we were completely wrong in our estimate of the workers' moral and intellectual level."

Much of his life that was not taken up with politics centred round Minna von Lilienthal, of whom he wrote to his sister in Vienna: "She exercises an enormous appeal to my senses and to my sensual fantasies. But that is all. She, as far as I can make out, thinks about as much of me as I think of a pair of old trousers. But she knows I am in love with her and is determined to force me to marry her by moral resistance."

This was not the case. Minna had no intention of marrying him; and intermittently he himself seems to have wished to break off his futile and undignified pursuit. In his next letter to his sister he writes: "I am so worn out that I must have recreation—and by that I only mean a crowd of pretty women. Could you find me any in Vienna? If so I will probably come and stay with you. Otherwise, no. It is a long journey and doesn't fit in with my other plans. But I have a hunger for recreation and for attractive women, like an ogre has for human flesh. . . . I gather from your letter you have a beautiful Olga for me, but only if my intentions are serious. If she really is good looking enough, and fulfils certain other conditions I wouldn't exclude the possibility of marriage . . . but somehow your letter gives me the impression she isn't very beautiful."

It was not only Lassalle who had moods of depression that spring. With the Countess staying on in Germany, becoming more and more immersed in Lassalle and the Association, Rüstow, alone in his exile in Switzerland, grew unhappy and jealous. He wrote to the Countess: "Your letter contained nothing but your admiration of Lassalle. Two-thirds of all your letters have been in the same strain. For sixteen years Lassalle has been hammering his Hegelian ideas into your head. But in spite of his corrupting influence I cannot see why you should seize on the slightest excuse to get excited about his doings, why you should see his 'triumphs' through his eyes, why you should repeat everything he says to you. You sometimes complain I never talk to you about my own interests; if ever I do I can be certain you will call me an idiot or else take no notice at all. When I compare the fiery enthusiasm you show for everything that concerns Lassalle with your indifference towards me and mine, I can only conclude that you care for Lassalle and do not care for me."

5

LASSALLE's arrangements for his spring campaign provided for a meeting at Leipzig on the 9th May, to be followed by a tour of the Rhineland. He planned then to go to Ems for a cure—his general health was bad and his throat especially troublesome. At the end of June he was due to return to Düsseldorf for the hearing of his appeal.

Before he left Berlin there arrived in the capital a delegation of weavers from the textile factory of Wüstegiersdorf in Silesia. This was one of the areas most affected by the American cotton blockade. There were wage cuts, mass unemployment and considerable local distress. The factory was owned by Reichenheim, a cotton magnate and influential member of the Progressive Party; and it was partly to embarrass the Progressives that the local officials—themselves of course Conservatives—facilitated the delegation's departure. In Berlin the men were looked after by Wagener; editor of the *Kreuzzeitung*. A young journalist on this paper, one Preuss, put them in touch with Lassalle. It was also Preuss who drafted their petition to the Throne. On the 6th May (at Bismarck's instance) the weavers were received in audience by the King, and next day the following statement was issued to the Press:

"Yesterday afternoon His Majesty the King graciously received a deputation of poor Silesian weavers who presented a petition. The weavers carried their complaint to the steps of the Throne so as to plead to the highest quarters for help in their sorrows. Owing to the pressure of their employers their wages are insufficient for their subsistence. Their complete destitution prevents them from travelling elsewhere to seek support for their families. The three hundred weavers chose three of their number to undertake this mission.

"It is understood that His Majesty received the delegates very graciously. He informed them he had instructed his Ministers at once to take such practical steps as the law might allow to aid them. . . . The King dismissed the deputation comforted by the thought of an early settlement of the points at issue and of succour in their distress. The Royal promise will have a cheering and stimulating effect throughout the Riesengebirge and will give new hope and new strength to thousands of anxious families."

This communiqué was issued on the eve of Lassalle's departure for Leipzig. What he thought of it comes out in a letter to the Countess dated the 11th:

"It is easy to guess Bismarck's real intention. As I told you last year he has always wanted to put through the social part of our workers' programme, but not the political part. I would not agree, so he is now trying to put it through himself, direct. It is obvious what he stands to gain if he could make this separation—he would have complete power. . . . But for a thousand reasons he will not succeed. He is not yet the man who can eat cherries with the Devil. Whether he wants to or not he is now acting as my agent for Silesia. . . . A request. I was fairly hoarse when I left, and now, after a two-hour speech, completely so. Please get Frerich's prescription and send it to Lewy's in Düsseldorf where I arrive to-morrow."

Ten days later he wrote to her from Düsseldorf describing how with bandages and grog he had been able to keep to his programme. "Physically I'm in a poor way. On the other hand morally, I'm in high fettle. I have had the most overwhelming experiences. . . . In Wermelskirchen the whole population was in an ecstasy. I did not show it, but I could not get over my astonishment that my campaign could take such hold of a country town. It was like the birth of a new religion. In these parts if we ever get universal suffrage we shall be elected unanimously. . . . Both doctors agree that after our cure at Ems I shall have to take a milk cure at the sanatorium at Rigi. I hope you will come too."

He had meant to hold his first Rhineland meeting in Düsseldorf on the 13th May. But owing to the influence of big business and the hostility of the landlords he was unable to get a hall till the 23rd. Meanwhile he spoke at Solingen (14th), Barmen (15th), Cologne (16th), Wermelskirchen (18th) and Ronsdorf (22nd). He was not exaggerating unduly when he described the warmth of his reception. Along the Rhine the movement was beginning to take hold. He had established himself with the Rhineland workers as a local hero. For every ten men willing to become paying members there were hundreds, if not thousands, ready to attend his meetings, and his superb showmanship had its effect. Crowds met him at the stations. Simple songs were composed in his honour:

> "*We greet you, our Herr President,*
> *In this our German Union,*
> *For unto you is honour due*
> *In this our great mass Union.*"

Outside the halls were banners with slogans:

> "*Welcome, oh welcome to Dr. Lassalle,*
> *A thousand times welcome in Ronsdorfer Tal.*"

6

HIS SPEECH at Ronsdorf was the most striking of the campaign, and one of the most remarkable of his whole career. Last autumn his words had been aimed at "one or two people in Berlin". On this occasion he told Lewy: "This time I shall dwell on internal matters, to arouse and strengthen the proper spirit within our ranks . . . it will be a review for our own people, whereas last time it was a revue designed for outsiders." The speech was in fact a flamboyant build-up of the General German Workers' Association. Willms, the new Secretary, who was thoroughly disgusted at the atmosphere he had found in the capital had reported from Berlin on the 18th May: "The masses in this *Bummelnresidenz* can't think. It would be a pity to spend a single groschen on our propaganda here." And again, "You may feel it wiser to give the people in Solingen a rosier picture of our progress here than is really the case."

Lassalle declared to his Ronsdorf audience: "Berlin is one of the greatest proofs of our success. We have now the kernel of a group in Berlin, whose intelligence and zeal, if not its numbers, make it one of the most important." He announced the formation of new branches elsewhere. He claimed credit for the outcome of a dispute over working hours in a factory at Hamburg. He proclaimed that working men's clubs in London and in Switzerland had adhered to the Association's policy in the Schleswig-Holstein and Polish questions. He claimed the conversion of the Bishop of Mainz, who, in a recent pamphlet on "Labour and Christianity" had sharply attacked the *laissez-faire* doctrine of the Progressives.

He then worked up to his climax. He explained social conditions in the Silesian textile industry, described the arrival of the delegation in Berlin and read the communiqué of its reception by the King. This communiqué, he declared, was the recognition "that the working-class question must be solved by legislation, that is to say, it is the recognition of the main principle for which the Association has been striving. . . . We have forced not only bishops but even Kings to recognise this principle." But this was not all. The King had promised help by legislative means. That, however would never be forthcoming from a Chamber elected under the Three-Class voting system, but only from a Chamber elected by universal suffrage. "The King, by his promise of a legal solution of the workers' question has, by implication, promised direct universal suffrage. Thus an irrevocable and formal guarantee for all further aspirations is promised you by the logical content of that royal promise!" Amid terrific applause he continued: "What Association, since the beginning of the world, has been able to show such results in the course of one year? Workers, people, the learned, Bishops and now the King have been forced to bear witness to the truth of our principles!"

He closed on a personal, almost Messianic note. "I have received notice of a sentence to imprisonment *in contumaciam.* In spite of a medical certificate that I needed a cure in a watering-place the Court refused an adjournment. Sentence was passed in the absence of myself and my witnesses. Well, I shall upset that Court decision as I have so many others. But, however strong a man may be, some enemies are too strong for him. I am not deterred by that. As you well realise, I did not raise this banner without foreseeing that it may mean my death. When such thoughts come to me I remember the words of the Roman poet—*exoriare aliquis nostris ex ossibus ultor*—an avenger will arise from my bones! Let not this great national movement perish with me, but let this torch that I have raised blaze on and on, while any one of you still breathes!"

7

EXHAUSTED by the strain of his tour he went on to Ems for his cure. The Countess went with him and on the 29th May he wrote to his mother, who was also ailing, to come and join them: but Frau Lassal was unwilling to face so long a journey. News reached him that Minna von Lilienthal had also gone to a watering-place, and he wrote urgently to Bucher for her address. Bucher, who did not know it, applied to von Bülow. "If I don't answer him at once I shall be woken up every night by a telegram from Ems." When he at last obtained the address Lassalle is credibly reported to have written to Minna that she would be responsible if he threw himself into the arms of the first good-looking girl he met in Switzerland.

Otherwise we find him concerned with the issue of his Ronsdorf speech in pamphlet form. Bucher corrected the proofs in Berlin. On the 5th June Lassalle wrote Willms to make the printer hurry. On the 15th he wrote again:

"Put all possible pressure on the printer so that there shall be no delay with the Ronsdorf speech. It would be better not to send the two copies to Bismarck in a wrapper. Send them in an envelope, as a letter, to the Wilhelmstrasse. Mark it 'personal'. They are not nearly so likely to forward anything on to him, even if marked personal, if it is in a wrapper and can be seen to be printed matter. The papers say Bismarck left Berlin on the 14th. He will certainly have left by the time the pamphlets are ready."

8

WE HAVE Paul Lindau's account of him at the time of the hearing of his appeal:

"He arrived in Düsseldorf on the 26th June. Ours was the only table to be occupied in the dining-room of the Hotel Domhardt. The Countess, who accompanied him, was smoking. Lassalle seemed very happy about the speech he was to make in court next day: he was in the best of spirits and did nearly all the talking. The Düsseldorf Representative [i.e. Lewy] listened respectfully to the words of the Master with half-open mouth. . . .

"The 27th was very hot. The President of the Court was kind enough to allot me a special seat as well as the Countess who sat next me and allowed me full use of her flask of Eau de Cologne. This was a real blessing in the low, narrow court-room, designed perhaps for a maximum of sixty members of the public and now holding at least 150. The corridors were also packed, and workers were standing all along as far as the street entrances. Lassalle had strictly forbidden any noisy demonstration, but they wanted at least to be able to see him arrive.

"At nine, as the Prosecutor was chatting with Lassalle's counsel Bloem, there was a stir: Lassalle came in followed by his *Fidus Achates*, the Düsseldorf Representative. Lassalle had a pile of books under his left arm, fifteen or eighteen volumes—almost more than he could manage, and the Representative was bent under an even heavier burden. Bloem smiled, but the Prosecutor looked quite alarmed and said (loud enough for us to hear) 'Good God'.

"Lassalle bowed to the Prosecutor and arranged his library on a table which the court attendant brought him. Then he greeted the Countess and shook hands with Bloem. In honour of the Court he had put on evening dress, tails and a white tie. When the judges appeared he went to the dock and made them a very low bow, to which they politely responded. The President declared the session open whereupon Lassalle asked for permission to sit behind his table so as to be near 'certain academic material' which he needed for his defence. The request was granted. . . .

"It was half-past eleven when Lassalle began his speech. The court adjourned at one, and in the afternoon Lassalle spoke from four to half-past six, so that in all he spoke for four hours. His speech gave the effect of spontaneity, but it had evidently been carefully thought out and arranged beforehand. He had a sheaf of notes in his right hand at which he glanced from time to time: then, for a period, he would seem to extemporise. He spoke with admirable clarity, and with great rhetorical force. The variation in tone, which I had noticed in his private conversation, was even more apparent. His delivery was extremely effective, though not without some trace of theatricality.

"He adapted his tone to the impression he wished to convey: but it all gave the impression of being done deliberately, of having been thought out and rehearsed. Whether he was evincing irony at his judge's ignorance, or confidence in his own views, or pathos at the persecution of which he was victim, in spite of the admiration provoked by his trenchant thought, forceful expression and high eloquence it was not possible entirely to forget the actor; all the more so because of the constant play of his features and gestures. . . . He would strike out in front of him, as if boxing, beat the air as if conducting a prestissimo movement, or raise his hand in a threatening attitude, and shake it so violently that his sheaf of notes came apart and fluttered to the floor. This last happened two or three times, always at the end of a period when the interlude required for collecting and rearranging his notes was most effective. I could not exclude the thought that he did it on purpose. . . .

"I was with him for several hours on each of the three days [between the close of the proceedings and the delivery of the Court's judgment]. I reported his speech—almost complete—in the *Düsseldorfer Zeitung*. Luckily he had spoken very slowly and with the aid of my private system of shorthand I was able to reconstruct the greater part of his speech. But there were passages where I had been too preoccupied with the personality of the speaker, and to fill up these gaps I applied to Lassalle himself. . . . I read him what I had written; he made a few small corrections and then dictated the missing passages. It took some hours. I sat at the table and took down some twenty pages so that in the end his speech alone filled more than twelve columns of my paper. Lassalle walked up and down as he dictated. He repeated exactly what he had said in Court, down to the dotting of the i's and the crossing of the t's. I noticed that although I was his sole audience, so that he had no need to strive for rhetorical effect, he used exactly the same modulations of voice and the same gestures as he had before."

In the closing words of his speech Lassalle declared: "It is hard for a man of my age and of my way of life to spend twelve months, twelve days even, in prison. I am no longer as I was in my youth when I would go to prison with the same indifference with which another would go to a ball. But, in spite of this, I would rather go to prison and stay there for the rest of my life than have pronounced judgment against me in this case." These brave words to the judges are not borne out by what he said in a fit of depression to Lindau: "I cannot endure a year in prison, or even six months. I cannot stand it. I would prefer to go into exile. My nerves are completely broken."

The Court did not reverse the finding of the Court below. It merely reduced the term of imprisonment to six months. There was of course a right of further appeal to the Supreme Court in Berlin. But it was in the shadow of the sentence of the Düsseldorf Court that Lassalle spent the last two months of his life.

Chapter 19

RIGI

1

From Düsseldorf Lassalle and the Countess went on to Frankfurt. On the 3rd July he addressed a meeting of the Association's local branch. In Frankfurt he met the composer Weissheimer who invited both him and the Countess to spend a few days at his home in the country. It was a cheerful party. Lassalle volunteered to write the libretto for Weissheimer's next opera, and they sat up half the night discussing the project. On the 8th Lassalle and his party went to Neustadt-an-der-Hardt to meet Schweitzer. Together they examined a proposal to found a party newspaper with Schweitzer as editor. Evenings were spent discussing philosophy and literature. One night Lassalle entertained the company by repeating his speech in the Casket Trial.

On 15th July the party broke up. The Countess went to Wildbad, Lassalle to his cure at Rigi-Kaltbad. From there he sent a series of letters and instructions to counter what he feared might grow into an opposition movement within the Association.

The statutes laid down that a general meeting should be held during 1864. Lassalle, fearing that controversial questions might be raised, decided that the meeting should take place in Düsseldorf and that branches unable to afford the expenses of a delegation should be represented by members in the Düsseldorf area. (Lewy could be counted on to ensure the amenability of the members so chosen.) Dammer, who was acting as Vice-President in Lassalle's absence, sent out a circular to that effect. But Vahlteich objected. He advocated a special levy to enable all branches to send delegates, and he called for a meeting of the Committee to reconsider the matter.

Dammer reported this move to Lassalle at Rigi and Lassalle at once drafted a circular, twenty pages long, with a view to the expulsion of Vahlteich.

"What I have said shows Herr Vahlteich to be an inveterate intriguer, of whom it would be idiocy to hope that he can ever mend his ways. Systematically, increasingly and by every means in his power he strives to provoke friction and disunity, to undermine the statutes of the Association and to aggravate in every possible way the difficulties of directing the Association's affairs. . . . If such activities continue and if the Committee do not take energetic steps to protect me from their recurrence I shall simply resign my post as President and return to my old role of a lone independent champion of the interests of the working class. . . ."

This he sent to Willms, the Secretary, with a covering note: "Have this printed at once and sent to all Committee members. We shall want at least 100 copies, as we shall have to show it later to the Branch Representatives. But you need not send it to Vahlteich till you have been yourself to Dresden; otherwise Vahlteich may forestall us there. . . . Go to Dresden and tell Försterling about it so that he can inform not only the Dresden Branch but all the other branches in Saxony about Vahlteich's intrigues. Talk to the people yourself, see how they feel. Exert your influence. If you find Försterling has the right ideas I will put him on the Committee. This journey is essential, as otherwise Vahlteich will be making trouble in the local branches. Charge up your travelling expenses. . . ."

There was also an unsatisfactory report from Willms on the behaviour of the Berlin Branch, and upon the 27th July Lassalle wrote back:

"You are entirely correct in saying that Branch Representatives are there to direct their Branches as instructed by Headquarters—not to take orders from the Branches. What surprises me is that you raise the point at all. Whenever I attended Branch meetings there was never any idea of the Branch passing a resolution unless I myself took the initiative. . . . Why is it being allowed to happen otherwise in Berlin? I suppose because there one is nearer the heart of Parliamentarianism! . . ."

2

LASSALLE was unhappy on Rigi. His fellow inmates at the sanatorium were uncongenial and the weather was vile. His main outlet was his correspondence with the Countess.

"You maintain", he wrote on the 22nd, "that the intrigues of my lady friends have caused trouble between us. 'Lady friends' is a ridiculous generalisation. You can only mean Frau Duncker. The others, Agnes, Frau Dohm, etc. always got on well with you. I insisted that Frau Duncker should do the same, and, when it came out that she couldn't, I dropped her. What more do you want? . . . No one has ever treated a woman so much as a friend as I do you. This is not affected by my making love to young women—that is something entirely different. It is wrong to say I need a woman friend. That I have in perfect form in you. Apart from you my relations with women are only for a specific purpose. . . ."

The Countess wrote that her maid was getting married and had given notice. He replied: "I was sorry to hear your news. It is bad luck for you. If you had thought of dismissing her I would rather have had her in the now vacant post of my girl from Gerson's than see her married in Elberfeld. It was only my scruples about not stealing your servants that kept me from putting an offer to her!"

The Countess was anxious over the pending sentence of imprisonment, and had gloomy presentiments. She wrote:

"I can't explain why but I am very worried about you. Are you really determined to go back to Berlin? Remember your enemies will do everything possible and impossible against you. . . . The role of a martyr is stupid and futile. What has it done for Blanqui beyond making him forgotten and useless? . . . Abroad, even in Naples, though there would be a lot of difficulties, you would still be there and working for people who can only be stirred to action by knowing you are there. . . ."

Lassalle replied in a cheerful vein rallying her on her "*clairvoyance*". He explained the points of procedure connected with his final appeal to the Supreme Court. "They can't lock me up before November, and I don't think before December." In any case even if he did decide to go into exile he would have to go first to Berlin to wind up his private affairs. He went on: "One thing more. I have to go to Hamburg where I intend to bring off a big *coup*, a very big *coup*, perhaps of real importance."

The projected *coup* was concerned with Schleswig-Holstein. The Danes had by now been driven out by the Prussian and Austrian armies, but the future of the provinces was still unsettled. The alternatives appeared to be their incorporation into Prussia or the addition of yet another petty State to the German Federation. Marx, writing some time later, thus sums up Lassalle's intentions: "In late September 1864 he was to go to Hamburg and there, with the half-wit Schramm and the Prussian police spy Marr, force Bismarck to annex Schleswig-Holstein. That is, Lassalle was to proclaim its incorporation 'In the name of the Workers' etc. In return for which Bismarck promised universal suffrage and a few socialist charlataneries."

Marx, of course, had no inside knowledge of Lassalle's relations with Bismarck. He was dependent on the incomplete and probably distorted information he received from Liebknecht. There had been no meeting between Lassalle and Bismarck since the outbreak of the Schleswig-Holstein war, and there was no bargain or understanding between them. Lassalle's intention, we can be pretty certain, was here again to claim credit for a step which he felt circumstances would force Bismarck to take.

3

THE SAME LETTER in which Lassalle gives the Countess a hint of his plans for Hamburg goes on to say:

"Then there has been this episode. The day before yesterday the weather was vile—as always though to-day is rather better. I was in my room, writing. A peasant boy comes in and says a lady is asking for me. Who can it be? I took my hat and stick and hurried down. There upon a horse, with an Englishwoman, an American woman and a Frenchman was—Helene, the Golden Fox! She had heard from Holthoff that I was at Rigi and had organised an expedition. Naturally, off I went with them to Kulm where we spent the night. Unhappily the Englishwoman has a child at Berne recovering from scarlatina, and in spite of the appalling weather she refused to stay even one more day. I could have killed her. Poor Helene, ill and with chest trouble, had to start off (and the rest of us) in ghastly fog and rain at 10 o'clock next morning."

Helene's memoirs gives a fuller account of what happened. She had been ill. The doctor had recommended fresh air as an aid to convalescence, and she joined up with a tour on horseback organised by an English friend, a Mrs. Arson. (Helene, who liked any sort of title, always calls her Mrs. D'Arson.) The main objective was to watch the sunrise from Kulm. Just before starting Helene got a note from Berlin that Lassalle was at Rigi for a cure. As the party approached the Rigi sanatorium a storm came on and they took shelter. Helene saw a boy and told him to find out if "Dr. Lassalle" was in the sanatorium. Lassalle appeared, made himself pleasant, and was co-opted to go on with the company to Kulm. That night, in the Kulm hotel, he proposed marriage. "We are", he told her, "each other's fate. To-day has proved it."

Helene has recorded her feelings:

"I loved and respected the man, but he was the first and only person I had met whom I could not master. It made me very uncomfortable. He took possession of me completely, without limit. Up till then I had been used to giving only what it suited me to give. Men were only too delighted at the smallest mark of favour. Here was one who was not content with halves. He must have all or nothing.... I felt I would have to make up my mind and I saw battles and struggles ahead. It was my nature then to avoid any unpleasantness....

"I did not sleep at all, so the 'blast of doom' from the horn of the nightporter did not frighten me as it did the others. We got up in the usual hurry of a Rigi sunrise, wrapped ourselves like ghosts in rugs, shawls and bedspreads, hurried out into the mist, and found nothing whatever to see. Lassalle thought I looked divine in my woollen wrappings. Tired and haggard as I was he compared me with the goddesses on Olympus. But he was furious with disappointment at having no sunrise to show me."

After breakfast they went on with their serious talk. Helene said: "You can ask what you like from me, but don't ask for energy or strength of will. Remember, I am *la femme la plus femme de l'univers*, and that means capricious and unaccountable. And I'm only a girl." Lassalle answered: "Your part is easy. Give me a clear and honest yes, and *je me charge du reste.*" They talked about Jewish-Christian marriage, about the Countess, about past love affairs. It was agreed that Helene should write to him to give her final answer. Then Mrs. Arson insisted on departure, and the company set off, in the rain, to the Rigi sanatorium where they left Lassalle and went on towards Berne.

4

LASSALLE, alone again in the sanatorium, spent half his time in the telegraph office sending wires to Helene—the tapping of the machine, he said, soothed his nerves—and the other half writing to the Countess. On the 28th he wrote:

"You think I cannot live without politics? You do not know me. Nothing would please me more than to retire to my books and my friends and to nature. I am sick and tired of politics. True my enthusiasm would flame up again if I had power, or saw my way to attaining power. Without real power one can get nothing done and I am too old and too big for children's games. . . . Politics means actual immediate effectiveness. Everything else one can get from books. At Hamburg I shall try and apply some pressure on events. But I can not say how effective that will be, and I am not making myself any promises.

"If I could only retire—I had got as far as this when a letter came from Helene. It is serious now, really serious. The weight of it all will fall on me again. Anyhow I cannot back out, and I do not see why I should want to back out. She is beautiful. As to personality she is the one woman who really suits me, the only one you would think suits me. So forward, across the Rubicon!

"It is another big complication and things are complicated enough already. I am curious to know if I shall pull it off. It is the same impersonal curiosity I had when I was fighting your cases. As if I was reading a novel. Well, I still have my strength and I still have my luck. . . ."

Helene had written:

"I intend to be your wife. You asked me for a 'yes *et je m'en charge*'. Here is my 'yes', *chargez-vous*. I have only two small conditions. First that we do all we can to arrange things normally, that is that you call on my parents and try to win their consent. If they finally refuse, *eh bien tant pis*, and off we go to Egypt. My second condition is that we get it settled and finished as soon as we can."

Lassalle's next letter to the Countess, dated 30th July, was from Berne:

"Here I am in Berne. Yesterday up to midnight I was with Helene at her friends' villa. I still do not know what our plans will be for the next fortnight, but on or after the 15th August I can come to fetch you. Helene entirely agrees. I must tell you that she has a great liking for you, a necessary condition, of course, of my liking for her. She is not at all like other women, not a trace of envy or jealousy. . . . Her one, but great fault is that she has no strength of will; though once we are man and wife that will not matter as I have enough for two."

The idyll in Berne, pending the formal assault on Helene's parents who lived in Geneva, lasted five days. Mrs. Arson, Helene's hostess in Berne, took to Lassalle as did their circle of friends. These included the American Consul and his wife and some French and Italian artists. Helene wrote to break the news to Yanko von Rakowitza who, she felt, "would keep his promise to care more for my happiness than for his own". Meanwhile in Berne there were parties and excursions and interminable talks. Lassalle promised Helene a day would come when she would "drive through Berlin behind six white horses, the first lady in Germany". Helene was still preoccupied with thoughts of the Countess. She records:

"He showed me photographs of more or less pretty women, and one of the Countess. I gave it back to him and said: 'That

Casket affair happened ages ago, almost before I was born. So I'll forgive you, for the Countess certainly isn't good-looking.' He laughed and said that might be true now, but twenty years ago it was quite different. 'She is old now,' he said, 'she was born in 1805.' 'In that case', I said, 'she should have had an affair with Napoleon.'"

But Helene faced up to the fact that the Countess was bound to play a big part in her future married life. She made the first approach in a letter of 1st August:

"Dear and Honoured Countess, now that I have my lord and master's permission to introduce myself I come, *le cœur et la main ouverts*, to beg a little of your friendship for him for his devoted wife. . . . I shall be shy and nervous when first I meet you. I am an insignificant little creature; all I can do is to love and adore him, try to make him happy, try with my childish play to smooth the wrinkles from his brow, do all I can to appreciate his lordly soul and his vast intelligence, and, in joy and in sorrow, stand firm and true by his side. For all this, dear Countess, I need your help and counsel. . . . Don't blame me for interrupting his cure. I could not help it. It was fate. . . ."

In due course Countess Hatzfeldt's reply to Lassalle's first announcement was forwarded on from Rigi. The Countess, who, so very recently, had known Lassalle to be infatuated with Minna von Lilienthal, recommended caution and patience. "Would it not be wiser to arrange with Helene to work for a *rapprochement* with her parents and await the final outcome of your Court cases before formally asking for her hand?" The Countess too had her own troubles. "My new maid was hopeless, in spite of her good references. She ruined everything she touched and I had to dismiss her at once. So here I am without a maid."

Lassalle's reply was brusque. "Any advice would now be too late. My decision is irrevocable. But in any case you would only advise me to do as I have done. Of that I am sure. You speak of my recently being 'madly in love' with another woman. As to that, firstly, I do not admit the conception of being 'madly in love'. Secondly even now, on the purely physical side, I think Minna more attractive than Helene which shows I am not blinded by physical urge. It is Helene's personality that is the complete counterpart of mine...."

Next day he wrote again: "The bourgeois, Philistine and unutterably wearisome procedure that you suggest cannot even be thought of.... Helene, who loves you, will find you a maid in Geneva."

It was arranged that Helene should leave for Geneva by a morning train, and should, at first, say nothing to her parents. Lassalle would travel two hours later, go straight to a hotel, and await word as to a suitable time to call. Their departure was postponed for twenty-four hours by a curious incident. They were returning with a party of friends from a country walk when they were set on by a group of peasants. In the consequent *mêlée* Lassalle laid about him with his Bastille-headed stick. He was, Helene records, the one real fighting man of their side, the others being merely 'the puny little American Consul, an elderly Frenchman and an Italian who might be classed as male.' The ladies joined in with their parasols and the battle fought itself to a standstill. It then transpired that the tourists had been trampling down some young seedlings. A few francs passed and goodwill was restored.

But Lassalle bore marks of the battle and felt it would be undignified to make his first call on his prospective father-in-law with a swollen nose. It was not till the 3rd August that Helene, and later Lassalle, left Berne for Geneva.

Chapter 20

GENEVA

I

To appreciate the attitude of the von Dönniges family during the next few weeks it is necessary to remember that Helene's father was a German tutor who had, thanks to the favour of royalty, succeeded in becoming a diplomat *de carrière*. His race, his profession, the mid-nineteenth century atmosphere in which he lived, all induced an acute sense of social position. The prospect of a son-in-law of the notoriety of Lassalle could not fail to fill him with horror.

Helene's memoirs give a convincing account of what happened on her return home. Her father was out, the rest of the family were at home jubilant over the recent engagement of Margaret—Helene's younger sister—to a Count Kayserling. This made Helene forget her promise and she announced that she herself was engaged to Ferdinand Lassalle. There was consternation. After a furious scene Frau von Dönniges sent Helene up to her bedroom where she burst into tears and started a letter to Lassalle. "You, my lord and god, have you arrived yet? The thought gives me courage—I must feel my master near me in all his strength so as not to be to others the child that I am to you. But I feel you near me and I feel your love and I'm afraid of nothing and am now and always your wife, your child, your adoring slave. . . ."

In the middle of it her father appeared, pale with anger. There was another noisy scene and he stamped out, locking the door behind him. Time passed. All became quiet in the house. Then Thérèse the maid—Helene's old ally in her childhood days—unlocked the door and told her the coast was clear. Helene slipped out and made her way to the Pension Bouvet where Lassalle had arranged to stay.

He had just arrived (having missed an earlier train) and was seeing to his luggage. He was angry when he heard what had happened, angry that she had not done as he told her and that he should thus be involved in the consequences. Helene, naturally, was hurt at this attitude. She gave him her letter to read. Her record goes on:

"After a little he said:

" 'Never mind. That doesn't matter. You have made a mess of things but I will put it right. And now, what are we going to do with you?'

"I stared at him in astonishment. 'With me?' I said. 'Why, the same as with you. We'll go to France by the next train.'

"His answer decided our fate.

" 'No. I will not be party to an abduction. Do your parents think I am the sort of man to be turned away like this? They will have to give their consent to the marriage. I will force them to do so. I shall telegraph at once to my mother, my sister and the Countess. Until one of them arrives you will have to stay with some friend.' "

Helene, in tears, implored and entreated, but Lassalle was adamant against any idea of elopement. Her memoirs continue:

"In the middle of all this, Thérèse, very out of breath, burst in and shouted 'In the name of all the Saints, get away! They're looking for you. Your Herr Papa is furious and has sent for the police. It's all been discovered. I've a cab outside and the next train goes in a quarter of an hour. You have only just time!' I looked hopefully at Lassalle, but he would not relent. 'We will use the cab,' he said. 'Where does your friend live? You, Thérèse, will go back to the house and report to me regularly what goes on. Later on you will of course join us and stay with us. Come along, child, we will go together to your friend.' "

The friend in question was a certain Mme. Rognon, who at once agreed to take charge of Helene. The three of them were still discussing their arrangements when Helene's mother and sister were seen coming to the door.

" 'Heaven has sent them,' said Lassalle. 'I will see them and talk to them.' We tried to dissuade him. Caroline (Madame Rognon) explained it would be much better not to let my mother in, and just say nobody knew where I was. But Lassalle insisted and we all went down to the drawing-room. The scene that took place between Lassalle and my mother—my sister said nothing—was frightful. In that hour I lost my mother, and she lost me, for ever.

"As soon as she saw us she called out: 'I cannot tolerate that man in my presence. Send him away!' Lassalle approached her with great dignity, assured her of his respect for her and his love for me and finally asked: 'But tell me what you have against me.' She turned her back on him and screamed: 'I am not obliged to tell you that. My husband will tell you. And now go away, get out of my sight!' I was furious. I laid my hand on Lassalle's arm and said: 'Let us go. I will not have you spoken to like that in my presence.' He took my hand and said to my mother: 'Madame, you can say and do what you like. Nothing can prevent my regarding you as Helene's mother.'

"This only made my mother more angry and when Lassalle went on to say he would go at once and see my father she said: 'My husband will not receive you. He will tell the servant to throw you out.' 'He will not do that,' said Lassalle calmly. 'I am not the type of man who is thrown out. But if Helene's father is not beyond making such an attempt to discredit all of us, then I will write to him.'

"'He will return your letters unopened.' 'In that case, Madame, even my patience will be exhausted. We will then be justified in taking our own measures.' 'You have done that already. You are a scoundrel, you have stolen our child!' 'No,' I broke in, 'he did not. I went away because I saw your heartlessness, because I wished to escape from my father's curses and threats.' My nerves were in a turmoil. My whole being yearned to leave my mother and cleave to the man whom I loved with such passion. But he smiled calmly. 'Madame,' he said, 'You say I have stolen your child. You will see how wrong you are. Helene, is there any sacrifice you would not make for me? Will you do any and everything that I ask?' 'Yes,' I said, with an anxious heart, 'I will do anything except go back to my parents.' 'But it is just that which I am asking, the greatest sacrifice you can make for me. Will you do it?' 'If

worry, they can obstruct, but in the end they cannot prevent. People don't get shut up nowadays, it isn't allowed, and a girl isn't lost like a pin. Much better take things quietly for two or three days. I shall arrive on the 10th. This sort of problem is in my province and I can handle it far better than you can. . . . There is only one point I think really important: will Helene stand firm? It all depends on that. If she holds out nothing is lost. But if not, then, my dear child, while I understand and share your pain, it is only the pain of disappointment for she is not worthy of you."

Lassalle meanwhile was pouring out a series of letters to Helene, in the frantic hope that through Mrs. Arson, Lesley, or some other intermediary they would eventually reach her. On the 7th he wrote: "I love you with a passion compared to which my love before was just a beginning. Since Wednesday night I love you to the point of madness." In a number of letters he explained the respective procedure to be adopted under Swiss and Bavarian law when parents attempt to oppose a marriage. Some of the letters are paragraphed, like official documents, with legal explanation interspersed with declarations of his love. By the 10th he was dreading that there might be some truth in what Arndt and Kayserling had told him on the 4th. He wrote ". . . Para. 9. It is impossible for there to be truth in what they tell me of your having given me up. You have no right to break your vows. You have no right to make so shameful a return for that excess of delicacy which led me to restore you to your mother. You have no right to compromise me. . . . Helene, my wife whom I adore with the madness and torment of despair, send me one line to show you stand firm and true."

None of these letters ever reached Helene. She remained locked up in her bedroom in her parents' house, with the key in her father's pocket. Then she heard they were going to remove her from Geneva and wrote a letter to Mrs. Arson:

"My dear and very loved friend, I'm leaving, or rather they're making me leave, in a few hours' time. I have no strength left. We are going to Evian and then Baix or Bex or whatever the name is. I am terribly unhappy. I have no news of my Eagle and don't know where he is. I am almost mad. . . . Send me my boots. They will let me have them. If you write don't mention his name, or even allude to him. Don't try and console me. I am inconsolable. I know you love me more than my parents do and may God reward you. . . . Remember me to our good friends and ask them to keep a little place in their hearts for your unhappy and broken but resigned

"HELENE.

"PS.—Margaret is engaged to Count Kayserling."

This letter Helene pushed under the door to the faithful Thérèse on the one occasion that the maid had the chance to come to her keyhole. It was then that Thérèse whispered the rumour—at that time quite untrue—that Lassalle had gone. Helene records she was so upset by this news that she did not pass out her other letter, one which she had written to Lassalle. "Lassalle had gone, had left Geneva. I thought and thought and saw no end to it, no way out, no ray of hope."

That night her family took her away by boat across the lake. Lassalle heard rumours that she had gone, which were confirmed by a letter from Lesley that reached him on the 12th. That day he wrote to Helene. "I will only accept your verbal, not written, assurance that you have given me up. If you stand firm, as I believe you will, no power on earth can separate us."

He drew up a power of attorney for Rüstow to represent him for the moment in Geneva and left for Germany. For the past week he had been exchanging a stream of telegrams with the Countess, with ever-changing arrangements as to where they should meet. He joined her in Karlsruhe on the 15th August.

3

IN KARLSRUHE there was some plain speaking by the Countess and a long and heated discussion. The following day, the 16th, Lassalle left for Munich. The Countess went to Mainz to enlist the support of the Bishop, who, as we have seen, was already interested in Lassalle's movement. That same evening the Countess made her report:

"My Dear Child,

"I arrived at three and at five made my call. I was admitted at once. . . . After long explanations and entreaties, which, as you know, came from the depth of my heart, and enquiries on his part as to what I felt he could do, he said: 'Yes, if the girl is a Catholic and appeals to the Church for protection and for the maintenance of the sanctity of the sacraments, then, perhaps, action on his part might be justified. But as for yourself and your appeal, the fact remains you are not a Catholic.' He referred to you in appreciative terms. . . . He expressed complete approval of your honourable behaviour, and considers you took the only course worthy of you. He approves of your plan to establish your rightful claim through the proper channels in Munich. . . . Goodbye, my dear and good child. I cannot forget your pale sad face on the platform when my train moved out. If you thought I was cruel in talking to you as I did, remember I was more forlorn than you. I feel my inner being is joined, physically, to yours; and if that cord is cut it is I who bleed. For my sake as well as for your own, be calm, give yourself rest, take care of yourself.

"Sophie."

The Countess then went to Switzerland. It was not till she had been there some days that either she or Lassalle discovered that Helene was a Protestant. The appeal to the Bishop of Mainz had been based on a false assumption.

Lassalle's business in Munich was facilitated by his friend Bülow providing introductions. One was to Richard Wagner who did not like him. Lassalle seems to have been far too preoccupied to notice this, and built some hopes on Wagner inducing the King of Bavaria to intervene. He made more tangible progress when he called on Baron von Schrenk, the Bavarian Foreign Minister. Schrenk was obviously interested in meeting Lassalle and the interview was a friendly one—Lassalle wrote long accounts of it both to von Bülow and to the Countess. "He [i.e. von Schrenk] said, 'In these circumstances I would not refuse to let you marry my daughter, though it might be embarrassing to have a son-in-law of such political importance. There might be a revolution and it would be disagreeable if one's son-in-law were hanged.' I replied that there might be no revolution, and that even if there were it would not be our party who would go to the gallows." Von Schrenk deprecated reference to the King, but suggested that Lassalle should call again, bringing a lawyer with him, to draw up some plan of action.

The Countess's first letter from Berne was not discouraging:

"I have just come back from Wabern where I found them all. They all deeply sympathise with you and admire the way you behaved: you have acted as a man of honour, and that you will never regret. I liked the two Lesleys best. Mrs. Arson too kept asking me to tell you how willing she is to help, but only for *your* sake. . . . They are all very angry with the Dönniges family, including Helene. . . . They suggest I should go straight to Geneva and do not think I will have any difficulty in seeing Helene. But don't you be in a hurry to come. Let us prepare the ground. . . . The Vlach whom they sent for is a silly boy, younger than Helene, who hasn't yet passed his examinations, which does not make their behaviour look any better. So be calm and patient. We have done the most difficult part. We have located Helene and can get access to her. . . ."

This crossed a letter from Lassalle. Baron von Schrenck had made the proposal that Dr. Haenle, the lawyer, should proceed to Geneva as his official representative with the task of securing an amicable settlement. Should that be impossible he was to insist that Helene should make a declaration of her wishes before a notary public and in Lassalle's presence. "This development," Lassalle wrote, "is marvellous. I do not count on it breaking old Dönniges' resistance. But if Helene stands firm it means that victory is ours."

But was Helene standing fast? Holthoff in Berlin (who throughout the dispute kept in touch with both parties and played a somewhat ambiguous role) wrote to Lassalle that she had given in to her parents. Even worse news reached Munich by the next post. Helene was now back in Geneva, Rüstow had seen her and she had given Rüstow a letter for Lassalle which said, "As I am now completely reconciled with my fiancé Herr Yanko von Rakowitza I declare of my own free will that there can never be any relationship between myself and you."

Lassalle sent frantic letters and telegrams to the Countess and Rüstow, now together in Geneva. He tried to persuade himself that Helene's declaration had been made under duress, but the bitter alternative was forever biting into his soul. "If this woman, for whose sake I am suffering so much, were to desert me it would be a blasphemy against mankind." And again: "Should Helene say no, then everything is lost and this official *démarche* I have brought about with so much difficulty will produce nothing but ridicule; Dönniges will be justified and every hope for me will be cut off. This faithless woman will be thrusting a dagger into my heart."

All depended on Helene. There was nothing more Lassalle could do. His one hope was that the Countess might find some means of influencing her resolve. In his despair he wrote to the Countess: "If Helene could only picture one thousandth part of my misery she could not have even the thought of being faithless. My hope is in you, arrange to see her, read her this letter, tell her how I was in Karlsruhe, use all the persuasiveness you can. . . ."

But on the 22nd Sophie von Hatzfeldt and Rüstow sent him a joint telegram:

"Helene's conduct unbelievably shameless. Impertinently and arbitrarily refused to reply to Sophie. No question of compulsion. Legal proceedings designed to establish compulsion would only confirm her negative attitude. . . . Main aim must be to frighten father. Best course you obtain letter from his chief as follows: evidence exists justifying Lassalle and proving Helene's unbelievable conduct; open scandal incompatible with public service; father must therefore reach satisfactory settlement with Lassalle. When this letter obtained come at once with Haenle."

4

HELENE's account of what happened to her during these three weeks is confused, as was, no doubt, the unfortunate girl's own state of mind. How far she was ill-treated is difficult to say. Dönniges *père* was pompous and bullying by turns. Her brother, who was more frank, told her straight out she was imperilling their father's career and his own prospects as an officer. It is clear that her resistance eventually broke down. That is all we know. When Yanko arrived she claims to have said to him:

" 'I swear to you that if ever I see Ferdinand Lassalle I will go to him and stay with him, over all your dead bodies if need be. With my own hand I would help to kill you all, strangle you or poison you, in order to be with him. Get that into your head, and now take me if you want to.'

" 'Is that true?'

" 'True? If you and all my relations and all the people I had ever cared for lay dead here at my feet, I would not turn an eyelid. I should be glad because I could go back to him over your dead bodies.'

"He shuddered.

" 'You have no pity,' he said.

" 'Who has pity on me? Who saw my side? From now—my head is aching. There is no need to go on with this.'

"He went out. But he was satisfied with the curious admission I had made to him and from that moment he did all he could to protect me from my family."

While at Bex she was, she says, continually expecting some sign or message from Lassalle. When none came she began to believe he had deserted her. When, back in Geneva, she saw Rüstow, he appeared to her cold and hostile. Nothing, she felt, could be gained by an appeal to him, so she handed over the letter her father had dictated.

That Rüstow should appear so is not surprising. He resented having been drawn into this tiresome and discreditable business on behalf of a man whom he disliked. And though the Countess may have arrived in Geneva with the sincere intention of winning back Helene for Lassalle she seems fairly soon to have felt it would be best to liquidate the affair with as little loss of face to him as possible.

Helene had, as already noted, written to the Countess before leaving Berne at the beginning of the month. The Countess had answered in very friendly terms: "Let me say at once what real pleasure I had from your kind letter, and how touched I was that you should write so soon. . . . When we meet, which I hope will be soon, I am afraid you may think I am rather grim, that I am old, peevish, dictatorial and jealous. . . . But this is only the outer shell. My heart is neither hard nor bitter, and perhaps I find it easier than other people to understand and sympathise with the young."

Helene was in captivity when this letter arrived and her father did not give it to her. He did, however, give her the letter which the Countess, in a very different frame of mind, sent by messenger on the 22nd. This referred to "Herr Lassalle's not only honourable but admirable behaviour," to "Herr Lassalle's preeminent political position," and went on to say: "You will therefore realise that after all that has happened it is as much in your interest as in that of Herr Lassalle that your relationship should be brought to an end in the manner most considerate to him." Helene records, not unconvincingly, that she felt this missive to be another sign that Lassalle had deserted her and that his friends were her enemies.

Helene scribbled a slip: "*Reçu la lettre, Helene de Dönniges.*" This was given to the messenger who brought it back to the Countess and said there was no answer. The Countess was very annoyed at this rudeness, and Rüstow sent a letter of protest to von Dönniges. "All Lassalle's friends," he wrote, "including myself, feel that after what has happened it would be a mistake for him to marry Helene." At the same time it must be made very clear that "people like the Countess and Lassalle are not to be treated like gipsies." Von Dönniges replied with a long self-justification, and a pompous and inconclusive exchange of notes went on for the next two days. It was still going on when Lassalle arrived from Munich with Dr. Haenle.

Chapter 21

CAROUGE

I

Lassalle came back to Geneva still fully determined to marry Helene; and there is little doubt that it was chiefly as a means of forcing her father to grant him access to her that he valued the presence of Haenle.

The fact that Haenle had credentials from his Minister of Foreign Affairs put von Dönniges on the defensive. He at once agreed to receive Lassalle and the latter called on him on the 25th. The matter being now an official one von Dönniges drew up a note on the interview which he sent to Dr. Haenle that same evening:

"I received Herr Lassalle in my house at 2 p.m. In the course of a conversation which lasted several hours he did not revert to the proposal in Baron von Schrenck's letter, i.e. 'to arrange that in the presence of yourself and of Herr Lassalle, in my house, my daughter Helene should give a formal expression of her decision in the prescribed form and before a notary public.' On the contrary, Herr Lassalle demanded that Herr Yanko von Rakowitza should be removed from my domicile while he, Lassalle, should be allowed freedom of access; as this was the only proof he would accept that my daughter Helene had voluntarily renounced his hand. I was naturally unable to entertain any thought of this senseless and impossible proposition. I replied that my maximum concession could only be to facilitate a free expression of my daughter's views in front of both parties concerned.

"Herr Lassalle refused to agree; and in the course of several hours persistently returned to allegations of moral compulsion or force exercised upon my daughter. I branded these as false and when he sought to base his allegations on statements by my cook, I called her into the room where she maintained that they were a tissue of lies. Herr Lassalle proceeded to name my landlord Colonel Vaucher. I at once called on Colonel Vaucher who expressed supreme indignation and who intends to-morrow to take legal advice in the matter of redress against Herr Lassalle."

Lassalle made a formal declaration in reply to this note on the following morning, 26th August. (Incidentally his letter to Holthoff to which he refers was written from Munich. This letter has not been preserved, and we do not know why Holthoff sent it on to von Dönniges.)

"Having yesterday vainly endeavoured to secure Herr von Dönniges' agreement to an amicable settlement of the question at issue; Having on this occasion been repeatedly accused by Herr von Dönniges of falsehood and slander over the matter of compulsion brought to bear on his daughter; and this notwithstanding his daughter's written statements—'*on ouvre toutes mes lettres*'—'*il y a eu des scènes affreuses*', etc., etc., which establish clear proof; and notwithstanding my express reservation in my letter to the lawyer Holthoff that the statements of the cook 'that Herr von Dönniges physically mishandled his daughter' reached me only at second hand; And since Herr von Dönniges has subsequently repeated his accusations in writing, which makes clear that they were made not merely in the heat of the moment,

"I declare:

"That I expressively reserve the right to take all proper steps to obtain redress from Herr von Dönniges for these defamations.

"In the matter at issue, however, seeing that Herr von Dönniges in his letter to Dr. Haenle advances the ungrounded assertion that I am unwilling to pursue the course suggested by Baron von Schrenck, I herewith declare in conformity with the Baron's proposal and in consequence of Herr von Dönniges' refusal of an amicable settlement that I make the following demand:

"Herr von Dönniges shall allow me, for the period of fourteen days, access to and facilities for unrestricted conversation with his daughter in his house.

"Failing this my minimum demand is that;

"Herr von Dönniges shall facilitate a formal declaration by his daughter before a notary public. Before this takes place however, I shall, in an anteroom of the notary's office, have a conversation of not more than two hours' length with Helene, either alone or in the presence of Colonel Rüstow, so as to ensure that her formal declaration shall be free, uninfluenced and true. Such a proviso is all the more essential as in our conversation of yesterday Herr von Dönniges was forced to admit, following a direct question from myself, that he was unable to asseverate that Helene had withdrawn her promise of marriage of her own free will and under no moral influence or compulsion.

"The notorial act shall take place in the presence of one relative or family friend to be designated by Helene's parents: but not of the parents themselves, as events have shown that the presence of her parents denies to Helene all freedom of choice."

Haenle, accompanied by Rüstow, at once took this document to von Dönniges and there ensued a meeting destined to be decisive. It is described in a protocol drawn up by Rüstow and Haenle.

"Herr von Dönniges expressed his consent to the minimum demand set out in Herr Lassalle's note on condition that his daughter also agreed. In spite of our refusal to accept this condition, he summoned his daughter. At Herr Lassalle's wish we put on record the following account of our conversation with the daughter which took place in Herr von Dönniges' presence.

"She appeared to us to be undisturbed and carefree, and displayed conventional flippancy rather than traces of a past or present emotional crisis.

"Colonel Rüstow explained, clearly and calmly, why Herr Lassalle was insisting on a conversation limited to two hours, either alone with her, or, if the proprieties so demanded, in the presence of a third person who would not, however, put limits to the freedom of the discussion. She declined the proposal, using the words: 'What is the point? I know what he wants. I am sick and tired of the whole thing.'

"When reminded of her vow she said: 'Vow? I don't make vows.'

"On our remarking that such words were inconsistent with her previous behaviour, for instance with her visit to Lassalle in the Pension Bouvet, she said: 'That is true, but all that happened on the spur of the moment.'

"Finally, Colonel Rüstow suggested that one of her remarks implied a fear that a meeting with Lassalle would bring her back to her former state of mind. This she denied, and declared the proposed conversation would be quite useless. Dr. Haenle suggested that the meeting would not necessarily last as long as two hours, since Lassalle would not wish it to continue after she had made her meaning clear. She replied:

"'He likes talking. Two hours will not be enough for him.'

"Colonel Rüstow put it to her that on her own admission she had done Lassalle a wrong and that she therefore owed him satisfaction. She smiled and said:

"'For his vanity?'

"Colonel Rüstow corrected her:

"'No. For his manly self-respect.'

"Dr. Haenle maintained the view that two considerations should move her to agree to the proposed conversation—firstly because she owed Herr Lassalle some satisfaction for the wrong she had done him, and secondly because this meeting might mitigate the possibly unfortunate consequences of the publicity which the whole affair was causing. She replied that she did not contest the force of these considerations, and would, after due reflection give Dr. Haenle an answer in writing."

The short account of this interview in Helene's memoirs gives a different picture. She talks of Rüstow's "hostility" and says she was hoping for a further interview with Haenle (whom she liked) which might have led to her being restored to Lassalle. These memoirs date from long afterwards, and were aimed at presenting her affair with Lassalle as a *grande passion*. They may have been written in complete sincerity, and yet, in view of the time factor and her lack of emotional balance, present a distorted picture. On the other hand, while Rüstow and Haenle may well have drafted their protocol in the hope that it would make Lassalle give up the idea of marriage, we may accept it as a reasonably accurate account of how Helene then appeared to an outside observer.

2

THE EFFECT on Lassalle was decisive. His romance was completely and finally shattered, and he found himself, as his nightmares had foreshadowed, exposed to the "unlimited ridicule" of his friends, his party, his enemies and the world at large. The heat of bewildered passion gave place to cold fury and he set himself to the task of winning back his self-respect.

There was no further need of Haenle, and Haenle that same day announced the end of his mission in a letter to von Dönniges:

"The report, which Colonel Rüstow and myself were compelled to make on the contents and tone of to-day's statements by your daughter Fräulein Helene, has made so deep an impression on Herr Lassalle that the notorial act which it was proposed your daughter should execute and, indeed, any further formalities, seem now to be superfluous. I am therefore leaving Geneva. I avail myself of this opportunity of taking leave of you and of assuring you of my highest esteem."

Lassalle himself drafted a telegram to Richard Wagner, whom he imagined to be still trying to interest the King of Bavaria: "Have myself withdrawn from affair owing to complete unworthiness of person concerned. Thank you for your good will but take no further action."

This telegram was not dispatched.

That same afternoon Lassalle wrote to von Dönniges: "It is clear from the report submitted to me by Colonel Rüstow and Dr. Haenle that your daughter is an abandoned prostitute. I have no longer any idea of dishonouring myself by marrying her. I have no longer any motive to delay my demand for satisfaction for your various insults, and insist therefore that you make the necessary arrangements with my two friends who are bearers of this note."

3

RÜSTOW has left a full account of subsequent developments. The Colonel Becker to whom he refers was Johann Phillip Becker, the well-known political *émigré* who had served under Garibaldi. Lassalle had for some time been in friendly correspondence with him.

Rüstow writes:

"Lassalle asked Colonel Becker and myself to be his seconds. When Becker refused on a question of principle Lassalle asked the Hungarian General Bethlen to act in his stead. Becker's refusal resulted in the letter to Dönniges being sent to him by a commissionaire and not taken personally by Becker and me. That same evening I twice went to see Dönniges but did not find him at home. On the morning of the 27th I called for General Bethlen; he was unable to come with me to Dönniges, so I went back to the Hotel Victoria. There I found Lassalle, in Countess Hatzfeldt's private sitting-room. He took me to his own room and asked me to promise not to mention the matter to the Countess. This I refused to do. He then told me that on that morning Count Kayserling and Dr. Arndt had called on him to present a challenge in the name of Herr von Rakowitza I explained to him he could not accept this challenge until old Dönniges had given him satisfaction. It was against all procedure to allow von Rakowitza to intervene. Lassalle implored me in the name of our friendship not to delay matters. Kayserling and Arndt were due back at twelve noon in order to meet us.

"I protested, but on seeing that Lassalle had made his mind up I finally agreed. The two gentlemen arrived within an hour. Lassalle left us and I emphasised the priority of Dönniges, but was told that he had fled to Berne in great haste, leaving his future son-in-law to defend the family's honour. We came to no decision and arranged to meet again at my rooms at three.

"I then reported the conversation to Lassalle, reiterated my point of view and urged him to refuse the challenge of von

Rakowitza. Lassalle would not listen to me and insisted that the duel be arranged for the following morning."

Helene records that she heard the von Dönniges side of the story from Yanko.

"My father had shown him the provocation, and explained that he himself was a middle-aged man and father of a family; he could not possibly take part in a duel. But yet this stain on the family's honour must not be allowed to remain. My mother had been talking in the same strain, only rather more openly. He, Yanko, had never handled a gun—he had been too delicate to take part in field sports, and as Lassalle was known to be a good shot he had had a couple of hours' pistol practice that same morning. My brothers were too young, so obviously it was for him to represent my father. In fact it was obvious, the traditional code of honour demanded it, it ought to be quite clear to me.

"Was it clear to me? I cannot tell. It is true I was brought up on all these ideas of honour. But I sincerely believe I never thought of that.

"My thoughts were along another line. Lassalle would kill Yanko. That was self-evident, as obvious to me as the necessity of the duel was to the others. I felt no sorrow about Yanko, my only friend. It seemed inevitable: he had to die. And in this way I myself perhaps would find my way to happiness. . . ."

Rüstow's account continues:

"I called on General Bethlen, and at three o'clock he, Count Kayserling and Dr. Arndt arrived at my rooms. Our opponents demanded as their conditions that the initiative should come from Lassalle, and that he should return the letters from Fräulein von Dönniges. These conditions we could not accept. However I still hoped for a settlement, and so arranged that we should meet again at 8. Meanwhile we arranged the conditions, in case the duel should take place. Our opponents proposed pistols with rifling but we succeeded in getting their agreement to smooth-bore pistols as proposed by us.

"I returned to the Hotel Victoria and advised Lassalle to take some pistol practice. He declared that this was 'nonsense'. I later learned that Herr von Rakowitza took a different view.

At least it was generally believed in Geneva that during the afternoon he visited a range and fired 150 practice rounds.

"At eight o'clock we had a second meeting in my rooms. All attempts to reach a settlement were in vain. The duel was arranged for the morning of the 28th.

"Towards nine o'clock Becker arrived with the gunsmith, and said that one of the pair of pistols we had chosen had a broken spring. I demanded that the spring should be repaired and in order to make sure I accompanied the locksmith to his quarters. Once arrived there he informed me that as a state of siege had been declared in Geneva he could not work at night. I admit that this difficulty nearly caused me to lose my temper, as I was, in any case, in a state of extreme nervous tension.

"It must have been then about ten. I went on to the Hotel Victoria where I had booked a room in order to be with Lassalle. I explained to him what had happened and he forced me then and there to write a letter to Dr. Arndt explaining that he agreed to pistols with rifling should no smooth-bore pistols be available, and that in the event of General Bethlen making difficulties he would engage Herr von Hofstetten in his stead. Herr von Hofstetten took this letter to its destination at 11 o'clock.

"I sat talking to Lassalle till midnight. I told him we had arranged that the parties in the duel might take up any position they choose; but that he must not take too long an aim—which was an unfortunate habit of his—as he was not the only one to shoot, etc.

"At midnight, I went to bed. I got up three hours after, dressed and went to my rooms to fetch a few small articles that I needed. From there I went to the locksmith, found him—at four o'clock—already at work, took one pistol with me and went back to the hotel. At five I called Lassalle, who was sleeping peacefully. He happened to see the pistol. He took it, put his arm round me, and said 'That is exactly the thing I wanted.' At half-past five I went again to the smith's and collected the other pistol.

"Then I fetched Bethlen.

"After half-past six we drove to Carouge, a suburb of Geneva, together with Hofstetten, whom Lassalle wanted to have with us. It was arranged that the parties should meet here at 7.30. Before we started Lassalle gave me his will: if things turned out unhappily I was to hand it to the Countess for presentation to the Geneva authorities. We arrived at Carouge before seven. On the way Lassalle kept asking me to arrange for the duel to take place on French soil, so that he could stay on in Geneva and settle with the old 'absentee'. While I was glad to see him confident I felt this was going rather far. I reminded him that it takes two to fight a duel and that every bullet can find its billet: one must never despise an opponent. My words made no impression on him.

"The other parties had not yet arrived in Carouge. Lassalle showed no trace of excitement and drank a cup of tea.

"The others arrived at 7.30. They had with them a Doctor Seiler who knew of a suitable place. They drove on ahead and we followed. We left Hofstetten in Carouge to come after us in a cab. On arrival near the place that Dr. Seiler had in mind we got out of the carriages and walked on foot through the trees.

"We drew lots and it fell to me to load for the first shot and to give the orders. I was advised, quite superfluously, to do so clearly and loudly. Twenty seconds were allowed for each shot. At zero, the second in charge was to call 'One', after ten seconds 'Two' and after twenty seconds 'Three'. I took the precaution first of all of calling 'Get ready'.

"I gave the command 'One'. Barely five seconds later the first shot rang out—fired by Herr von Rakowitza. Lassalle replied immediately.

"He missed. He had death in his body. It was a wonder that he could fire at all.

"After firing he stumbled two paces to the left. I heard—I had to keep my eyes on my watch—some one, either General Bethlen or Dr. Seiler, ask 'Are you wounded?'

"Lassalle answered: 'Yes'.

"We laid him on a blanket and administered first aid.

"Our opponents left us. Dr. Seiler and I helped Lassalle into a carriage. We drove with him and supported him as well as we could. Bethlen went back with Hofstetten in the cab.

"I made the driver keep off metalled roads, which he was able to do except for some two hundred metres.

"Lassalle kept very quiet. It was only when we came to the cobbles that pain made him speak: he asked if we would soon be back.

"I knew from my experience that the wound was dangerous. That it was mortal I first learned from Dr. Seiler whom I met as I was going to fetch a lawyer at Lassalle's urgent wish."

Lassalle lingered on, heavily drugged with opium, for three days. He died on the morning of 31st August.

EPILOGUE

It is not within the scope of this book to do more than touch very briefly on events after Lassalle's death.

The requiem service at the Geneva synagogue was attended by four thousand people. Switzerland, in Marx's phrase, was "the Coblenz of the European revolution", and Herzen and Bakunin were among the distinguished political *émigrés* who were present.

Countess Hatzfeldt had the body embalmed and took it in solemn progress down the Rhine. The emotional hold of Lassalle's name on thousands of the Rhineland workers and the sensational rumours current as to the circumstances of his death brought vast crowds to every halt. As Lassalle had said of his last Rhineland tour it was indeed "like the birth of a new religion".

The popular excitement was such as to alarm the authorities. Finally they intervened at the instance of the Lassal family. The body was taken to Berlin and thence to Breslau, where it was finally laid to rest in the Jewish Cemetery. Lassalle's oldest friend, the aged Professor Boeckh, composed the epitaph:

Here lie the mortal remains
of
Ferdinand Lassalle
Thinker and Warrior.

Countess Hatzfeldt wrote to Lassalle's mother: "I took Ferdinand's cold hand and swore an oath that I would take vengeance on his murderers, defend his memory against his enemies, and carry on his work. . . . All I want is to be able, should there be life after death, to tell him I have done my duty to him."

The Countess made every effort to have Yanko von Rakowitza extradited and tried for murder. She was persistent in her attempts to foster what amounted to a personal cult of Lassalle, both inside and outside the Association. She was protagonist in most of the legal, political, personal and literary disputes and vendettas that were his immediate legacy. She died, a lonely but undaunted woman, in 1881.

Rüstow had then been dead three years. A few months after Lassalle's death he had written to her: "I have long realised that compared to him I meant nothing to you. This I have felt a great and undeserved injustice. What I did [in August] I did for your sake. I would have saved him for you if he would have let himself be saved." This letter did not bring about a reconciliation and the two drifted apart. Rüstow's financial and other troubles accumulated. Frau Herwegh became anxious about him and made an appeal to the Countess. There was no answer. In August 1878 he shot himself.

Helene in due course married Yanko. Her memoirs finish with these words:

"My one feeling that survived those terrible days was hate, deep implacable hate, against my parents whose cruel selfishness had been the cause of all this misery; and also a lasting shame for my own weakness of will. This shame I feel still, and still admit my weak-mindedness to have been unforgivable. But I do not think I wronged Lassalle's memory when, half a year later, I became the wife of the already dying Yanko and cared for him devotedly until his death five months afterwards. Right to the end he had shown himself to be my truest and most unselfish friend."

After Yanko she married two other husbands, and went on the stage. In the end she too committed suicide.

Sonia Sontsev married a man called Arendt and went to live in the Crimea.

Lothar Bucher accepted a post under Bismarck which led to a highly respectable and not undistinguished official career.

The news of Lassalle's death came as a shock to the *émigrés* in London. On the 4th September Engels wrote to Marx:

"You can imagine how the news surprised me. Whatever Lassalle may have been personally, or as a thinker or man of letters, he was undoubtedly one of the most important men in Germany . . . what rejoicings there will be among the factory owners and the Progressives—Lassalle was after all the only man they were afraid of in Germany itself."

Three days later Marx replied:

"Lassalle's misfortune is very much in my head these days. After all he was one of the old stock and the enemy of our enemies. . . . I am sorry that for the last year or so our relations were clouded, though the fault was his. I am glad I resisted provocation from various sides and made no attack on him during his jubilee year."

To the Countess, for whom he always had a real regard, Marx wrote: "I know what he was for you and what his loss will mean. But take heart over this—he died young, in triumph, like Achilles." And later: "You are right in feeling that I, more than others, can appreciate his greatness and importance. . . . So long as we were in correspondence I always expressed my warmest appreciation of his achievement; and always very frankly criticised any point that seemed to me wrong. He told me, in his own forceful way, how pleased he was at this. But quite apart from what he did I loved him as a man. The trouble was that we kept in hiding from each other, as if we were going to live for ever."

The Countess was indiscreet in her handling of these letters and Marx was annoyed. In addition, he was confronted with the rapid growth of the General German Workers' Association after its founder's death. Bernhard Becker, Lassalle's nominee to succeed him as President, soon showed himself to be incompetent and had to be replaced by Schweitzer. But within a year the membership of the Association had doubled and the prestige of Lassalle's name had correspondingly increased. Marx made his attitude clear in a letter to Kugelmann in February 1865.

"Lassalle: during his agitation contact between us was suspended because of (i) his vanity, braggadocio and shameless plagiarism of my writings; (ii) I condemned his tactics; (iii) I explained to him here [in London] that direct socialist action by the Prussian State was nonsense. . . ."

Three years later he wrote to Schweitzer, who had invited his co-operation:

"Lassalle's Association was founded in a period of reaction. Lassalle, and this is his immortal service, re-awakened the workers' movement in Germany after fifteen years of slumber. But he committed great mistakes. He let himself be too much controlled by the immediate circumstances of the time. . . . He was forced into concessions to the Prussian monarchy, the feudal party and even the clericals."

The name of Lassalle, however, maintained its hold on the movement in Germany. In 1875 the General German Workers' Association united, in a congress at Gotha, with the younger and rival movement under Liebknecht and Bebel to form the German Social Democratic Party. In spite of all the pressure that Marx and Engels could exert the new party officially adopted a programme largely based on the theories and slogans of Lassalle; and only in 1891, eight years after Marx's death, was Engels able to secure its radical modification. It was on this occasion that he wrote to Kautsky:

"If people do not know that Lassalle's whole greatness rests on this, that for years Marx allowed him to parade the results of Marx's research as his own and, owing to defective education in economics, to distort them into the bargain, then that is not my fault. But I am Marx's literary executor and as such I also have my duty to perform.

"Lassalle has belonged to history for twenty-six years. . . . The legend that conceals and glorifies the true stature of Lassalle cannot become an article of faith of the party. However highly one may estimate Lassalle's services to the movement, his historical role in it remains an equivocal one. Lassalle the socialist is accompanied step by step by Lassalle the demagogue. The Lassalle of the Hatzfeldt case appears everywhere, showing through Lassalle the agitator and organiser; the same cynicism in the choice of methods, the same tendency to surround himself with noisy and corrupt people . . . demanding that the workers should take the part of the monarchy against the bourgeoisie and intriguing with Bismarck—one of his own kidney—in a way bound to lead to the betrayal of the movement, if, fortunately for him, he had not been shot in time. . . . Should I be forced to it I would have no choice: I should have to clear away the Lassalle legend once and for all."

Kautsky's verdict however was: "The standpoint of Marx towards Lassalle is not that of German Social Democracy. . . . How could we forget the man from whose writings all we old party comrades, and some of the younger ones too, derived our first knowledge and inspiration as socialists?"

BIBLIOGRAPHICAL NOTE

The most convenient edition of Lassalle's collected works is that of Eduard Bernstein (Berlin, 1919), which contains some useful notes.

Lassalle's early diary was published with notes by Paul Lindau (Breslau, 1891). Although a good many of his letters had, by the end of the First World War, been collected and published by Bernstein, F. Mehring, H. Oncken, Gustav Mayer and others, the bulk of his posthumous papers remained in possession of the Hatzfeldt family. These were recovered by Mayer during the French occupation of the Ruhr, and issued by him in six admirable and scholarly volumes—*Ferdinand Lassalle: Nachgelassene Briefe und Schriften* (Stuttgart, 1921–1924). This series contains passages from the diary not included in Lindau's edition; and also corrected versions of various papers relative to the final episode previously published by Bernhard Becker in his *Enthüllungen.* However, Becker's pamphlet, written in the course of his vendetta against Countess Hatzfeldt, remains of interest as a monument of spitefulness and bad taste. The correspondence with Bismarck, which was not discovered till some years later, was also published by Mayer—*Bismarck und Lassalle, ihr Briefwechsel und ihre Gespräche* (Berlin, 1928). A good introduction to Lassalle is afforded by the selection of documents, with short but adequate notes, edited by Stefan Grossmann (Berlin, 1919).

Of considerable interest and importance are the relevant passages in the Marx–Engels correspondence. Then there are Helene von Rakowitza's memoirs (*Meine Beziehunger zu Ferdinand Lassalle*, 1879), which give a convincing picture of the heroine of the final tragedy.

Biographies include works by G. Brandes, Bernstein and Herman Oncken. That by Oncken is the outstanding one. But the enlarged edition came out in 1924, since when a good deal more material has become available. A subsequent life by Arno Schirokauer (*Lassalle: The Power of Illusion and the Illusion of*

Power, 1931) would be more satisfying were it not so insistently clever.

The literature available in English is somewhat meagre. Volume 11 of the *Cambridge Modern History* makes no mention of Lassalle, and refers to Marx only once, as a member of a "light skirmishing corps of young Radical writers". There is an abridged translation of an early edition of Oncken's biography, also translations of the lives by Brandes and Schirokauer. There is of course George Meredith's *The Tragic Comedians*, which gives the final episode in the guise of fiction. It has received high praise from competent judges; but to some of us, familiar with the vivid vitality of the records left by Lassalle, Helene and Sophie Hatzfeldt, it seems to-day a little dim and bogus.

INDEX

INDEX